Education and Society Today

CONTEMPORARY ANALYSIS IN EDUCATION SERIES
General Editor: Philip Taylor, University of Birmingham

Contemporary Analysis in Education Series

Education and Society Today

Edited by
Anthony Hartnett
and
Michael Naish
University of Liverpool

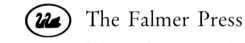 The Falmer Press

(A member of the Taylor & Francis Group)
London, New York and Philadelphia

6766

UK   The Falmer Press, Falmer House, Barcombe, Lewes, East Sussex, BN8 5DL

USA   The Falmer Press, Taylor & Francis Inc., 242 Cherry Street, Philadelphia, PA 19106-1906

First published 1986

EDU

Library of Congress Cataloging in Publication Data is available on request

ISBN 1-85000-132-4
ISBN 1-85000-133-2 (pbk.)

Jacket design by Leonard Williams

Typeset in 11/13 Garamond by Imago Publishing Ltd, Thame, Oxon

Printed in Great Britain by Taylor & Francis (Printers) Ltd, Basingstoke

Contents

Contents

Acknowledgements

We would like to thank the following people all of whom have, in different ways, provided invaluable help in the preparation of this book. John Vaughan, tutor-librarian of the Department of Education Library, University of Liverpool, and his staff provided us with books, articles and photocopies. They did this as efficiently as ever, even though they were working under trying circumstances with the library being restructured and rebuilt around them. Mrs. Helena Cross has continued to act as our research assistant although she has formally retired from the University. She has helped us in many ways, particularly by her tenacity in tracking down often recondite publications. Mrs. Kath Moore typed all the drafts of the introduction and of the chapter which we have contributed to the book. We have relied on her great skill to enable us to read what the other has written and, occasionally, what we have written ourselves. Her work in translating rough, cut-up and amended manuscripts into clear typescripts has been indispensable. Professor David Jennings, Chairman of the Research Committee of the University of Liverpool, has shown continued interest in the book and has provided us with a series of vital research grants. These played an important part in our preliminary work on the book and on its shape and contents. They enabled us, too, to explore relevant literature in more depth than would otherwise have been possible. Professor Philip Taylor of the University of Birmingham suggested the idea of the book to us and gave us advice, help and interesting references while the book was being written. Malcolm Clarkson of the Falmer Press provided support and his invaluable professional skills.

In times like these, which are especially difficult for educational studies, we have taken sustenance from the work of a group of people who combine intellectual commitment with a concern for the serious moral and political issues that are inseparable from education. We have used (and perhaps even misused) what they have written or said. Among those who have been of particular importance to us are: Mike Apple, Basil Bernstein, Waltraud Boxall, Wilfred Carr, Frank Coffield, Tony Edwards, Douglas Finlayson, David Hamilton, Maurice Holt, Fred Inglis, Ruth Jonathan, John Kekes, Nicholas Maxwell and Bill Reid. Neville Bann has provided us with a great deal of material from the archives of the Conservative Party and we have quoted from it at the beginning of the chapter that we have contributed to this book.

We are indebted to our students, in particular those on our Master of Education, Advanced Diploma in Special Education, and Postgraduate Certificate in Education courses. They have constantly reminded us of how much, given the current state of educational studies, still remains urgently to be done.

The contributors to the book deserve a special word of thanks. They agreed to follow the detailed procedures that we suggested and to see their own work in the context of the book as a whole. They allowed their fellow contributors to read and comment on their work in draft, and they made our editorial task less onerous by producing work on time.

All of those mentioned above have made this book possible, Sir Keith Joseph made it necessary. Although he tried hard to persuade people that his own educational policies left politics far behind, his tenure of the office of Secretary of State for Education and Science raised political, educational and other issues which require a sustained and intellectually informed debate. This book is intended to be a contribution to that debate.

Anthony Hartnett and
Michael Naish
University of Liverpool
September 1986

General Editor's Preface

This is not a happy book but it is a good one. In large part it seeks to answer from a variety of standpoints a sobering question:

> When a government loses patience with its
> educational system and the system loses
> faith in its government, what then?

The book does more than offer answers to this question. It documents the death of that mutual respect which could mean the end of democracy in education as we have known it and the rise of the tyranny of manpower needs defined by a centrist bureaucracy. Almost every aspect of education, it would appear, is caught up in a struggle to see its contemporary history as more than an exercise in futility. Educationists are hurt and angry, feeling unfairly blamed for political not educational ills and inadequacies, and are bullied into adopting policies over which they have had no say. But angry though the book is, it has its positive side and contains much sober analysis and constructive thought. It offers solutions as well as criticism and is not without hope.

Anthony Hartnett and Michael Naish are to be congratulated for bringing this forceful reader into being; in orchestrating its several contributors, addressing a wide range of issues into a collective coherence. *Education and Society Today* deserves to be widely read and studied. More than this it should provide valuable understanding for those who sense that much is amiss in education but are not sure what.

Philip Taylor
University of Birmingham
September 1986

Introductory Essay: Conceptions of Education and Social Change in a Democratic Society

Anthony Hartnett and Michael Naish

'At a meeting of the Universities Council for the Education of Teachers (UCET) Dr. H. Judge asked the Permanent Secretary at the Department of Education and Science (Sir David Hancock) whether it was "not important for the universities to maintain a constructive and critical role outside the immediate concerns of a government's policy" ... Sir David Hancock attacked the question as "aggressive and political" and flatly refused to discuss it' (*Times Educational Supplement*, 22 November 1985, p. 6)

We hope that this book combines the advantages that multiple authorship has in such an area as education with an element of intellectual coherence that is greater than is often found in books of articles. In this introduction, we try to indicate one or two ways in which the articles are related and one way in which the book might be read. There are, of course, other ways, and what we offer here is simply a personal account.

The Debate about Education: Two Approaches

Education, and particularly state education, is under attack. It is not simply that there is talk of creating more direct grants schools, of enlarging the private sector, and of denationalizing the school system so as to 'create a system of separate and independent schools responsive to market mechanisms' (Hargreaves, p. 148).[1] It is, too, that education is believed to have failed to deliver the economic goods which it should have done in the 1960s and 1970s, and, therefore, to have been responsible for economic and industrial decline and for unemployment. Education is also blamed for what is taken to be an increase in violence, in permissiveness, and in lack of respect for authority.

One result of these pressures has been a marked increase in the central control of education. Lawton (pp. 19–36) describes this well, and the extent of this centralization can be judged from the quotation in Edwards that central government has created through the Manpower Services Commission 'a nationalized youth training industry without counterpart in any non-communist country' (p. 122). Centralization has restricted the autonomy of the local education authorities in dealing with their local educational problems; has removed much control over the curriculum from teachers; and has reached deep into the curriculum of teacher education. The effect of this has been to make the technical and administrative issues about education (such as how to get better value for money or how to relate schools more closely with industry) appear to be the central ones. By concentrating on these issues, the political issues raised by education have been pushed into the background. A consequence of this has been that almost all of the debate about education has been focussed on issues about the day-to-day running of schools and other educational institutions. It is as if the debate about crime concentrated exclusively on the day-to-day issues that arise within prisons or as if the debate about energy sources concentrated exclusively on how to run Sellafield. Such wider issues as to whether prisons, as they are currently constituted, are either an efficient or morally justifiable way of dealing with criminals or as to whether there should be nuclear power stations at all are not raised.

The concentration on the technical, administrative, and related practical issues in education has restricted the debate about the ends, point, purpose, and nature of education to professionals in the higher echelons of the educational hierarchy, and has removed them from classroom teachers and from the public in general. These issues, it is assumed, are uncontentious and, in any case, can be safely left to the politicians and their aides in the Civil Service and elsewhere. This view of education might be called 'a management view writ-large'. Just as, say, in a large industrial firm which produces cars, the top management decides how many cars are to be produced, how many are to be saloons, hatchbacks and vans, and so on, and then sends instructions down the line, so in education the top management (the government of the day, their advisers, and top civil servants) decides what the output of the education system is to be and then sends instructions down their line. This is one view about the nature and scope of the debate about education and about those who have the right or competence to take part in it.

There is, however, another view. It is seen perhaps most explicitly in the articles by Jonathan, Reid and Holt, P. and J. White, and Hartnett and Naish, among others in this book. Here the debate is taken to be a political debate about the nature, quality, and direction of society. As such, it is a debate about contentious issues about which there is no last word. Education, on this view, is a political term in much the same way as are, say, liberty, equality, and social justice. Just as debates about these terms, and the societal arrangement they sanction, are inseparable from questions about the quality and nature of society, so are those about education. Moreover, because the debate about education's purposes is political, it is one in which all the citizens of any adequately institutionalized democracy have a role to play. This book is meant to be an exemplification of this position. It is, accordingly, not a book which focusses on practice, where practice is taken to cover simply the day-to-day running of educational institutions. It focusses, rather, on some issues about the relationships between education and society but in a way, we hope, which shows that these issues have quite specific consequences for practice (down to choice of text books and curriculum content, for example) and which shows that issues about the justification and improvement of practice cannot be adequately resolved (in so far as they can be resolved at all) without taking some view about these wider issues.

Education and Conceptions of Education

One way of seeing how impoverished any debate about education is which concentrates solely on technical, administrative, or practice focussed issues is to consider the issue about conceptions of education.

The general problem to which the enterprise of education is addressed concerns what preparation should be given to a society's young to enable them to become full members of society (however this is defined) and, accordingly, to enable them to lead valuable and satisfying lives in it. This general problem is an enduring one (Hartnett and Naish, p. 188) in that it has to be addressed continuously as generations in a society succeed each other and in that the particular form in which the general problem presents itself varies over time. The form in which the problem of giving an appropriate preparation to the young presented itself in, say, 1885 is not the same as in 1985. The development of new areas of knowledge and of technology and changes in the structure of society are, among other things, responsible for this. The enterprise of education, then, can have no specific definitive form but is one which has to be created and recreated, sustained, changed and developed in response to changes in the form in which the general problem presents itself. To say this is to say that education is an enterprise that admits of different conceptions.

The multiplicity of conceptions does not arise, however, simply because circumstances render one of them inappropriate and require its replacement. They arise, too, because at any particular time, different groups in a society will each have their own view of the form education should take, depending on its own political, cultural, religious and other views as to how the particular form of the general problem should be addressed. Each of these groups will, that is to say, develop, advocate and demand the institutionalization of its own conception of education. These conceptions and the arguments in their support depend on particular political views about the nature of the good society and about the role of citizens in it. As Hollis (1971) puts it, 'the principles for deciding the merits of educational proposals relate to the general aims of the community' (p. 166). To defend a particular conception of education (to defend the form it should take at a particular time) involves defending a view about how a society is best and most justly organized. The relationship holds the other way too. Any political view about the good society will embody a conception of education, since it will need to lay down the kind of preparation the young require if such a society is to be created and sustained.

Conceptions of education, then, involve issues about the nature and characteristics of the good society and hence of the good life as well as those about what Inglis (1985) calls 'the good, the true and the beautiful' (p. 27); they involve issues about how the distribution of power, wealth, and status is to be justified or changed; they involve issues about social change in general but particularly about those changes that are required if the conception in question is to be given the place it claims is justified and if it is to flourish. A cursory glance at the history of education and of educational ideas will show how these conceptions vary between societies (Chinese literati and Plato's philosopher kings); within societies over particular historical periods (the gentleman classicist, the entrepreneur, the technologist);

and within societies at any given time (liberal education, education as largely work-related, Muslim education and so on).

To argue for a particular conception of education is to argue for a particular political position involving issues about how society should be organized. This applies, equally, to conceptions coming from the Manpower Services Commission as to those from Muslim parents discussed by Troyna and Ball (p. 41). In a democracy all competing conceptions need to be on the public agenda and to be given whatever institutionalization the arguments in their favour merit. A necessary condition for this is that there should be a sustained and informed public debate about them.

The issue about conceptions is seen in a number of articles in this book. Bullock, in his discussion of public schools, outlines a particular conception of education largely focussed on examinations with a social experience which is taken to be a useful preparation for the higher professions and work in multi-national companies at managerial level. He notes how the institutional practices of such schools encourage an 'emotional dependence on institutional life' and loyalty to institutions as well as the development of 'affective neutrality' (pp. 184–5). He notes, too, how, in spite of attacks on them, the public schools, and the conceptions of education institutionalized in them, have adapted to change.

Public school conceptions of education profoundly affected the state system, particularly after 1902, as Reid and Holt's discussion makes clear. These conceptions, seen at their purest in the sixth form of public schools, and related, by means of a particular view of what knowledge was and where it was to be found, to a particular conception of democracy, were stronger than those derived from the elementary school tradition. The result was a system of education where what went on at the top determined what went on at the bottom, and right at the bottom it stopped anything going on at all. As Reid and Holt put it, the only scholars who did stay on at school till 16 were in public and endowed schools, and their experience with 'its text-based literary curriculum' determined 'what should be learned in secondary schools by 11-year-olds who might stay there for two or three years' (pp. 97–8).

Public school derived conceptions of education still play a part, as Edwards (p. 128) makes clear, in educational provision for post-16-year-old students, even with the current emphasis on education for jobs. The proposal by Sir Keith Joseph to have a distinction and merit grade for the GCSE confirms that high grades in these examinations will be the pinnacle of, and *raison d'être* for, secondary education. Success in them is the mode of selection for higher education and part of the pre-vocational training for high status jobs and professions. The evidence is that employers are happy with these examinations and they recruit from their products (Edwards, p. 127). Students themselves are aware that successes in such examinations can lead to 'the more prestigious professional and managerial occupations' (Edwards, p. 127). For conventionally defined able pupils, then, the dominant conception of education is largely a traditional academic one, with little 'reference to vocational relevance, applied knowledge, or new technology' (Edwards, p. 128). Reform has been 'concentrated on what should be done for the rest' and what this consists of, above all at post 16 level, is an education constituted by training for jobs which are usually of low status and which, though on their way, are still well below the horizon. The result as Edwards (p. 128) shows, is that the 'old academicism' is preserved (for the élite) alongside the 'new vocationalism' for the lower orders.

Contrasted to public school derived conceptions of education are those implicit in Troyna and Ball's discussion of ethnic minorities and education in the UK. Some Muslim parents, for example, have a conception of education that is largely derived from their own cultural and religious backgrounds, and one they wish institutionalized in schools of their own (p. 39). They and other ethnic and religious groups may well argue for a conception of education which, as Troyna and Ball put it, encompass 'the provision and maintenance of ethnic minority community language in schools as part of the mainstream curriculum' (p. 42).

Tomlinson shows how conceptions of special education for those 'with learning and behavioural difficulties' have developed over the past 100 years or so, and have become institutionalized. She notes how the particular conceptions can only be understood against the background of 'a technological society' and its demands for 'academic and technical élites and a smaller flexible work force' (p. 47). She points out, too, how the conception of education related to those with special educational needs is meant to address the problem of how to deal 'with large groups who will never be considered suitable to acquire the education or training which will allow them incomes above subsistence level but who, nevertheless, will need training for some kind of self-sufficiency and controlled social behaviour' (p. 59).

Acker draws attention to a number of ways in which schools

have institutionalized different conceptions of education for girls from those for boys (pp. 61–75). Schools may well embody conceptions of education that lead to women being socialized 'to give a high priority to domesticity so that they participate in the labour market intermittently, for low wages and with poor prospects, with mostly female colleagues but under the direction and domination of men' (p. 66). The concern expressed by Sir Keith Joseph about the relative lack of access girls have to maths and science in schools is another sign of conceptions of education that differ for boys and girls (p. 70). Acker cites the 1985 Equal Opportunities Commission Annual Report which draws attention to how in education 'girls and women become scarcer as the qualification level rises' and, where they are found, it is in 'arts, languages, domestic, and commercial subjects rather than in physical sciences, craft subjects and engineering' (p. 64). This clearly will have consequences for earning power and status in the wider society.

Politics and Power: Keeping Competing Conceptions in their Place

Just as conceptions of education involve political issues about the nature of the good society, so does the question of which conceptions of education are to be allowed institutional form. This question is part of a central political issue about, as Dworkin (1978) puts it, 'what it means for a government to treat all its citizens as free, or as independent, or with equal dignity' (p. 127).

The less power is diffused and the more it is centralized (for example in government departments), the less likely it is that the variety of viewpoints about justifiable conceptions of education and their institutionalization will be respected and, hence, that citizens be treated as 'independent or with equal dignity'. This is because the exercise of power by the centre will need to be legitimated by a claim that it knows better than the citizenry at large or than particular groups what is in their interests and what conceptions of the good life and of education are suitable for them. In order for this claim to be sustained views from the grass roots about conceptions of education will, in one way or another, need to be discounted. This is seen most clearly in societies where power, wealth and status are very unequally distributed. In such societies, it will be extremely difficult for those without power to develop their views or to have them taken seriously (Geuss, 1981).

An important consequence of the possession of power is that those with it are well placed to keep off the agenda issues and critiques that they believe are threatening to them (Bachrach and Baratz, 1963). Some examples of this are the 'Great Debate' from 1976 (see Lawton, 1980, pp. 34–41); University Grants Committee and Department of Education and Science policies on universities since 1980; and the processes involved in the closure of the Schools Council (Plaskow, 1985). The more the agenda is controlled, the less public participation there is likely to be in the debate, since any attempt to control the agenda rests on some view about who has a legitimate voice in the matters at issue. Groups who have well argued critiques of current educational policies and of current institutional arrangements, who believe that they are not taken seriously, and who are determined to be taken seriously, will be kept at the periphery. They may be offered 'consultation', when what they want is to influence and change policy and practice and the distribution of resources. The chapters by Troyna and Ball, and by Acker illustrate these points well.

Troyna and Ball show that various ethnic groups want 'a greater say in the orientation and content of their children's education' (p. 39). This involves issues about separate and supplementary schools, about ethnic minority languages, and about the use and control of funds under Section 11 of the Local Government Act of 1966 (p. 42). Troyna and Ball show how consultation was managed, and was seen as 'the process by which those authorized to make a decision convey the nature of their proposals or the facts underlying those proposals to those affected by them' (p. 40). Ethnic minority groups' views on curricular matters were discounted, since they were not compatible 'with the notion of "Education for All" which provided the ideological framework within which the (Swann) Committee's arguments and recommendations were situated' (p. 43). Moreover, such talk as there is of partnership with parents is concerned with 'the surveillance' and 'social control of youth (especially black youth after the urban disturbances of 1980 and 1981)' (p. 44). What it is not concerned with is the form of the educational provision such youths should receive. A number of similar points about social control and children classified as having behavioural or learning difficulties (the heirs of the 'social problem classes') are made by Tomlinson in her discussion of special educational needs (pp. 47–61).

Acker argues that the educational system in the UK is less favourable to girls/women than to boys/men, and that gender codes ensure that cultural ideas about masculinity and femininity are reflected in the practices and classificatory schemes of schools. She notes that there are no 'legitimized pressure groups with an interest solely in women and education' and that, consequently, the government believes it has no reason to take heed of the many unofficial groups and individuals who have something to say about sexism in education (p. 68). Educational policies (and documents on which they are based) are 'sex blind' and have nothing specific to offer women (see, for example, *Better Schools*, Acker, p. 70). Other policies (for example, cuts in teacher education) may reduce disproportionately the opportunities for women.

The history of education is partly the story of how different conceptions of education come into being, of how some are institutionalized or some not; and of how, when they are, they are sustained or of how they are replaced. One test of an open society, and of one that gives equal respect to all of its citizens, is how far those who support different conceptions are allowed the space and opportunity to argue their case; how far they have access to the best material and intellectual resources to help them do so; and how far the merits of their conceptions result in their institutionalization and in changes in what education is taken to be.

It is possible, therefore, to regard some conceptions of education (for example those contained within public schools) as 'insider' ones which have been institutionalized. The assumptions, significance and consequences of these conceptions may be taken for granted. Other conceptions (for example from women's groups and ethnic groups) may be regarded as 'outsider' views and discounted by the processes outlined by Troyna and Ball. These processes are likely to lead to an official agenda for the debate about education which is apparently apolitical, bland, technical and of interest only to those professionals who derive a living from it.

Centralization and Competence: The DES — A Case in Point

The theme of centralization is seen in various places throughout the book and is discussed most fully by Lawton. We take centralization to be the process whereby departments of state (especially the DES, but also the Department of Industry) through the distribution of resources and other means attempt to control the debate about education and the activities of educational institutions.

Lawton describes how the DES has increased its power and influence (largely at the cost of that of teachers, LEAs, and schools) over the school curriculum, and then (largely at the cost of that of the training institutions) over teacher education. The assumption behind such an increase is that the problems faced by the educational system are better solved by central control than by having autonomy diffused throughout it. Whether this assumption is justified is an open question, and one that cannot be answered without an adequate understanding of the role of the centre, of the grounds on which it makes its decisions, and of the quality of them. This would require public scrutiny of the DES. It has however put its own activities beyond the reach of argument. Lawton, who describes himself as 'a DES watcher' reveals that much of his account is based on guesswork, speculation and inference from often small and scattered clues. The successful DES campaign against the Schools Council (Plaskow, 1985) was secret and its 'yellow book' (which contains the views of the DES on the Schools Council) has not been published. No one outside the DES knows how the DES works and probably some people within it do not know either. The most recent account of it (Pile, 1979) is that of an ex-insider, and relying on this as an unbiased or adequate account of the DES' workings is rather like relying on an account from a deputy headmaster as to how schools work. If the DES is a key institution in education this is surely an extraordinary situation.

All of this might be a matter of less concern if there were grounds for thinking that there was little wrong with the DES. There are, however, some grounds that point the other way. As Lawton's discussion makes clear, the DES was the subject of major criticisms in the two reports on it, that of the OECD (1976) and of the Expenditure Committee of the House of Commons (1976). The fact that these are the most recent reports on it is itself worth noting, above all in the context of demands for *teacher* accountability and assessment. The DES reply to the House of Commons Committee Report was all of thirteen pages long and suggested that action had already been taken and that the Committee 'did not really know what it was talking about' (Lawton, 1980, p. 37). But how, without public scrutiny of its decisions and workings, can the citizenry at large know whose view of the DES workings are best founded — that of the DES itself or that of the Expenditure Committee or indeed some other third view? If solutions to educational problems are to be as adequate as possible and are to be seen to be so, is it satisfactory that an institution, whose power is increasing and, hence, whose power to do damage to the quality of these solutions is also increasing, is beyond the public scrutiny of those whose interests it is allegedly supposed to serve? For, as Edmund Burke (speech on the Middlesex election, 1771) put it, 'The greater the power, the more dangerous the abuse'. Further, institutions and individuals at the centre may well set the tone for LEAs and other parts of the educational system (schools, colleges, and so on). They, too, may become closed, secretive, and allow at best only token consultation. As J. and P. White (p. 179) suggest, some teachers, taking their cues from educational and other institutions that they believe work in this way, 'may well unreflectively assume that a certain amount of secrecy and even cover-up are necessary to a smoothly functioning society' — a view that may also be part of the hidden curriculum for their pupils. This raises issues about secrecy, power, and political morality in a democracy. (Some relevant discussion can be found in Arendt, 1962; Bok, 1978 and 1982; Michael, 1982; Nagel, 1978; Williams, 1978).

Education, the Definition of Problems, and Proposed Solutions

One current and highly visible problem that provides both a background to much of the work in this book and that, at the same time, is a major focus of at least three contributions to it (Coffield, Edwards and Jonathan) concerns the relationships between education, work, and unemployment. It is this problem particularly, that raises issues about the quality of centralized thinking (and hence about competence) and about the quality of solutions proffered to educational problems. There are strong suggestions in some of the work in this book that many current educational policies neither rest on an adequate or grounded analysis of the problem nor provide a solution which addresses it. Halsey's comment (quoted by Troyna and Ball, p. 37) that education is seen as a 'waste-paper basket of social policy' where problems that are not taken seriously are 'dubbed "educational" and turned over to schools to solve' draws attention to the fact that problems whose solution lies entirely or largely in other areas of social policy are even so assigned to educational institutions for solution. This general point gains plausibility from the discussions by Apple, Coffield, Edwards, Jonathan, and Reid and Holt.

Apple (p. 164) argues that many of the current proposals for educational reform in the USA are offered in response to what is taken to be a decline in the quality of teachers, of discipline and so on, although it is 'unclear whether all of these conditions *are* getting significantly worse'. Coffield (p. 111) notes that under-lying MSC policy is what he describes as 'a new economic law ... to the effect that it is mainly skill shortages which cause unemployment'. Edwards (p. 129) also notices this diagnosis in David Young's remarks about 'with skills young people can get jobs'. But overall, as Coffield (p. 116) notes, Britain has ten out of the (European) Community's fifteen most disadvantaged regions. It is, surely, an ostentatious triumph of ideology over informed judgment to believe that why parts of North-East England are in the bottom twelve out of 131 regions in Europe and are (with parts of Merseyside, the Midlands and elsewhere) in the same company as 'Calabria, Sardinia, Sicily, and Northern Ireland' is because of a lack of skilled manpower. There is some evidence that this is not the case. Coffield's discussion suggests that the actions of state and other industries in the North-East, through deliberate policy decisions, have resulted in the closure of works and loss of jobs (pp. 111–2). This suggests that the problem is not a failure of supply of labour but a lack of demand for it, brought about by deliberate policy decisions, that the problem has been inadequately analyzed, and that current educational policies designed to address it are irrelevant to its amelioration. Quite different solutions from those currently advocated in the UK are available, even in *educational* policy, to the problems raised by unemployment and technological change, as Reid and Holt's discussion of the Victoria Ministry of Education discussion paper (pp. 105–7) makes clear.

Whether the failure to offer an adequate analysis of these problems and of the solutions proposed to them is because of a lack of competence at the centre or is because of a deliberate strategy undertaken for motives of expediency (noted by Edwards, p. 121) or is because of a combination of these factors or is even because of some other factors cannot be clearly known in advance of investigation. But expediency and lack of competence are at least as initially plausible ways as others of explaining the failure. What is clear is that by focussing the debate on education blame has been shifted, here as in the USA, *from* 'economic, cultural, and social policies and effects of capital *to* the school and other public agencies' (Apple, p. 162). Yet, as Jonathan's discussion argues, without changes at the economic and other related levels changes at the educational level are likely to be ineffective — paregorics at best and not panaceas. And the educational policies will involve vast sums of public money being misspent and will constitute 'an immoral trick played on the young' (Coffield, p. 113).

Where the diagnosis of problems and the generation of solutions to them is left to the centre or relevant part of it and, hence, where the diagnosis and solutions are not put to the test of sustained and informed public scrutiny, failure in diagnosis and in problem solving is most likely. Moreover, where the centre determines what happens throughout the country, then the consequences of any failure are more serious than if a locality or region had got it wrong. The error is generalized and is more difficult to check.

Education and Politics: Educational Studies, Teacher Education, and the Wider Public

The discussion so far should have done enough to show that the central and prior issues about education are political issues and that how these are resolved will have quite specific effects on the quality of citizens' lives and on the quality and worth of the experiences that children and young people have in their classrooms, schools, colleges, and universities. These issues are political in that conceptions of education are located in particular political theories about how a society should be organized so as to yield its citizens the possibility of living lives that they find valuable and satisfying. They are political, too, in that they raise issues about social justice and fairness and about whose conceptions should be institutionalized and how these are to be financed. They are political in that they raise issues about how the enterprise of education is to be controlled, and they are political in that any educational proposal makes demands on other areas of policy — economic, social and so on.

Such a view has important consequences for teacher education, as J. and P. White argue, and, indeed, for the school curriculum. As they put it, 'both teachers and, as they become capable of understanding the issues involved, also pupils, have the moral right to know how a particular curriculum content ... fits into the wider political plan, and the moral duty not blindly to accept this plan and its constituent parts, but to reflect on its moral acceptability' (p. 173). This, as they show, has important implications for the way teachers should conceive their roles and their work and, more generally, for the way schools are run and for the role of pupils in them. It is, they argue, when teachers 'try to *disclaim* a political dimension to their work that their attitude becomes suspect', since, whether they like it or not, their work cannot avoid having such a dimension (p. 180).

Yet it is clear, from some of Lawton's discussion, from that of Hartnett and Naish, as well as from the comments of J. and P. White themselves (pp. 172–3), that the whole tenor of current educational policy is one of suppressing its political dimension. Schools, colleges of higher education, universities (above all their departments of education) are to train their pupils, students, student teachers and so on to produce what the centre wants, or what the centre says industrialists or parents want (even though its judgement in these latter two areas are suspect [cf. Troyna and Ball, and Edwards, p. 127]). The inadequacies of this view of education are discussed in Hartnett and Naish. A central objection to it is that the issues about the aims of education are fundamental, political, and enduring, and, hence, are controversial and beyond the professional expertise of the centre to decide, that they do not admit of closure, and that they are the legitimate subject of public debate (pp. 186–9).

Hartnett and Naish (pp. 192–7) argue further, that the role of educational studies is not simply to help teachers and other professionals address the political and other issues involved in education but that they ought to constitute an intellectual resource, directed towards this purpose, for the public at large. They go on to argue that educational studies have not really taken on either of these roles. They suggest, too, that as the institutions of teacher education are increasingly incorporated into the centre, so the contributions of these institutions to the debate about education's prior and central problems are likely to be even smaller and poorer.

Legitimacy and Social Violence

The final issue we raise here is one about the legitimacy of educational institutions. We take institutions to be legitimate or have legitimacy when they have the justifiable support of those whose interests they are, allegedly, there to serve. In this sense what are conventionally described as the 'forces of law and order' have probably ceased to have legitimacy in the eyes of some groups in Northern Ireland. The extent to which a society's institutions are legitimate is one measure of how genuinely democratic it is. It is also true that institutions that are not legitimate are likely to be ineffective.

Hargreaves' chapter is concerned with this issue as it bears on comprehensive schools. He outlines a number of strategies by which he hopes that the legitimacy of these institutions can be sustained. He suggests that it is a failure in legitimacy that is 'the single most important factor' in explaining 'the under-achievement of pupils between the ages of 14 and 16.' This is perceived by pupils as a 'lack of a collaborative partnership between teacher and learner over what is to be learnt, over how it is to be learnt and over how it is to be assessed' (p. 153). This is an interesting point in the context of effectiveness.

The chapter by J. and P. White, too, raises issues about legitimacy. It is clear that the kind of political understanding they advocate on the part of teachers and pupils is vital to the legitimacy of schools in the eyes of pupils. They argue more generally that schools, in which political, moral and other issues about children's and others' interests are *explicitly* taken seriously, can serve 'as a model of how a community can work relatively harmoniously together — not a tension-less or conflict-free community ... but one in which conflicts are contained and compromises struck within generally agreed procedures' (p. 181). Jonathan notes, in her defence of an education designed to enable people to make informed choices for themselves and not simply to equip them to carry choices out, that if society 'makes choices for the individual' perhaps seeing him or her primarily as someone to be slotted into a niche (decided elsewhere) of a given socio-economic order, he or she is likely to become 'a victim of circumstance — a cog in a machine either of collective irrationality or of cynical vested interests' (p. 144). And where this happens institutional legitimacy is, again, likely to be lost.

The chapters by Apple, Coffield, and Troyna and Ball all support the view that the issue of legitimacy is of urgent practical concern. Apple (p. 162) notes how, in the USA, parents and children are voting with their feet and are setting up their own schools. Troyna and Ball raise similar issues about the legitimacy of the official state institutions of education for ethnic minorities. It is almost certain that the 'unofficial' schools discussed in their chapter have greater legitimacy, in the eyes of their sponsors and of parents whose children go to them, than the official state schools. Further useful discussion of this is to be found in McLean (1985). Coffield's chapter also raises issues about the legitimacy of youth training scheme programmes as these are perceived by those young people who go on them (p. 109). Bullock shows how public schools have retained and extended the confidence of those who use them and have in their eyes, at least, retained their legitimacy.

A number of explanations might be given for the loss of the legitimacy of institutions. It is almost certain to occur when they are captured by a particular section or sections of the population; where the actions of the centre are beyond public scrutiny and beyond genuine accountability; where the public agenda and public participation in the debate about particular groups' interests is restricted; and where the debate has no effect on political action. When there is a loss of legitimacy and when there is no debate of a kind that makes acceptable compromise and mutual adjustment possible, then those groups whose interests, concerns, and advice are given no weight may eventually resort to violence to gain, in the only way they can, that to which they believe, no doubt in many cases quite justifiably, they have a right. The riots and disturbances on the mainland of the UK during the 1980s raise the question of how far such action is likely to become the norm rather than the exception.

Conclusion

The implications of these introductory comments are that the debate about education must be rescued from the banalities of some party politics and from the technicalities of the professionals. It needs to become a properly public debate in which the central political issues raised by education are continuously addressed in an informed and serious fashion. The outcomes of this debate need to have a genuine bearing on policy, practice, and on the control of resources and institutions. Outsiders' conceptions of education need to be brought in from the periphery, and those in the middle need to be seen to deserve their place there by passing the test of publicly conducted critical scrutiny. To achieve this is to begin to put the tradition of education 'in good order' (Reid and Holt, p. 91). It is, too, part of what Raymond Williams (1961 and 1983) has called 'the long revolution'. This book is meant to be a contribution to that debate, to the renewal of that tradition, and to that slow, complex and difficult revolution.

Note

1 Unless otherwise stated, all references thus indicated are to authors' chapters in this book.

References

ARENDT, H. (1962) 'Truth and politics' in LASLETT, P. and RUNCIMAN, W.G. (Eds) *Philosophy, Politics, and Society*, Third Series, Oxford, Basil Blackwell, pp. 104–33.

BACHRACH, P. and BARATZ, M.S. (1963) 'Decisions and nondecisions: an analytical framework', *Political Science Review*, 57, pp. 632–42.

BOK, S. (1978) *Lying: Moral Choice in Public and Private Life*, Brighton Harvester Press.

BOK, S. (1984) *Secrets: On the Ethics of Concealment and Revelation*, Oxford, Oxford University Press.

DWORKIN, R. (1978) 'Liberalism' in HAMPSHIRE, S. (Ed.) *Public and Private Morality*, Cambridge, Cambridge University Press, pp. 113–43.

GEUSS, R. (1981) *The Idea of a Critical Theory: Habermas and the Frankfurt School*, Cambridge, Cambridge University Press.

HOLLIS, M. (1971) 'The pen and the purse', *Proceedings of the Philosophy of Education Society of Great Britain* Supplementary Issue, 5, 2, pp. 153–69.

INGLIS, F. (1985) *The Management of Ignorance: A Political Theory of the Curriculum*, Oxford, Basil Blackwell.

LAWTON, D. (1980) *The Politics of the School Curriculum*, London, Routledge and Kegan Paul.

McLEAN, M. (1985) 'Private supplementary schools and the ethnic challenge to state education in Britain' in BROCK, C. and TULASIEWICZ, W. (Eds) *Cultural Identity and Educational Policy*, London, Croom Helm, pp. 326–45.

MICHAEL, J. (1982) *The Politics of Secrecy*, London, Penguin Books.

NAGEL, T. (1978) 'Ruthlessness in public life' in HAMPSHIRE, S. (Ed.) *Public and Private Morality*, Cambridge, Cambridge University Press, pp. 75–91.

PILE, W. (1979) *The Department of Education and Science*, London, Allen and Unwin.

PLASKOW, M. (1985) (Ed.) *The Life and Death of the Schools Council*, Lewes, Falmer Press.

WILLIAMS, B. (1978) 'Politics and moral character' in HAMPSHIRE, S. (Ed.) *Public and Private Morality*, Cambridge, Cambridge University Press, pp. 55–73.

WILLIAMS, R. (1961) *The Long Revolution*, London, Chatto and Windus.

WILLIAMS, R. (1983) *Towards 2000*, Chatto, London and Windus.

The Department of Education and Science: Policy Making at the Centre

Denis Lawton

The Historical Background

It is impossible to understand the Department of Education and Science (DES), as it is now, without knowing a good deal about its historical background. As with many British governmental (and other) institutions, the present form of the DES is, to a large extent, the product of its history.

The early central authority was weak — in some respects, deliberately weak. The first government grant to education was in 1833 when Lord Althorp, the Chancellor of the Exchequer, included in the Report of the Committee of Supplies, a sum of up to £20,000 for education. The money was packaged in this way in order to avoid yet another Education Bill being voted out by the House of Lords. The £20,000 was allocated not to any government department, but was to be distributed to two religious societies (the National Society and the British and Foreign Schools Society) to supplement their own funds for school buildings. The payment of the grant was controlled by Treasury rules, but there was no intention, at this stage, that the state should control the schools themselves.

The reason for this caution (and sensitivity) was connected with philosophical views then current about the nature of government. The prevailing political philosophy was laissez-faire, but the voices of the radicals were beginning to be louder and more numerous. The question of education for the poor was central to the debate about government intervention.

The 1833 grant was a typical English compromise: yielding on one principle (giving money), but maintaining another (not interfering). Within a few years the annual grants to the religious societies had increased to such an extent that some kind of central organization was clearly necessary. In 1838 a Select Committee on Education had demonstrated the need for extending education for the poor beyond the capacity of the two religious societies, and, in the following year, the Committee of the Privy Council on Education was established. This was to be a very small body comprising the Lord President, the Lord Privy Seal, the Home Secretary and the Chancellor of the Exchequer, who were charged with the duty of superintending the expenditure voted by Parliament for the purpose of promoting public education. The weakness of this central authority has often been commented upon by historians. Bishop (1971) claimed that the Committee of the Council became at first an irrelevance, then an anachronism and, finally, a laughing stock.

Nevertheless, a very able administrator was appointed Secretary to the Committee, Dr. James Kay-Shuttleworth. One of his early decisions was to issue a minute making the award of grant dependent on inspection. Two inspectors were appointed for this task, the first of Her Majesty's Inspectors. Initially, the role of HMI was seen in terms of making sure that public money was spent in accordance with regulations, but even this was condemned as dangerous state interference by some advocates of laissez-faire.

Hostility to state intervention in education continued throughout the nineteenth century, and was intensified from time to time by events such as the 1870 (Forster) Education Act which extended the participation of government. However, W.E. Forster, Vice-President of the Council, who introduced the Bill in the House of Commons, refused to consider the idea of elementary schools directly controlled by the central authority rather than by local school boards. He feared that it would give the central authority far too much power.

Another reason for the weakness of the central authority in education was that there was no unified control over the developing education system. After the 1851 Great Exhibition, it was increasingly recognized that there was a need for scientific and technical instruction of 'the industrial classes'. Grants were given to schools whose pupils were successful in a range of scientific and technical subjects. These grants were controlled, not by the Committee of the Privy Council but by a new body, the Science and Art Department, which was officially under the control of the Board of Trade until 1856. Even after that date, when it became part of the

Education Department, it maintained a semi-independent status, and a separate group of inspectors.

By 1858, the amount of public money being spent on elementary schools had increased far beyond that envisaged in 1833 or even in 1839. Those who had opposed public education became increasingly concerned with the principle of value for money. A Royal Commission was set up under the chairmanship of the Duke of Newcastle. Its report, published in 1861, was highly critical of elementary education. One of the results was the 'Revised Code' of 1862, which involved an extreme form of central financial control by means of a centrally devised curriculum, enforced on teachers by the dreaded system of 'payment by results' supervised by HMIs. Although payment by results survived in a modified form until the end of the century, and, in the short term, gave HMIs and the central authority very great powers of control, in the longer run it served to diminish central influence.

Payment by results was hated by the majority of teachers. It was not welcomed by many others, including such HMIs as Matthew Arnold, who saw the 1862 Revised Code as ruining the cooperation between HMIs and teachers. One result of this kind of central control was the development of the National Union of Elementary Teachers (NUET), which later became the National Union of Teachers. This was a professional organization of teachers opposed both to payment by results, in particular, and to central control, in general. The policy survived as a major plank of NUT policy, and was connected with the NUT's decision to oppose the continuance of the Curriculum Study Group in 1962.

After a series of committees, commissions and education acts in the nineteenth century, many of which increased educational provision and the budget for it, the Board of Education was eventually established in 1900. But the fears expressed in 1833 and 1839 had not entirely disappeared. State control of education was still viewed with disfavour, and even with alarm. Section IV of the 1899 Board of Education Act made provision for a Consultative Committee on Education, consisting of 'not less than two-thirds of persons qualified to represent the views of universities and other bodies interested in education'. The setting up of this Consultative Committee (succeeded in 1944 by the Central Advisory Councils) reflected the feeling that too much government control was distinctly unhealthy, and that some kind of independent watch-dog was needed to guard against governmental excesses. The same traditional dislike of too much concentrated power may have been behind the more recent parliamentary reforms of Norman St. John Stevas, resulting in the establishment of a number of parliamentary select committees, including one on education. The scrutiny by select committees is supposed to ensure both a critical review of government policies and a continuous analysis of the exercise of power by civil servants and in the case of Education, HMIs. This is another survival of nineteenth century attitudes: bureaucrats and inspectors were to be distrusted almost as much as politicians!

The 1902 Education Act also served to extend state education, especially by making possible, for the first time, public expenditure on secondary schools. But by now another feature of the current 'system' was developing: *local* education authorities, and the important notion of 'partnership' between central and local government. The very considerable powers of local education authorities (LEAs) also owe much to the nineteenth century distrust of state control and over-centralization. The LEAs, which came into existence with the 1902 Act, were much more powerful than the school boards they replaced. They were made responsible for voluntary schools, secondary and technical education, as well as elementary schools. The idea of balancing central power with local democratic control developed strongly in England, and is connected with the importance attached to local choice and decision-making. The 1902 Act was a very important landmark in the development of the idea of a national system locally administered. But part of the function of local administration is the critical interpretation of national policies. The 1902 Act created a more coherent national system, but, at the same time, guarded against central excesses by strengthening local authorities.

Although the 1944 Education Act has often been hailed as a major innovation and reform, in many respects it is simply a development from nineteenth-century ideas and very much in line with the 1902 changes. A possible exception is in the field of curriculum control. The elementary school curriculum was controlled by codes from 1862 until 1926, when the code lapsed to be replaced by a series of national reports. However, central control of the secondary curriculum survived for another twenty years.

The 1902 Act was followed, in 1904, by the Secondary Regulations — a set of precise curricular requirements which officially remained in operation until the 1944 Act. Whether the absence of curriculum control in 1944 was a deliberate Machiavellian policy (White, 1975) or simply a thoughtless omission, (Raison, 1976) has not been completely resolved, although the balance of evidence, as usual, is on the side of muddle and mistake rather than conspiracy. The effect of the 1944 Act, however, if not the intention, has become quite clear: much control (especially curriculum control) passed from the centre to the local authorities. It was local authorities who were to be responsible for efficient education in the schools.

The 1944 Education Act also transformed the Board of Education into a Ministry. A Minister of Education replaced the President of the Board of Education. This was an apparent elevation of the importance of education within government, but not necessarily an increase in power at the centre. The Act stipulated that public education should be organized in three progressive stages — primary, secondary and 'further' — and gave LEAs the responsibility for providing these three stages (but with universities remaining under central, if indirect, control). The 1944 Education Act is of particular importance in considering the role of the DES today, but the terms of the Act, and the intention behind some of its wording are puzzling not to say ambiguous (Aldrich and Leighton, 1985).

Aldrich and Leighton focus on the notion of partnership as the major feature of the 1944 Education Act. They ask a series of very important questions. 'Was the partnership established in 1944 an effective one?'. 'Were the various parties clear as to their respective functions?'. 'Was the framework of the partnership able to cope with the changing social, political and economic circumstances?'. 'Was it an effective blueprint for education in the post war world?'. 'Was it properly implemented?'. 'Is it relevant to the 1980s?'. The result of Aldrich and Leighton asking these questions suggests that the 1944 Act is now out of date and should be replaced by new legislation. But the analysis they make of the 1944 Act is equally useful in demonstrating the weaknesses of the Ministry of Education and its successor, the DES. The Act, they suggest, failed adequately to define the role of the central authority. Moreover, the status of the Ministry of Education (and the DES) has been low in terms of the calibre of politicians in its top posts. The Ministry, and later the DES, also tended to be regarded by civil servants as a Department without its own policy and without the means to implement policy. The central authority in education had been weak and remained so.

Some educationists have seriously doubted whether there is an educational *system* in England and Wales. Forty years after the 1944 Education Act there is still no regional organization of the central authority, although some of its policy branches are organized on a territorial basis. Since 1944 a number of significant changes have taken place in education, but the 1944 Act is still the central legislative machinery, although modified in minor ways by more recent Acts.

Change in Style in the DES

The Ministry of Education became a Department of State in 1964, after the Robbins Report, but that has not significantly altered its functioning as a central authority. The DES, unlike ministries of education in most other European countries, does not run schools, colleges or universities, or employ teachers or operate public libraries. In view of this uniqueness, it is surprising that so little has been written about how the central authority functions and almost nothing 'from within'. One important exception is the book *The Department of Education and Science* written by a former Permanent Under-Secretary, Sir William Pile. This book was written in the late 1970s (after his retirement) and published in 1979. It may be interesting and productive to look at some of the statements made by Pile and to analyze the changes that have taken place since then. The purpose of this exercise will be to show that in recent years there has been a very marked change of style at the centre; a change of style through which politicians and civil servants have sought to increase power at the centre and hence to weaken the position of the other 'partners' in the education service.

Pile's book is particularly interesting, since it was written at 'the end of an era'; an era of decentralisation and of little intervention. What has emerged in the last ten, and above all in the last five, years is the beginning of something quite different, the growth of centralization.

In order to demonstrate this process of increasing centralization, it will be useful to examine what has happened in the following areas:

(i) partnership with LEAs;
(ii) the school curriculum;
(iii) the Schools Council;
(iv) higher education, including teacher training.

Let us begin each case with a quotation from Pile, and then assess the changes that have occurred since 1979.

Partnership with LEAs

Pile has a whole section devoted to 'the role of the Department's partners in policy formation'. He has this to say:

> In the discussions that take place ... in the preparation of the major report, it is frequently the representatives of the local authority or teachers' associations, or individual chief education officers or teachers, who make major contributions. 'If we look to the past', a past President of the Society of Education Officers has remarked, 'we must certainly recognize that during the course of this century most of our major educational advances have been due to the initiative and experiment of individual Authorities. This is probably no exaggeration, and indeed what might be expected, since it is individual chief education officers and individual teachers who have the experience that comes from working at the coal face; and this experience is reflected in the contributions that their representatives make as members of advisory bodies. (Pile, 1979, p. 39)

In Pile's time the DES was clearly non-interventionist and continued so with the possible exception of some degree of coercion following the issuing in 1965 of Circular 10/65 requiring LEAs to submit plans for comprehensive schooling. But in 1975–6 when two important events followed in quick succession.

First, the OECD Report on the DES; second, the Expenditure Committee Report on Policy-making in the DES. The task of the OECD experts was to examine the 1972 White Paper 'Education: A Framework for Expansion' as a piece of policy-making. One of their more significant criticisms was to comment on the almost complete neglect of the 16–19 age group, but the major criticism was of the way that the DES was run as a 'Ministry of Education'. The experts commented on the high standard of civil servants, but were critical of their inability, or unwillingness, to develop educational policy. The chief features of its policy formation process seemed to be a desire to minimize controversy; to reduce possible alternatives to matters of choice of resource allocation; to limit the planning process to those parts of the education service and and to those functions controlled by the DES; and to exploit as fully as possible the powers, prerogatives and responsibilities given to the DES under the 1944 Education Act; and, at the same time, to undertake as much as possible the full role of the government in the determination of the future course of educational policy, and to minimize it in the eyes of the general public. All of this constituted an interesting appreciation of DES style.

During the same year (1975/76) the DES was also subjected to the scrutiny and criticism of the House of Commons Expenditure Committee, which made a general study of policy-making in the DES. One complaint was that the DES was excessively secretive; another was that it lacked adequate planning techniques and organization. The DES was again accused of reducing policy-making to a matter of resource allocation.

Since 1976 there has, however, been a change in attitude by DES officials. They have been more willing to develop central policies and pursue them vigorously. Since 1979 with its change of government, they have been helped both by the fact that Margaret Thatcher's Conservative administration has had a clear financial policy, and also by the fact that the longest serving Secretary of State for Education for some time, Sir Keith Joseph, has had firm views about education, many of which have been compatible with the developing centrism of the civil servants in Elizabeth House. This is most clearly illustrated by the willingness of DES officials to use financial control as a means to save money as well as to effect other kinds of change. Having been criticized for having only a policy on resource allocation, they now use their well developed fiscal skills to enforce other centrist policies. The old slogan that 'power is where the money is' may not be the whole truth, but it is certainly a large part of it.

Local authority expenditure is financed partly out of rates and partly by a grant from central government, the rate support grant (RSG). Local expenditure is constrained in two ways: by local resistance to rate rises, and by the amount that central government is prepared to provide from taxation. In 1983, central government sought further control over local government expenditure by legislation which would give central government power to limit the rates in any authority where the level of expenditure was too high. The effect on education of this 'rate-capping' policy in 1984/85 has been very serious. Education is both one of the big spenders in local authorities and has also been singled out as a major cause of overspending. LEAs, thus, now have less control over their educational expenditure, with the final decision about some kinds of expenditure in the hands of the DES. All this comes at a time when LEAs have greater need for discretion in dealing with local problems arising from such factors as falling pupil rolls in schools and the consequent need to maintain a broad curriculum.

The DES has taken advantage of the changing financial situation in order to implement aspects of a central policy. The Education (Grants and Awards) Act of 1984, for example, has enabled the government to pay education support grants to LEAs for specific 'innovations and improvement' that the DES wished to encourage. This is a major departure from the policy of allocating money to LEAs and of allowing them to decide for its expenditure on their own local priorities. Two points about the 1984 Act should be stressed. First, it does not provide extra money for these innovations, but withholds about £47m. (or 0.5% of the total) from the general grant; second, it involved LEAs in bidding and competing against each other for the withheld money which was to be allocated according to DES priorities. Such priorities were 'management training', 'business studies', 'mathematics teaching', 'computer studies', and 'new examinations'. These priorities may or may not have coincided with those of the LEAs.

More serious is the conflict between the DES and HMI over financial policy. Successive HMI reports on LEAs have demonstrated that the financial constraints imposed by central government have had an adverse effect on the provision of education in many local authorities. The Secretary of State for Education has, however, continued to maintain his stance that factors other than the finance available are the really important ones. The important general issue here is that LEA autonomy means little unless adequate funds are provided. However, the rate-capping policy means that LEAs are not free to add to their funds for education by increasing the local rate. Central government decides what money is to be spent on education, and imposes that limit rigidly and harshly.

The School Curriculum

'A traditional feature of the English system, which gives responsibility for determining the curriculum of the schools to the LEAs and teachers and not to the central department ...' (Pile, 1979, p. 35)

'The Department's role in relation to the school curriculum has traditionally been strictly limited. The Education Act

> 1944 specifically provided that 'secular instruction' . . . in the schools shall be under the control of LEAs. As a rule, LEAs delegate the responsibility to heads of individual schools. In practice this has meant that the teachers have been within limits free to determine their own curricula.' (*Ibid*, p. 94)

> 'In practice, the Department has traditionally been reluctant to intervene in curriculum matters . . .' (*Ibid*, p. 95)

Control of the curriculum probably marks the most dramatic change in the swing of power from LEAs to the DES. An account of this is given elsewhere (Lawton, 1980 and 1984), but a brief summary and updating will be useful here. 1976 is again a significant year for the beginning of the story, although the major events come later.

1976 was the year of the 'Great Debate in Education' which followed the then Prime Minister's (James Callaghan) speech at Ruskin College, Oxford. After a series of national discussions, the agenda for which was set in somewhat narrow terms by the DES, a green paper on education was produced in July 1977, which argued that much more central interest in the curriculum was appropriate and necessary. It was suggested that LEAs, taking account of local circumstances, should coordinate the curriculum. Furthermore, warning was given that the Secretaries of State proposed to invite LEAs and teachers to take part in consulations about a review of curricular arrangements.

The DES Circular 14/77, which followed, asked for very detailed information about the curriculum, and went far beyond what might have been expected from the original green paper. The publication of *Local Authority Arrangements for the School Curriculum, Report on Circular 14/77*, (DES, 1979) indicated that the DES was not satisfied with the kind of curriculum control being exercised. It asserted that LEAs did not have adequate information and lacked a curriculum policy. In 1979 the election of the Conservative government under Margaret Thatcher, intensified the move towards centrism. The critical report on what LEAs were doing was followed by the DES's own solution *A Framework for the School Curriculum* (DES, 1980a). This was openly centrist in tone, and extremely bureaucratic in style. At the same time, Her Majesty's Inspectorate (HMI) issued *A View of the Curriculum* (DES, 1980b). This was important for two reasons: first, because it was fundamentally different from the DES document; second, it indicated the growing tension between HMI and the DES on curriculum questions. By 1981 attempts had been made to manage the tension, and *The School Curriculum* (DES, 1981b), was discussed with HMI. *The School Curriculum*, however, still displayed a greater commitment to bureaucratic efficiency than to professional commitment and educational quality. This document was followed by circulars 6/81 and 8/83 which reminded local education authorities of their responsibilities on curriculum policy. LEAs are now regularly instructed on national curriculum policy, and are requested to show how much progress they are making towards meeting national criteria.

Much of this central initiative was not only necessary but long overdue. A well thought out policy to relate curriculum response at national, local and school level is essential in the 1980s, and would, had it been done, have improved comprehensive school organization in the 1960s. Unfortunately, the policy has not always been clear; in fact, at times, it has been confused because there is lack of coordination between DES officials and HMI. The confusion has arisen because civil servants fail to make proper use of the professional expertise of HMI, and that available elsewhere in the education service.

Another, much less welcome initiative has been the tendency of ministers to make pronouncements on the curriculum which are overtly political. In March 1982 Sir Keith Joseph, for example, addressing the Institute of Directors, stated that 'schools should preach the moral virtue of free enterprise and the pursuit of profit' (*Times Educational Supplement*, 26 March) and, in 1983, Sir Keith continued to discuss the need for simple economics as part of a core curriculum. This latter may well be a sensible view, but one which ought to be argued in educational, not in political, terms.

Another controversial intervention in the curriculum arose from a reaction to the popularity of CND and the growth of peace studies in schools. On 22 June 1983, Rhodes Boyson, then Parliamentary Under-Secretary with responsibility for schools, stated in the House of Commons, in reply to a question from a Conservative member, 'I share my Honourable Friend's concern about the growth of peace — or rather appeasement — studies, because that is basically what they are'. Schools were, in fact, encouraged to make use of the Central Office of Information pamphlet *A Balanced View* (1982) which outlined the case for retaining nuclear weapons. Furthermore, in March 1983, Sir Keith expressed disapproval of national criteria in physics which included the political and social implications of the subject. This would be less worrying if the Secretary of State did not have the power to withhold approval of 16+ examinations where they do not meet national requirements. What concerns many educationists is the combination of the exercise of power by the DES with party political interference.

Sir Keith Joseph has taken a great deal of interest in examinations, especially the new 16+ GCSE. This examination is to be much more closely controlled from the centre than any in recent history, and each examining board must adhere to nationally agreed criteria. Most educationists realize how complex and delicate the task of producing national criteria is, and how important it is not to go too far in the direction of control from the centre. For the Secretary of State to take an interest in the national criteria and make interventions of a political kind in what amounts to syllabus writing is a matter for concern. It may be no more than a harmless eccentricity, but it could be a dangerous precedent.

Central control of the curriculum and of national criteria for examinations has come about rapidly and is not unassociated with political bias. It represents more than any other centrist tendency a major shift of power in the educational system. It is, thus, unfortunate that it fails to represent a convincing educational policy.

The Schools Council

In 1962 a 'curriculum study group' was set up within the Department to explore the possibilities. In the event this unit did not prove acceptable as a permanent agency for curriculum development. It became apparent that to obtain the active support of teachers and LEAs an agency must be created that was independent of the Department and whose constitution reflected the primacy of the teachers in the curriculum field. (Pile, 1979, pp. 101–2)

That agency was the Schools Council and, in the years following its creation it emerged as a very important and not unsuccessful body in England and Wales concerned with the curriculum and examinations and their development. However, by the 1970s it was increasingly subjected to criticism. Some of this came from the DES and some from HMI. One interpretation of the events of the 1970s and the early 1980s is that the DES and HMI resented the independence of the Schools Council and wished to exert more direct influence over curricula and examinations (Plaskow, 1985). The most blatant attack on the Schools Council came from the DES in the form of the secret, but extensively leaked, 'Yellow Paper' or 'Yellow Book' of 1976. Among other things, it said,

> The Schools Council has performed moderately in commissioning development work in particular curricular areas; has had little success in tackling examination problems, despite the availability of resources which its predecessor (the SSEC) never had; and it has scarcely begun to tackle the problems of the curriculum as a whole. Despite some good quality staff work the overall performance of the Schools Council has, in fact, both on curriculum and examinations, been generally mediocre.

From the time of the Yellow Book open season was declared on the Schools Council by the DES. In 1977, a review of the Schools Council's constitution was commissioned in response to the accusation that it was 'politically' influenced by the teacher unions. A number of very sensible streamlining reforms were suggested but despite undertaking them a Committee was set up to review the workings of the Council under the chairmanship of Mrs. Trenaman. The Committee reported favourably (DES, 1981a). But the DES made its own counter-recommendations and the Secretary of State announced that the Schools Council would be abolished and be replaced by two smaller bodies: the Secondary Examinations Council (SEC) and the School Curriculum Development Committee (SCDC). This decision by the centre was important for at least two reasons. Firstly, it separated the curriculum from examinations, contrary to professional opinion going back at least as far as the Report of the Norwood Committee, in 1943. Secondly, members of the two Committees are nominated by the Secretary of State, and do not serve as representatives of any organization or constituency in the education service. Attention has already been drawn to the fact that examinations were to be controlled by another subtle device, the national criteria which had to be approved by the Secretary of State for Education. It was thus the Secretary of State who was to confirm his controlling influence both of the curriculum and of examinations.

Higher Education, including Teacher Training

It is a much prized characteristic of British universities, modern as well as ancient, that they are self-governing in-

> stitutions, usually operating under the provisions of Royal
> Charters, with virtually complete academic autonomy and a
> large measure of administrative autonomy, which they have
> for the most part retained, despite their growing dependence
> on public funds. (Pile, 1979, p. 154)

The DES is, of course, concerned not only with universities, but
also with 'public sector' higher education in the polytechnics and in
other institutions which are nominally the responsibility of LEAs,
or voluntary (religious) bodies. Public sector higher education is
coordinated by the National Advisory Body (NAB) and the universities by the University Grants Committee (UGC). NAB, at a time
of severe financial constraints and with a declining amount of
money available for higher education, has increasingly become an
agent of central policy in higher education.

Similarly, the autonomy of universities preserved by the UGC
has been seriously eroded. This erosion and consequential increase
in central control has been achieved by financial means. The traditional independence of universities was weakened first by massive
cuts in funding starting in 1981, and more recently (1985) by the
announcement of further cuts at least until 1990. Universities were,
and are being, forced to implement cuts which they do not think
advisable with the UGC supervising the policy of university con-
traction as part of central policy.

This policy is enunciated in the 1985 green paper on *The
Development of Higher Education into the 1990s* which urges universities to be more efficient and to look for money elsewhere than
from government on the very dubious argument that money from
industry would give them more independence. Other policies being
forced on reluctant universities (and on a reluctant UGC) include
that of selective funding for research. Traditionally, universities have
maintained the principle that all university teachers are also researchers. Some do more (and better) research than others, but all
do research, since part of any university's rationale is what is taken
to be the necessarily close relationship between university teaching
and research. Whether this doctrine is true or false matters less here
than the fact that universities are being forced to abandon it and to
label some academics as teachers and others as teachers *and* researchers.

On teacher training, Pile (1979) writes:

> HM Inspectors also have a considerable role (in teacher
> training). Each college and polytechnic department of educa-
> tion has an HMI assigned to it, who advises on the general

running of the courses, on the curriculum and on related matters such as arrangements for teaching practice. HMI organize courses for serving teachers, which along with courses organized by LEAs and other bodies are an important element in the growing provision of in-service training. The university departments of education are not subject to the controls described above. (p. 123)

Since this paragraph was written, much has changed. Government policy has determined that the teaching force should be smaller, but better. The White Paper *Teaching Quality* set out a number of criteria which were to be insisted upon for all colleges and universities teaching Bachelor of Education degrees (BEd) and the Postgraduate Certificate in Education (PGCE) courses, both leading to qualified teacher status conferred by the DES.

In order to enforce this policy, the Secretary of State set up a new body the Council for the Accreditation of Teacher Education (CATE). The DES looks to this Council for advice on whether a course conforms to the criteria set out in the annexe to the Circular, 3/84 (*Initial Teacher Training: Approval of Courses*). The criteria require that:

(a) institutions should develop and run their initial teacher training courses in close partnership with experienced practising school-teachers;

(b) teacher trainers should have regular and frequent experience of classroom teaching;

(c) teaching practice and school experience together should amount to no less than fifteen weeks; the higher education and initial training for intending teachers should include the equivalent of at least two full years' course time devoted to subject studies at a level appropriate to higher education;

(d) students should be prepared to teach the full range of pupils which they might encounter in ordinary schools, with their diversity of ability, behaviour, social background, ethnic and cultural origins;

(e) institutions should carefully assess the personal and intellectual qualities of candidates for teacher training, and should involve experienced practising teachers in the selection of students.

There is, in addition, an overriding criterion that PGCE courses should be of at least thirty six weeks' duration. Most had been around thirty two weeks long.

These criteria are a strange mixture of truisms and unexamined assumptions. They serve, however, to increase the power of the DES and HMI. Both university departments of education and those in polytechnics as well as in colleges of higher education become subject to accreditation by CATE. CATE will act only on the basis of a report by HMI on a visit to an institution. Admittedly, universities do not have to be visited by HMI, who come in only by invitation. But if a university department of education is not visited, it cannot be accredited, and will lose its initial training courses and may have to close. The principle of autonomy remains, for what it is worth, but the authority of the centre has been significantly extended. Whether this is hypocrisy or a subtle compromise, the result is the same — more central control.

Toward an Analysis

Throughout this chapter I have referred generally to the DES as the central authority in education. This is not satisfactory. We must sub-divide the central authority into three separate powers at the national level: political, bureaucratic and professional. They may or may not be in accord on central policy. In fact it will be argued that the three central power groups will, to a large extent, possess distinct, even conflicting ideologies. The three groups are:

(i) Politicians who include not only the ministerial head of department (the Secretary of State for Education) and the Ministers of State and Parliamentary Under-Secretaries attached to the Department, but also their political advisers. These last have grown in number in recent years.

(ii) The bureaucrats are the senior civil servants who work in the DES. The most senior DES official is the Permanent Secretary who is assisted by a small number (about four) of deputy secretaries plus a chief legal adviser. Each of the deputy secretaries has responsibility for a group of branches of the DES. Deputy secretaries also act as chairmen of policy groups within the departmental planning organization. Working for them are assistant secretaries, and, ultimately, all the 2500 or so civil servants working for the DES. Only the most senior are likely to affect government policy in any significant way.

(iii) Finally, the professionals are the 450 or so HMIs. The Senior Chief Inspector has the rank of Deputy Secretary, but, significantly, does not necessarily report to the Permanent Secretary in the DES, but has the right of direct access to the Secretary of State. There have been interesting occasions when this right has been exercised and, in recent years, it has been jealously defended against ambitious permanent secretaries in the DES.

These groups will tend to subscribe to three differing ideologies. Reality will not be as neat as the following model suggests (table 1). Some DES officials may be more like the professionals, and some HMIs might well have views closer to the bureaucrats or even to Conservative politicians. But in general the categorization can be shown to hold.

Table 1.

EDUCATIONAL IDEOLOGIES

	Beliefs	*Values*	*Tastes*
Politicians	Market forces	freedom of choice	independent schools
Bureaucrats (DES)	good administration management system maintenance	efficiency	central control exams tests
Professionals (HMI)	professionalism experience of practice	quality	impressionistic evaluation

It may be reasonable to derive from these three ideologies differing views of issues and policies in education. On curriculum, we might well find that the politicians are addicted to such slogans as 'basics', the DES bureaucrats would be concerned with 'specified objectives' (there is even evidence for this in Pile, 1979), whilst the HMI would give professional support for a 'common curriculum'. Almost any issue in education will provide evidence of tensions and conflicting ideologies between the three groups — politicians, bureaucrats and HMIs. Evidence for this can be gleaned from the public utterances (written or spoken) of the three groups.

What is suggested here is that the DES as the central authority in education should be treated not as a consensual but as a 'tension system'. Part of the fascination and importance of DES-watching is to detect issues which are conflict-generating, and to see how they are resolved within the tension system. Elsewhere it has been suggested (Lawton, 1984) that such analysis needs more work of a detailed kind before the model can be verified. However ideologies can be assigned to particular groups by means of the content analysis of publications. This is not difficult — but is time-consuming. However, it may be increasingly important if we are to understand the depth of centrism. Only by knowing much more about the strength of support inside the central authority for various policies can those outside become more effective in moderating the dangers of central control.

References

ALDRICH, R. and LEIGHTON, P. (1985) *Education: Time for a New Act?* London, University of London Institute of Education.

BISHOP, A.S. (1971) *The Rise of a Central Authority for Education*, Cambridge, Cambridge University Press.

DEPARTMENT OF EDUCATION AND SCIENCE (1979) *Local Authority Arrangements for the School Curriculum*, Report on Circular 14/77, London, HMSO.

DEPARTMENT OF EDUCATION AND SCIENCE (1980a) *A Framework for the School Curriculum*, London, HMSO.

DEPARTMENT OF EDUCATION AND SCIENCE (1980b) *A View of the Curriculum*, London, HMSO.

DEPARTMENT OF EDUCATION AND SCIENCE (1981a) *Review of the Schools Council*, (The Trenaman Report), London, HMSO.

DEPARTMENT OF EDUCATION AND SCIENCE (1981b) *The School Curriculum*, DES Circular 6/81, London, HMSO.

LAWTON, D. (1980) *The Politics of the School Curriculum*, London, Routledge and Kegan Paul.

LAWTON, D. (1984) *The Tightening Grip*, London, University of London Institute of Education.

PILE, W. (1979) *The Department of Education and Science* London, Allen and Unwin.

PLASKOW, M. (Ed.) (1985) *The Life and Death of the Schools Council*, Lewes, Falmer Press.

RAISON, T. (1976) *The Act and the Partnership*, Centre for Studies in Social Policy.

WHITE, J.P. (1975) 'The end of the compulsory curriculum' in *The Curriculum*, Doris Lee Lectures 1975, Studies in Education, London, University of London.

Partnerships, Consultation and Influence: State Rhetoric in the Struggle for Racial Equality

Barry Troyna and Wendy Ball

The Era of 'Regressive Educational Offensives'

The history of political initiatives and interventionist policies in education in the UK reveals a tenacious commitment to the view that the school should be the principal site for the promotion of equality of opportunity. But as Professor Halsey pointed out in the early 1970s, such approaches are based on unrealistic, liberatory premises because they ignore the structural basis of inequalities in the UK. He suggested then that these policies and initiatives were embedded in a political ideology which treats,

> ... education as the waste paper basket of social policy — a repository for dealing with social problems where solutions are uncertain or where there is a disinclination to wrestle with them seriously. Such problems are prone to be dubbed 'educational' and turned over to the schools to solve. (1972, p. 8)

In the mid-1980s this manoeuvre constitutes a particularly important weapon in the present government's ideological armoury. For example, as the rate of youth unemployment accelerates, the inability of school-leavers to find a job has become increasingly interpreted as an educational problem. In turn, this has generated crude functionalist theories of education and, in its White Paper, *Better Schools*, a sharp reminder from central government to teachers that: 'Education at school should promote enterprise and adaptability in order to increase young people's chances of finding employment or creating it for themselves and others' (DES, 1985,

p. 3). This political and ideological sleight of hand also provides the government with a justification for the introduction of a series of measures designed to enhance compatibility between what students experience and learn at school and what is (supposedly) expected of them from employers. This ideological conception of schooling as a direct preparation for work has presaged a range of what Stuart Hall terms 'regressive educational offensives' (1983, p. 2). These crystallize around such notions as 'national needs', 'relevance', 'accountability' and 'competence' which, together, form the *leitmotiv* of *Better Schools*. In specific terms they have provided a legitimating gloss, on the one hand, to the greater involvement of central government and employers in decisions affecting the curriculum and examinations, and, on the other, a correlative decline of the role of teachers in these decisions. Two examples should be sufficient to sustain this argument. First, the introduction of the Technical and Vocational Education Initiative (TVEI) stemmed from the unprecedented involvement of a non-educational body, the Manpower Services Commission, in educational decision-making. In fact, the traditional educational policy-making community was not even consulted at the planning stage of TVEI (Moon and Richardson, 1984). Second, the abolition of the Schools Council and its replacement by the newly-formed School Curriculum Development Committee wrested influence over curriculum matters away from professional teachers' organizations and enhanced the powers of central government in this sphere. These developments are only the tip of the iceberg; nevertheless, they suggest that the distinctive mode of state interference in the education system, and the spurious rationale for intervention should be matters for serious concern for as Brian Simon points out:

> . . . involvement by the state in the restructuring and control of education for social/political purposes has been apparent at least from the middle of the last century and earlier. What is new are the modes of control now being developed and brought into play. Significantly, the state, instead of working through and with other social organisations (specifically local authorities and teachers' organisations) is now very clearly seeking a more direct and unitary system of control than has ever been thought politic — or even politically possible — in the past. (1984, p. 21)

This brief perusal of national developments on the educational landscape should provide some indication of the ideological and political context in which the struggle for racial equality in education is being fought. It is, of course, a struggle which assumes different forms, priorities and strategies; these vary from one locale to another and are likely to be informed and structured by different class, religious, gender and ethnic interests. Nevertheless, and at the risk of oversimplification, it is a struggle which coheres, more or less, around the demand from black parents and community groups for a greater say in the orientation and content of their children's education. For some groups, such as many Muslim parents in Bradford and Brent, the goal would be the establishment of independent and voluntary-aided Muslim schools which would allow for the retention and perpetuation of Islamic principles and mother-tongue learning in the British context (Sarwar, 1983). For others, it might mean greater day-to-day involvement in the running of their children's schools through their representation on governing bodies. Different, again, might be the demand that LEA officers and elected members consult with local black parents and groups in decisions affecting the curriculum, recruitment practices and promotion prospects for black teachers, the allocation of resources, and service delivery generally in the LEA. Of course these are not mutually exclusive demands; rather, they assume different priorities in particular contexts. In the rest of this article we want to look critically at what some observers might see as state concessions to these demands. After all, on the grounds of the recent increase in LEA multicultural and anti-racist education policies, the establishment of consultative structures between LEA administrators and local black organizations, and the commitment of the Secretary of State to ensure that 'parents of ethnic minority pupils ... play a more influential part in the affairs of their children's schools' (DES, 1985, p. 62) one might be tempted to conclude that important gains have already been secured. It is our conviction that this would be a premature judgment. After all, if there is to be effective power-sharing or participation at the local state level there must be effective *power* at the local level. And, as we have indicated, this is what is being eroded by central government. So even assuming the existence of a local education authority genuinely committed to participation (rather than to legitimation), the room for initiative has been constrained. It is against this background that we can more fully understand the way in which ethnic interests are handled in the arena of the local state.

Let's begin, however, by looking at the notion of consultation and examine the way it has been operationalized both in the local state and in relationships between the black communities and central government.

Consultation, Selection and Legitimation

The structural decentralization of the educational system does, of course, allow for some form of *relative* autonomy at the local level and it is in this available 'space' that the struggle for racial equality in education generally takes place. As we have already noted, this has led, amongst other things, to the publication of multicultural and anti-racist education policy statements in a growing number of LEAs, the establishment of associated support services and the setting up of procedures and mechanisms through which LEA officers and members might consult local black residents over their service delivery. However, the fact that consultation with black groups does not lead automatically to a reappraisal and reformulation of service delivery along the lines proposed by these groups can be accounted for, at least in part, by the way LEA policy-makers choose to define and operationalize the notion of consultation. Kenneth Brooksbank's observations are pertinent here because he makes the point that consultation,

> ... is not a process by which views are collected and the persons consulting are committed to the majority view ... In educational administration, consultation is the process by which those authorised to make a decision convey the nature of their proposals or the facts underlying those proposals to those affected by them. They do so while ready to change what they are doing, in response to what is said during the consultative process; but they are not committed to such changes. (1980, pp. 221–2)

This is an important corrective to popular understandings (and expectations) of consultation which are often based on the view that it implies participation in decision making on equal terms and is synonymous with the term 'referendum'. It is not and, from this perspective, we can see that the involvement of black groups and individuals in the consultative procedures concerning anti-racist education policies in such LEAs as Inner London and Berkshire does not denote, *per se*, their enhanced status in decision-making. Compared to (mainly white) policy-makers, they retain a position of relative powerlessness so that their views and proposals may or may not be accepted and represented in the ultimate formulation and implementation of policies.

The 'management' of consultation by policy-makers also allows for the selection, differential incorporation and legitimation of views expressed by various black community groups. In Bradford, for example, the 1982 and 1983 multicultural education policy documents are said by the LEA's Senior Policy Adviser to constitute the outcome of the first 'form of official contact between ethnic minority organizations and the Council' (quoted in Morris, *et al*, 1984, p. 9). In fact, they comprise a selective representation (and legitimation) of these views and demands. Thus while the policies recognize the right of parents to withdraw their children from assemblies and RE lessons, include regulations to cover dietary and clothing provision, and recommend that headteachers and their staff invite local religious and community leaders into their schools, they reject demands from the Muslim Parents Association (MPA) for independent, voluntary-aided schools, despite the MPA's appeals to relevant sections of the 1944 and 1980 Education Acts. Why? According to the LEA's 1982 policy document: 'The authority is greatly concerned to maintain a shared educational experience for all the children in Bradford'. What complicates this picture even further, and facilitates the process of differential incorporation, are the demands made by the Asian Youth Movement in Bradford, some of which correspond with those of other religious and parental groups, some of which are in contradistinction to them. Now, these debates and disputes in Bradford are by no means exceptional; they are exemplary of processes in LEAs up and down the country, and from them we can distil two significant conclusions. First, from a range of local black community group views LEA policy-makers are able to select what they want to include in their policies. In this process, white policy-makers are able to legitimate particular community interests and perspectives and discard others. Second, they highlight the futility of such policy-makers as those in Inner London, who refer in their documents to '*the* black perspective' (ILEA, *Multiethnic Education*, 1983, p. 16, our emphasis). Such a proposition obscures important and distinctive internal differences. To present these perspectives as homogeneous and buttressed by a common consensus is to reproduce stereotypes along those lines which have, traditionally, equated 'parental views' on education with those articulated in white communities by middle-class parents.

The diffuse, and therefore manipulable, status of the term 'consultation' can also be demonstrated in the selective representation and legitimation of black communities' views in *Education For All*, a report on the education of children from ethnic minority groups compiled by Lord Swann and his committee. The committee's enquiry took over five years to complete, and its evidence-gathering exercise comprised not only written invitations to various (black and white) groups but also arrangements for 'thirty "open" meetings or fora' to facilitate the involvement of 'parents and young people, particularly from ethnic minority organizations who might otherwise have been unlikely to make their voices heard through formal channels' (1985, p. x). Hearing and listening are not the same thing, however, and, as we will now show, the Swann Committee's conception of consultation adhered more to the former.

From the evidence represented in the Swann Report as well as from our own experiences as educational researchers looking into LEA policies on multicultural and antiracist education, it is clear that three substantive issues figure prominently on the agenda of black groups in their local and national campaigns for racial equality in education. To begin with is the matter of 'separate' and 'supplementary' schools. To a large extent, as we have already indicated, the former are demanded by certain South Asian organizations who are concerned that their cultures, languages and religions should be maintained in the UK. The latter are associated with some Afro-Caribbean groups who see supplementary (or Saturday) schools as the only feasible alternative to a mainstream education service which is racist. In the words of Nel Clark, founder of Dachwyng Saturday School, the imperative is clear: 'A community cannot be passive and allow a racist education system to disadvantage our children. We need to do something' (1982, p. 123). The second issue concerns the provision and maintenance of ethnic minority community languages in schools as part of the mainstream curriculum. This is especially a matter of concern to many parents of South Asian origin. Thirdly, there is the general and long-standing indignation about the use of Section 11 finance by LEAs. This section of the Local Government Act 1966 is the chief source of government funding for race-related initiatives in education and other local authority services. Many black groups insist that grants from this source have been misused routinely by LEAs to 'pump prime' existing staff resources. Black groups have demanded full involvement in decisions affecting the allocation of these funds. Some groups go even further. The Leicester branch of the Indian Workers Association (GB), for instance, insists that Section 11 funds should be used exclusively to meet the 'special needs' of black students, and that these needs should be defined by the black communities themselves. According to this argument, Section 11 grants should no longer be used to create 'posts such as race relations advisers, multicultural advisers, multicultural support services etc., . . . which bear little relevance to the specific needs of the blacks' (Kapur, 1984, p. 11). So how were these concerns represented in the Swann Report and what was their impact on future DES strategies for multicultural and anti-racist education?

In its final proposals to Sir Keith Joseph, the Swann Committee did not support either the call for separate and supplementary schools or for the maintenance and provision of community languages in the mainstream curriculum of state schools. Despite overwhelming support for these matters from those black groups consulted during the enquiry, they were rejected. The reason: they were incompatible with the notion of 'Education for All' which provided the ideological framework within which the Committee's arguments and recommendations were situated. This is not the place to appraise critically 'Swann's song' of 'Education for All' (but see Troyna and Williams, 1986). The point we want to emphasize is that consultation with members of the black communities failed to ensure that their arguments were accepted or legitimated by the Committee.

If these two issues highlight the gap between consultation and legitimation in the relationship between the black communities and the Swann Committee, then the debate over the use of Section 11 grants exemplifies how far the Swann Committee, itself, as a consultative body to the DES, was structurally peripheral to the core of educational decision-making. The Committee articulated the views of many black groups in recommending that funding from mainstream budgets, rather than Section 11, should be used to 'cover initiatives designed to prepare all youngsters for life in a multiracial society' (1985, p. 360). But this suggestion fell on deaf ears. Sir Keith Joseph made it clear in the Parliamentary debate which accompanied the publication of the Report that he would not change the present mode of funding.

The 'New Partnership'

It could be contended against our general argument that the government's intention 'to change the composition and entrench the powers of governing bodies' so that schools should serve more effectively 'the community from which it draws its pupils' (DES, 1985) constitutes an important victory in the struggle for racial equality in education. After all, it signifies a commitment to ensure that black parents have some say over the day-to-day running of their children's school. But, in ending this article, it is important to note precisely what role the government intends to assign parents in this apparently new scenario. It is important also to acknowledge the political and ideological imperatives associated with this development.

A critical reading of *Better Schools* would reveal that it is in the face of a growing legitimation crisis over the education system's relationship with black (and white) students that the government has seen it necessary to consult with local parents over matters of social control and discipline. We are told, for instance that 'parents should support the school on the question of attendance' (p. 58, para. 191) and, more specifically, that through their representation on school governing bodies parents will be able 'to exercise an important influence over the ethos of the school and ... with the school's contribution to the life of the local community, for example in the effect of the school's ethos on juvenile crime' (p. 68, para. 231). The designation of these roles to parents fits in well with the government's more general ideological typification of black (and white) youth as 'alienated', 'a social time bomb' and a threat to law and order. The rhetoric of the new partnership with parents simply conceals a long-standing concern with the social control of youth (especially black youth after the urban disturbances of 1980 and 1981) and the perceived responsibility of black parents particularly, to help in the surveillance of these youths. At the same time, black parents' influence over the school curriculum remains partial and constrained. At best the government will allow black parents and communities the opportunity to contribute to their children's education through 'the educational and cultural activities *which they themselves arrange*' (p. 62, para. 210 our emphasis).

We began this chapter by suggesting that in an era of 'regressive educational offensives' the part played by teachers in decisions affecting the UK's educational system was being eroded systematically by central government strategies. In blunt terms, their professional status and autonomy is under attack. The proposed composition of governing bodies outlined in *Better Schools* constitutes a further step along this road; another feather in the cap of the accountability movement. From this vantage point, it becomes easier to understand why, in the struggle for racial equality in education, LEA multicultural and anti-racist education policies have so far proved to be largely ineffective ammunition. As our research in 'Milltown' has shown, these policies have made a partial and limited impact on the routine practices, procedures and pedagogy of teachers. Those on the 'chalk face' believe they have neither the space or resources to develop initiatives along multicultural or anti-racist lines; they are also sceptical of their LEA's prescriptive calls for action at a time when the accountability movement is on the rise (Troyna and Ball, 1985a and 1985b). Their resistance is understandable, if not defensible.

It is against this antagonistic and dismal background that the struggle for racial equality in education takes place. At present it seems that any victories will have to be hard earned and will be, at best, highly localised and piecemeal. Or is even this a forlorn hope?

Acknowledgements

We are grateful to Robin Cohen, Anthony Hartnett and Michael Naish for their comments on an earlier version of this chapter.

References

BROOKSBANK, K. (1980) *Educational Administration*, London, Council and Education Press.

CLARK, N. (1982) 'Dachwyng Saturday School', in OHRI, A., MANNING, B. and CURNO, P. (Eds) *Community Work and Racism*, London, Routledge and Kegan Paul, pp. 121–7.

COMMITTEE OF INQUIRY INTO THE EDUCATION OF CHILDREN FROM ETHNIC MINORITY GROUPS (1985) *Education For All*, (The Swann Report), Cmnd 9453, London, HMSO.

DEPARTMENT OF EDUCATION AND SCIENCE, (1985) *Better Schools*, Cmnd 9469, London, HMSO.

HALL, S. (1983) 'Education in crisis', in WOLPE, A.M. and DONALD, J. (Eds) *Is There Anyone Here From Education?* London, Pluto Press, pp. 2–10.

HALSEY, A.H. (1972) 'Political ends and educational means' in HALSEY, A.H. (Ed.) *Education Priority*, Vol. 1, London, HMSO, pp. 3–12.

KAPUR, S. (1984) *Section 11 Posts: Review or More of the Same?* Leicester, Indian Workers Association G.B.

MOON, J. and RICHARDSON, J.J. (1984) 'Policy-making with a difference? The Technical and Vocational Education Initiative', *Public Administration*, 62, spring, pp. 23–33.

MORRIS, G., HUSSAIN, A. and AURA, T.G. (1984) 'Schooling crisis in

Bradford', *Race Today*, July/August, pp. 8–11.

SARWAR, G. (1983) *Muslims and Education in the U.K.*, London, The Muslim Educational Trust.

SIMON, B. (1984) 'Breaking school rules', *Marxism Today*, September, pp. 19–25.

TROYNA, B. and BALL, W. (1985a) *Views from the Chalk Face: School Responses to an LEA's Mutlicultural Education Policy*, Warwick University, Policy Papers in Ethnic Relations No. 1.

TROYNA, B. and BALL, W. (1985b) 'Styles of LEA policy intervention in multicultural/antiracist education', *Educational Review*, 37, 2, pp. 165–73.

TROYNA, B. and WILLIAMS, J. (1986) *Racism, Education and the State: The Racialisation of Education Policy*, Beckenham, Croom Helm.

Special Educational Needs

Sally Tomlinson

The education system in Britain is currently being restructured to meet the demands of a technological society which 'needs' academic and technical elites and a smaller flexible workforce. Higher levels of academic attainment, and vocational skills are now required, and adequate achievements in ordinary education are important in order to gain most kinds of employment. This leaves larger and larger numbers of young people who are increasingly being defined as incapable of, or unwilling to participate in, ordinary education or training. They are defined as having special educational needs, and a whole set of new policies and practices are developing to cater for these special needs.

Special educational needs has, in the 1980s, become an ideological justification for the expansion of a sub-system of education that leads many pupils ultimately to a 'special' life-style, characterized by low-status employment or a workless future and to relatively powerless social positions. As with much educational change, the purpose and direction of special educational change is not immediately obvious, particularly as this kind of education developed within a benevolent framework in which provision always was ostensibly for the 'good' (or the special needs) of the child. Assertions that increased percentages of pupils need to be separated, either within segregated or integrated settings, and offered a special curriculum that leads to a special post-school career, are coming to be accepted as part of a natural process, rather than as a social process. It is becoming difficult to probe behind the powerful ideology of benevolent humanitarianism and analyze the expansion of 'special educational needs' in terms of institutional needs, economic efficiency, or political requirements.

From a sociological perspective, a major interest in the expansion of numbers of pupils with special educational needs lies in consideration of the sort of pupils who are increasingly considered to have these needs. They are, as statistics can demonstrate (see Swann, 1985) and practitioners will testify, largely children with learning and behavioural difficulties, — children who pre-1981 were described as ESN-M (educationally sub-normal, mild or moderate) and remedial, maladjusted or disruptive. They are also, as much literature has documented (Stein and Susser, 1960; Stott, 1966; Gulliford, 1971; Ford *et al*, 1982) overwhelmingly children of manual working class parentage, with a disproportionate number of black, materially disadvantaged and male children among them. There is no increase, indeed there has been a decrease, in the porportion of children whom the general public would immediately agree had special needs, — the blind and partially sighted, the deaf and partially hearing, severely mentally or physically handicapped children, epileptic, delicate and those with speech defects (Swann, 1985, pp. 6–8).

This chapter traces the evolution of the child with learning and behavioural difficulties over the past hundred years and indicates that it is more likely to be the needs of the education system or social and economic needs that have contributed to the expansion of numbers, to the exclusion from ordinary education and to 'special' treatment for these children. Alternative reasons for the expansion of special education other than the rhetoric of special needs are examined, and dilemmas of integrating large numbers of children that special education was intended to segregate in some form or other are discussed. Just as special needs have become an ideological justification for the piecemeal development of a whole variety of intervention and provision, so integration has become a utopian ideal — an attempt to express egalitarian dreams within the reality of an inegalitarian, competitive education system.

Origins

The origins of the child with learning difficulty lie in the development of a mass elementary education system that necessitated the recognition of pupils who could not function satisfactorily within the system. How to define such pupils has always posed a problem, and the changing terminology of defect, disability, handicap or special need is an indication that such terms are social constructs developed within particular historical contexts. The 1886 Idiots Act provided a nice example of this. 'Idiocy', the Act decided, 'means a greater deficiency of intellect, and imbecility means a lesser degree of such deficiency'.

Educable imbeciles were considered worthy of exclusion from ordinary education, as were the group of children who appeared to be intermediate between imbeciles as defined by the Act, and normal children. This group were designated by Dr Shuttleworth, a physican at the Lancaster Royal Albert Idiots Asylum, as 'weak or feeble-minded' (Barrett, 1986). By the 1880s this group of children were causing considerable concern in the newly established elementary schools. Children who, before compulsory education, had functioned socially and often economically at an adequate level were now found to be educationally deficient, or 'incapable of sustained learning'. Payment by results, — the system by which teachers received remuneration based on the educational success of their pupils — was singled out by some school inspectors as 'over-pressing children'. These children began to loom large as a problem to the school system, and a Commission set up in 1885 to examine the blind, deaf and dumb, eventually examined 'such other cases as would seem to require exceptional means of education'.

In their 1889 report, the Commission recommended 'their separation from ordinary scholars in public elementary schools in order that they receive special instruction' (Report of the Royal Commission, 1889). The pupils who most concerned the Commission were variously designated as feeble-minded, educable imbeciles and those who were badly behaved in the elementary schools. It was these children who formed the clientele of the first special classes and schools set up in large cities in the 1890s. Other schools established and continued to use the standard 0 classes, for children who could not reach the required levels of what would now be called 'test performance'. These classes were necessary because of the numbers of children with learning and behavioural problems. As a London school inspector noted in 1897, 'of every seventy children in standard I, twenty-five were almost entirely ignorant, they misbehaved, learned nothing and truanted' (Pritchard, 1963, p. 117). Here, perhaps, in the 35 per cent of pupils whose presence impeded the smooth running of Victorian elementary schools, lie the origins of the 20 per cent of pupils targeted by the Warnock report (DES, 1978) as having special educative needs, or indeed the 40 per cent of 'less-able' pupils a recent DES curriculum innitiative is aimed at (DES, 1982). However, Barrett (1986) has demonstrated that even in the 1890s there was no unambiguous acceptance that it was the 'needs' of the children that required their special treatment. He quotes one inspector who wrote that 'dull children are manufactured by the cast-iron requirements of modern educational codes'. The social origins of pupils with learning and behavioural difficulties are traceable to the needs of ordinary schools to separate out their problem pupils to allow them to credential other pupils within a competitive system, as much as to any actual needs individual pupils might have.

The Social Problem Class

The commissions and committees who, pre-1900, considered the problems posed by feeble-minded and troublesome children, — variously described, from the 1890s, as dull, stupid, backward and deficient had a variety of motives. The smooth running of some schools was one, the employability of such pupils was another, and concern that the special education of such pupils should not be too costly was a third (Pritchard, 1963). However, by the turn of the century the feeble-minded and defective were coming to be regarded as a grave threat to the well-being of the population, and more stringent measures for the social control of what were referred to as part of the 'social problem classes' were under way. The Charity Organization Society, the National Association for the Promotion of the Welfare of the Feeble-Minded, and the Eugenics Society were all organizations which, from the 1890s to the 1920s, campaigned for the stricter segregation of feeble-minded and defective children, and of the 'morally defective child', — a forerunner of the maladjusted child, who was particularly thought to need 'custodial care'. Linkages between low social class, social vice and crime and educational backwardness or retardation became part of the common sense of experts and of educational practitioners. Even Winston Churchill, who was briefly Home Secretary in 1910–11, was in favour of the segregation and sterilization of the retarded, and petitioned the Prime Minister on the dangers of the 'multiplication of the unfit'. One influential practitioner addressed the North of England Education Conference in 1900 on the subject of 'Preventing the retarded affecting the moral and physical well-being of the race', and recommened permanent segregation for those 'not normal at age 13–14' (Dendy, quoted in Pritchard, 1963).

The notions of racial degeneration and the social problems

caused by a 'group' of feeble-minded pupils, who were thought likely to be unemployed or turn to crime, led to an increased search for the educationally defective and backward within schools, particularly via the work of the Royal Commission on the Care and Control of the Feeble-Minded which reported in 1908. This Commission appointed medical investigators in sixteen districts to indentify, amongst others, the feeble-minded and the 'morally defective or imbecile'. They were convinced that 'the numbers of feeble-minded whose training is neglected, over whom no sufficient control is exercised, and whose wayward and irresponsible lives are productive of crime and misery — causing much expenditure wasteful to the community' should be sought and segregated in special schools, classes and institutions (Report of the Royal Commission 1908, Vol. 8.).

By the late 1920s the notion of an expanding social problem class threatening society was well-established, as was the idea that it was the children of this 'class' who were candidates for special education. In 1929 the Wood Committee, representing the Board of Education, wrote of 'families of mental defectives — which contain ... a larger proportion of insane persons, epileptics, paupers, criminals, unemployables, habitual slum dwellers, prostitutes, inebriates and other social inefficients' (p. 80).

This Committee, as a result of its investigations, claimed that there was a much larger group of pupils in schools than those already categorized and segregated as feeble-minded, or defective, and that children in ordinary schools who were dull and backward should be 'envisaged as a single group presenting a single educational and administrative problem'. This group were, post-1944, termed the educationally sub-normal (Board of Education and Board of Control, 1929). Similarly, children, who between 1920–1944 were variously described as nervous, difficult, neuropathic, unstable, moral defectives or anti-social, became a statutory administrative category of maladjusted pupils after 1944. Post-war, the notion that there was an expanding number of pupils with learning and behavioural difficulties, whose presence was troublesome to ordinary schools and teachers, became a well-established truism.

The 1944 Education Act had sanctioned selection by ability, and had thus implicitly sanctioned selection by disability for some form of special education. The duty laid upon local education authorities to ascertain pupils who had any 'disability of body or mind' (Education Act 1944, Section 35) was vague enough to exclude any children who might conceivably upset the smooth running of normal education and certainly allowed for the separation of larger numbers of children whose learning and behaviour were considered problematic. Teachers at this time, certainly appeared to agree with Cyril Burt's assertions that it was impossible to teach normal children *and* backward and troublesome children in the ordinary school. Burt (1937, p. 576) wrote 'The teacher is doing a double duty. It is like asking a single shoe-maker not only to manufacture the boots and shoes for the whole neighbourhood, but at the same time take charge of all the repairs', and he recommended the segregations of problem pupils into 'auxillary schools or classes'.

Problem Pupils Post-1944

In the thirty years following the 1944 Act there was considerable expansion of segregated special provision for pupils where learning and behavioural problems were enough to warrant certified exclusions from normal school provision. Particularly in the 1960s and 1970s, there was also an expansion, of special provision for remedial and disruptive pupils, who were deemed to interrupt the work of ordinary schools, — particularly the newly developing comprehensive schools. It is no accident that the first moves to discover pupils with learning and behavioural problems occurred after the introduction of mass elementary education, and the second after the introduction of mass secondary education. Further, the labels attached to the pupils during this period owed more to administrative convenience than to anything else. They were not 'normative' categories, in the sense that there were agreed measuring instruments or agreed criteria to decide who was ESN, maladjusted, remedial or disruptive.

There would be, and was, considerable argument between professionals and practitioners over who should be categorized in this way. 'The answer to the question, what is an ESN-M child, or a maladjusted child will depend more on the values, beliefs and interests of those making the judgements than any quality intrinsic to the child' (Tomlinson 1982, p. 66). There is a paucity of literature which has questioned the epistemological status of these categories. However, Tomlinson (1981) has examined the social construction of the 'ESN-M child'; Sewell (1982) has traced the history of the 'remedial child'; Ford, Morgan and Wheeler (1982) have analyzed the 'maladjusted and disruptive' pupil as a product of the need for social control in education; and a series of chapters edited by Lloyd-Smith

(1984) have examined provision for the disruptive or disaffected pupil as a product of social, educational and economic crisis rather than as 'bad' behaviour originating within children.

The problems of categorization and labelling of children whose learning and behavioural difficulties posed problems for teachers in ordinary schools and classes can be particularly illustrated by the development of the statutory category of the ESN child and by the difficulty of differentiating this category from that of the 'remedial' child. The first guidelines on pupils considered to be 'educationally retarded' post-1944 were laid down in a Ministry of Education pamphlet in 1946. Such retardation was thought to be due to 'limited ability' or to 'other considerations' or by both together. Other considerations, in the 1946 guidelines, included late bed-times and over-indulgence and irresponsibility of parents, but 'one of the advantages of the new Act is that no decision as to the cause of retardation must be given before the child is given special educational treatment' (Ministry of Education, 1946).

ESN pupils were to have a 'low I.Q.' of between 55 and 75 but were not to be 'behaviourally troublesome'. The maladjusted category was to take care of such pupils. And the guidelines referred to a further 6–9 per cent of 'less seriously retarded pupils' who could be retained in ordinary schools for their special education. In fact, the numbers of pupils assessed and referred to ESN schools increased considerably from 1946. In the nine years up to 1955, 142 more ESN schools opened in England and Wales and although teachers were never issued with any guidance as to how to recognize an ESN child, they seemed to have no difficulty in doing so. However, teachers appeared to consider that an ESN child was one who was both retarded *and* behaviourally troublesome. A Ministry pamphlet in 1956 noted that 'it has become less difficult to place the really troublesome educationally subnormal boy or girl, whose mental disability is complicated by behavioural difficulties and perhaps a record of delinquency (Ministry of Education, 1956, p. 13).

During the 1960s a series of contradictory definitions emerged from the Department of Education and Science, and, by 1970, an ESN child

> could be educationally backward without requiring special schooling, or could be of above average ability and still require special schooling. No cause need be established for a child's retardation, but teachers were expected to distinguish

different degrees and types of backwardness. ... an ESN child may or may not be distinguished from a backward child who may remain in an ordinary school. In the 1940s the child was not intended to be a troublesome child, but troublesome children had tended to be referred as potentially ESN. (Tomlinson, 1981, p. 50)

By 1970, an Education Act had resulted in the sub-division of the category of educationally sub-normal into ESN-M (mild or moderate) and ESN-S (severe), and several enquiries had demonstrated that pupils categorized as ESN-M were almost entirely the children of semi- or unskilled working class parentage with an over representation of black pupils (Tomlinson, 1981). Whatever means teachers were using to recognize and refer potential ESN-M pupils, they were referring the children of the 'social problem class' that had always proved to be a perennial worry for educators. The distinction between the ESN-M and the remedial child was particularly difficult to maintain during this period. Although selection criteria for remedial classes often included psychometric testing, Nash (1975) found that teachers selected out children whom they disliked or found difficult to manage. The 'troublesome and badly behaved' who, as with the ESN-M, tended to be pupils of manual working class parentage, were the ones who found their way into remedial classes. Sewell (1982) has suggested that the development of large numbers of remedial classes post-war was functional for the education system 'where there was a large degree of psychometrically based streaming, and where the political and social basis of such educational judgements were considered unproblematic' (p. 72).

One of the major recommendations of the Warnock Committee (DES, 1978) was that the distinction between ESN-M and remedial pupils be abolished. The descriptive category of 'child with learning difficulty' was intended to encompass those segregated into ESN-M schools and those remaining in remedial classes in ordinary schools. In addition the concept of special educational needs was now intended to 'embrace educational help for children with emotional or behavioural disorders who had previously been regarded as disruptive' (DES, 1978, p. 46). Thus, children with learning difficulties could now be officially conceded to have behavioural problems and vice versa.

The category of 'disruptive' pupil was an unofficial label, developed on an ad hoc basis during the 1970s. An HMI survey of the variety of centres, units, and classes for behaviourally troublesome pupils, undertaken in 1977, showed that sixty-nine LEAs had established such provision, with 1974 being a peak year for developments. They reported over 239 such units, and by 1979 the Advisory Council for Education discovered 386 centres (Advisory Council for Education, 1980). The establishment of this unofficial category of special education was legally based on section 56 of the 1944 Education Act, which allowed LEAs to make provision for children 'otherwise than at school', and, in most cases, pupils remained on the roll of their ordinary school. Provision for disruptive pupils rapidly became an alternative to ESN-M or maladjusted provision, and no lengthy assessment procedures were necessary. Newell (1980) pointed out that the new 'sin-bin section of special education' had even fewer safeguards than the rest of the special education sector. Additionally, the Warnock Committee had reconfirmed the familiar assumed connection between learning and behavioural problems in schools and the working (or unemployed) class by noting that 'we are fully aware that many children with educational difficulties may suffer from financial or wider social deficiencies'. (DES, 1978, p. 4)

Special Needs and the Comprehensive School

The use of the terminology of 'special needs' has now become a rationalization to cover expanded provision for children considered to have learning and behavioural difficulties, who are also the children of an expanding 'social problem class'. It thus becomes particularly important to question why at this particular historical moment provision is expanding. Part of the answer lies in the contradictory expectations about comprehensive schooling and in the role schools now increasingly play in separating out and preparing larger numbers of young people for a workless future.

The expansion of special education cannot be understood without reference to developments and changes in the whole education system, particularly changes since the establishment of state comprehensive education during the 1970s. A common school, underpinned by egalitarian ideologies and attended by middle and working class children, was envisaged by supporters of comprehensive schools but comprehensive education is now dogged by a series of dilemmas. One dilemma which was slowly revealed during the 1970s was that, if selection by ability was inadmissible, so was selection by disability or inability. The 100-year-old principle of segregation gave way to notions of integration, and comprehensive schools were expected to incorporate many non-conformist and troublesome children who would previously have been candidates for exclusion. Other dilemmas involved the promise to offer equality of opportunity and having to explain away unequal outcomes; the pressure to raise standards and to credential more pupils by expanding the examination system while offering a suitable curriculum to the 'less able'; and the pressure to incorporate a subject-orientated traditional grammar school-type curriculum while incorporating secondary modern-type pupils.

Reynolds and Sullivan (1979) have argued that, initially, comprehensive schools were left relatively free to develop their own curricula, pedagogies and forms of control with little outside interference. One response to dilemmas posed by the 'less able' and the 'unwilling' (pupils with learning and behavioural problems), whose numbers increased after 1973 and the raising of the school-leaving age was to segregate them internally within the schools. Up to the beginning of the 1980s there was little evidence that comprehensive schools had solved the problem of providing a curriculum for the 'less able' or the 'remedial-special'. Evidence indicated that such schools preferred streaming, setting and banding to mixed-ability teaching, and that their curricula for the less able were narrow and inappropriate. Given the pressures to concentrate on the able and the examinable, this is not surprising. While the comprehensive school curriculum increasingly became subject to pressures from political and economic interest groups outside school, a major focus in the 1980s has been on the curriculum for the 'less able'. The DES 14–16 'lower attaining pupils programme', for example, is a direct but little publicized political incursion into this curriculum. DES criticism of the inappropriate curriculum offered to the less able up to the early 1980s was largely a criticism of the apparent slowness of schools to realize the social and political consequences of the disappearance of the youth labour market for less able and special leavers. The pupils at whom DES and other vocational and educational programmes for the less able are aimed are those who, up to the mid-1970s, could be minimally motivated to learn and behave at school by means of the carrot of possible employment. Programmes designed for the less able and special adolescents are part of a political response to the problem of dealing with larger numbers of young people who, despite new vocational initiatives, will probably never acquire employment. The expansion of special education to embrace larger numbers of young people, particularly at post-16 level, may provide both a rationale and a justification for the subsequent economic position of this group. 'To have received a special education — with its historical stigmatic connotations, even a non-recorded special education in an integrated setting, may be regarded unfavourably by potential employers' (Tomlinson, 1982, p. 177).

Integration — A Utopian Ideal

Given the hundred year-old history of segregating pupils with learning and behavioural difficulties, and given their continued stigmatization, which, less intense than during the first half of the twentieth century, still ensures even so that these pupils and their families are regarded as problematic, why has the notion of 'integration' become so popular in the 1980s? The Report of the Committee chaired by Fish (ILEA, 1985), which examines special provision in Inner London, argues that the aims of education for children with disabilities and difficulties should be the same as those for all other children, and that the process of integration and not segregation should be a major policy aim of those responsible for the education service. Booth and Potts (1984) have defined integration as the realization of the 'comprehensive principle'. 'It is the abolition of the distinction between ordinary, and both remedial and special education that is implied' (p. 6).

Supporters of integration use a variety of arguments to justify their position, but a major argument is that post-war egalitarianism is now firmly established in Britain, via a comprehensive education principle, and that overt selection by ability or disability is no longer permissable.

Many local education authorities are now proceeding with reorganization in the belief that the exclusion of fewer children from segregated special schools is evidence that they have accepted an integration principle. It is ironic, however, that authorities who failed to make segregated provision post-1945 can now claim to be in the forefront of an integration movement. Supporters of integration claim that, since all those with special needs should be able fully to share in the privileges and opportunities of the education system, all that is needed is the 'right' sort of curriculum and pedagogy, the 'right' sort of organization, teachers with the 'right' sort of skills, and sufficient resources, to ensure that barriers between special and ordinary education are broken down. It is likely, however, that, as far as children with learning and behavioural difficulties are concerned, much of the rhetoric of integration is utopian.

Mannheim (1936, p. 173) wrote that 'a state of mind is utopian when it is incongruous with the state of reality in which it occurs'. He argued that, although there are groups within society who, often for liberal humanistic reasons, consider particular social changes desirable, if their thinking is too far removed from current social structures and requirements, their beliefs will take on a 'wish-fulfilment' quality. The rhetoric of integration, as it is currently employed in Britain, and, indeed, in the USA, may be no more than romanticized liberalism, given the current 'needs' of education systems in technological societies, noted at the beginning of this chapter. The practice of separating pupils with learning and behavioural difficulties is becoming more, not less, necessary, for an education system more and more concerned with credentialing and 'raising standards'.

In the USA Madden and Slavin (1983), reviewing literature on mainstreaming, concluded that many regular class teachers felt poorly prepared or able to deal with the requirements of academically handicapped pupils, and they noted that 'questions about the value of mainstreaming have been raised in the press and in political debates with increased frequency' (p. 521).

Recent research in Britain appears to demonstrate a familiar and understandable reluctance on the part of teachers to deal with children with learning and behavioural problems in the ordinary classrooms without a good deal of extra help and support (Gipps and Gross, 1985). The flurry of activity directed towards the development of support services, resource units, peripatetic teams, remedial assistance, 'release' teachers, individual teaching programmes, special needs advisory teams, special needs screening projects and the like is not necessarily evidence of integration. It is evidence that, as the reply of the National Union of Teachers (1979) to the Warnock Committee pointed out, particular groups of pupils, especially the maladjusted and those of low ability, might present 'insupportable problems for teachers in ordinary classrooms' (NUT, 1979).

The teacher who told the Fish Committee that 'we feel that the dream of total integration is a dangerous fantasy which is being promoted in ignorance of the practicalities involved' (ILEA, 1985, p. 34) was expressing the real anxieties of many practitioners. The conflicts of interests that are developing in ordinary schools as moves to integrate, or, more correctly, to separate out more pupils with special needs, are becoming obvious as schools attempt to cope with new demands and expectations. For the first time in the history of state educational provision, remedial or special needs departments have become important, and can now claim resources, attention, expertise, higher status and a right to intrude into the practices of their colleagues. Those pressing for a 'whole-school' approach to the recognition of special needs have some way to go in convincing colleagues that such involvement is necessary. The development of 'special schools within ordinary schools' would seem to be a more likely scenario. Integration, along the lines in which it is presented by its supporters, is likely to remain utopian optimism, given the tasks and expectations laid on teachers within an increasingly competitive education system.

Conclusion

This chapter has suggested that the terminology of 'special educational needs' has become an ideological rationalization for the expansion of special education to embrace larger numbers of pupils with learning and behavioural difficulties. From an historical examination, it can be seen that feeble-minded, educationally subnormal, remedial, maladjusted and disruptive pupils are also largely the children of the manual working class or of the unemployed. These pupils present a problem to schools which are now required to train academic, technical, and vocational groups, unimpeded by pupils who cannot or will not reach the standards now demanded, and who are destined for sporadic low-skilled employment or for a workless future. Integration, presented as a mechanism for removing stigma and segregation and offering wider possibilities to all children in education, is in fact a mechanism for expanding the special education sector into a respectable sub-system of education rather than a poorly resourced area. It is part of a political response to crucial problems facing the education system, problems relating to dealing with large groups who will never be considered suitable to acquire the education or training which will allow them incomes above subsistence level, but who, nevertheless, will need training for some kind of self-sufficiency and controlled social behaviour. The ideology of special needs and the utopia of integration currently provide a framework within which differential education and training can be offered to the heirs of the 'social problem classes'.

References

ADVISORY COUNCIL FOR EDUCATION (1980) *Survey of Disruptive Units*, London, Advisory Council for Education.

BARRETT, M. (1986) 'From education to segregation — An enquiry into the changing character of special educational provision for the retarded in England 1846–1918', unpublished PhD thesis, Lancaster, University of Lancaster.

BOARD OF EDUCATION AND BOARD OF CONTROL (1929) (Wood Committee) *Report of the Joint Departmental Committee on Mental Deficiency* (Wood Report), London, HMSO.

BOOTH, T. and POTTS, P. (1984) *Integrating Special Education*. Oxford. Blackwell.

BURT, C. (1937) *The Backward Child*, London, University of London Press, 5th Edition 1969.

DEPARTMENT OF EDUCATION AND SCIENCE (1978) *Special Educational Needs* (Warnock Report), London, HMSO.

DEPARTMENT OF EDUCATION AND SCIENCE (1982) *14–16 Lower Attaining Pupils Programme*, London, HMSO.

FORD, J., MONGON, D. and WHEELER, M. (1982) *Special Education and Social Control — Invisible Disasters*, London, Routledge and Kegan Paul.

GIPPS, C. and GROSS, H. (1985) 'Do teachers have special needs too? Teachers perceptions of the role of new developments in provision for children with special needs', paper presented at the annual conference of the British Educational Research Association, Sheffield.

GULLIFORD (1971) *Special Educational Needs*, London, Routledge and Kegan Paul.

INNER LONDON EDUCATION AUTHORITY (1985) *Equal Opportunities for All* (Fish Report), London, ILEA.

LLOYD-SMITH, M. (Ed.). (1984) *Disrupted Schooling*, London, John Murray.

MADDEN, N.A. and SLAVIN, R. (1983) 'Mainstreaming pupils with mild handicaps — Academic and social outcomes', *Review of Educational Research*, 53, 4, pp. 519–69.

MANNHEIM, K. (1936) *Ideology and Utopia*, London, Routledge and Kegan Paul.

MINISTRY OF EDUCATION (1946) *Special Educational Treatment*, Pamphlet No. 5, London, HMSO.

MINISTRY OF EDUCATION (1956) *The Education of Handicapped Pupils 1945–55*, Pamphlet No. 3, London, HMSO.

NASH, R. (1975) *Classrooms Observed*, London, Routledge and Kegan Paul.

NATIONAL UNION OF TEACHERS (1979) *Special Educational Needs. The NUT Reply to the Warnock Committee*, London, NUT.

NEWELL, P. (1980) 'What are the alternatives', Conference on Disruptive Units, London.

PRITCHARD, D. (1963) *The Education of the Handicapped 1760–1960*, London, Routledge and Kegan Paul.

REPORT OF THE ROYAL COMMISSION OF THE BLIND, DEAF DUMB AND OTHERS OF THE UNITED KINGDOM. (1889) 4 vols. London, HMSO.

REPORT OF THE ROYAL COMMISSION ON THE CARE AND CONTROL OF THE FEEBLE-MINDED (1908) 8 vols. London, HMSO.

REYNOLDS, D. and SULLIVAN, M. (1979) 'Bringing schools back in' in BARTON, L. and MEIGHAN, R. (Eds) *Schools, Pupils and Deviance*, Driffield, Nafferton Books.

SEWELL, G. (1982) *Reshaping Remedial Education*, London, Croom Helm.

STEIN, Z. and SUSSER, M. (1960) 'Families of dull children — Social selection by family type', *Journal of Mental Science*, 106, 445, pp. 1304–10.

STOTT, D. (1966) *Studies of Troublesome Children*, London, Tavistock.

SWANN, W. (1985) 'Is the integration of children with special needs happening'. — An analysis of recent statistics of pupils in special schools', *Oxford Review of Education*, 11, 1, pp. 3–18.

TOMLINSON, S. (1981) *Educational Subnormality*, London, Routledge and Kegan Paul.

TOMLINSON, S. (1982) *A Sociology of Special Education*, London, Routledge and Kegan Paul.

What Feminists Want from Education

Sandra Acker

> Education is not only a children's issue. It also sets the limits of what is possible for women. (Rogers, 1983, p. 65)

What do feminists want from education? Naturally, there is no simple answer to such a question. Even establishing a definition of feminism is no easy task, and certainly no single group or individual can speak confidently for all feminists. This chapter is about the relationship of feminist theory and practice to educational policy. More specifically, I discuss the nature of feminism and its implications for educational reform, the role of feminist groups in promoting change, the response of the government, and the prospects for the future. I begin, however, with a brief identification of the major themes in the literature on gender and education.

Gender and Education

All feminist educational reform efforts start from an assumption that the education system, together with other social institutions, is less favourable to girls and women than to boys and men (Arnot, 1985). Some see the system as in need only of minor adjustments to improve equal opportunities, while others wish to replace it altogether with a woman-centred alternative. Between these positions are numerous others. There is a rapidly-growing literature on gender and education which provides a basis for feminist educational analysis and innovation.

Some of the literature concentrates on placing education in its wider social context, particularly on developing an understanding of how pressures from the economy and the state combine with cultural ideologies about gender to shape the content and outcomes of the education girls and boys receive. Most writers, however, examine the education system in relative isolation from its surroundings. Questions are asked about sex differences in access to and participation in the system and about gender differentiation as embedded in curriculum and pedagogy. I cannot undertake a detailed review in the space available here, but references up to 1981 can be found in Acker (1982), and there are useful bibliographies in Acker *et al.* (1984) and Walker and Barton (1983).

Those concerned with access and representation note the different patterns of subject specialization and qualification levels of the sexes in secondary, further and higher education, as well as in MSC training schemes. The appendix of the Equal Opportunities Commission's Annual Report (EOC, 1985) gives a good overall summary of these trends. In general, girls and women become scarcer as the qualification level rises. They are found in arts, languages, domestic and commercial subjects rather than in physical sciences, craft subjects and engineering.

Women's participation in adult and continuing education has received recent attention. Attempts are being made to provide courses for mature women returning to education or employment. There are also expressions of concern about the limited access of women teachers and lecturers to higher and more secure positions in schools and other educational institutions. A topic on which more work is needed is the interaction of ethnic minority status and gender in shaping educational access, experiences and outcomes (Fuller, 1984).

Studies of schools are accumulating and beginning to give us an understanding of the ways in which 'gender codes' (MacDonald, 1980) operate. The term refers to the process by which cultural ideas about masculinity and femininity are reflected in a school's practices and classificatory systems. Attention has been paid to option-choice systems which intentionally or unintentionally differentiate by sex; to routine dividing of the sexes in school organization, classroom procedures and teacher talk; to messages given to children by a teaching hierarchy with men concentrated at the top (headteachers) and women at the bottom (scale 1); to potentially detrimental effects of mixed-sex teaching on girls' academic achievements and self-esteem; to patterns in teacher-pupil interaction, including stereotyped teacher attitudes and extra attention given to boys; to sexism in learning materials. The most recent trends have been towards developing a more sophisticated knowledge of how gender identities, derived from out-of-school settings, interact with teaching styles and school practices to reinforce gender differentiation; towards understanding girls' perceptions of school and other aspects of their lives and their strategies for coping with or resisting subordination; and, finally, towards documenting and analyzing girls' and women teachers' experiences of sexual harassment, sometimes combined with racial harassment, in school.

Feminism and Education

What is Feminism?

The most generous definitions of feminism rely on self-designation or allow any group seeking advances in women's status to count as feminist. An alternative approach is to settle on some guiding principle (Randall, 1982). Janet Radcliffe Richards (1982), for example, describes a feminist as someone who believes 'women suffer from systematic social injustice because of their sex' (pp. 13–14). Others express a similar idea but more strongly, replacing injustice with oppression or subordination.

Virtually all accounts of feminist theory recognize at least three divisions within contemporary Western feminism (which is all I can deal with here). The most common — but not the only — categorization is socialist feminist, radical feminist and liberal feminist. Eisenstein (1984) describes these succinctly:

> ... recent analysts seem to agree on the distinction between radical feminism, which holds that gender oppression is the oldest and most profound form of exploitation, which predates and underlies all other forms including those of race and class; and socialist feminism, which argues that class, race, and gender oppression interact in a complex way, that class oppression stems from capitalism, and that capitalism must be eliminated for women to be liberated. Both of these, in turn, would be distinguished from a liberal or bourgeois feminist view, which would argue that women's liberation can be fully achieved without any major alterations to the economic and political structures of contemporary capitalist democracies. (pp. xix–xx)

Some attempts to categorize run a serious risk of depicting a fossilized feminism suitable for the textbooks but unrecognizable on

Sandra Acker

the street, where, as Eisenstein (1984) remarks, 'feminist practice outstrips feminist theory' (p. xx). Although I shall use the three categories above in my analysis, it is important to realize that there are alternative classifications (some give black feminism or lesbian feminism or cultural feminism a separate place; others list such campaigns as the women's health movement, the women's peace movement and so on). Moreover, there are sub-divisions within each main group (Randall, 1982); there are unaligned feminists (for feminism is a social movement, not an organization); and there are people who do not regard themselves as feminists but who nevertheless work for the improvement of women's lives.

An interesting recent attempt to find a better way of classifying feminist positions has been made by Maggie McFadden (1984), who suggests feminists can be divided into two groups according to the position they take on the importance or otherwise of sex/gender difference. *Minimizers* are 'concerned to de-emphasize difference and press for the integration of females into masculine systems' while *maximizers* 'stress disparity and ... seek to transform or abandon masculine systems' (p. 498). Each can be seen as a continuum moving from minor alterations in the status quo to revolutionary upheaval. McFadden discusses theories and theorists along each continuum and suggests ways in which they might be linked.

It is not difficult to find criticisms by one 'type' of feminist of others. But as Midgley and Hughes (1983) observe, 'In general, urgent remedial issues centering on gross injustices tend to unite the movement' (p. 26).

Feminist Approaches to Education

Although few writers on feminist theory have given extensive attention to educational issues, it is possible to trace the educational implications of each of the three main strands of feminism. Socialist-feminist approaches to education focus attention on the role of the education system in producing a labour force differentiated by sex, as well as by class and race. Women will be appropriately socialized to give a high priority to domesticity, so that they participate in the labour market intermittently, for low wages and with poor prospects, with mostly female colleagues but under the direction and domination of men. The large number of girls who receive secretarial and domestic qualifications rather than scientific or technical ones is unremarkable in this model. Socialist-feminist writers note

66

the ways in which schools reinforce motherhood to the exclusion of other options and the support schools give to the sexual division of labour in the economy and the family (David, 1984). They are conscious of the persistence of inequality in the wider society and argue that there are limits on reform through education alone (Deem, 1981). As yet, however, they have written relatively little specifically on educational reform strategies.

Radical-feminist approaches to education also acknowledge powerful outside forces influencing educational outcomes. They detail the ways in which men benefit from women's economic and psychological dependency. Particular attention is paid to sexist text-books, to sexual harassment and to other practices in schools which confirm boys/men as dominant and girls/women as dependent or subordinate. An emphasis is put on the social construction of knowledge and the ways in which women's contributions to history and culture have been trivialized or ignored. The women's studies movement gains much (though not all) of its impetus from radical feminism.

Providing girls with 'equal opportunities' in education is the major aim of liberal feminists. Girls are thought to receive less than a fair share of teacher attention, of school resources and of prepara-tion for well-paid jobs. The situation is, in principle, capable of amelioration. One strategy is to increase public awareness. Another is to encourage girls to 'seize opportunities' when they arise. Still another is to work through established channels — unions, political parties, pressure groups — often with male allies.

Liberals take exception to the gloomy theories of the others that threaten to paralyze all action in the face of towering structures of capitalism and patriarchy. In turn, radicals and socialists criticize liberals' tendency to ignore structures outside education and other sources of inequality. Liberals are said to blame girls for 'feminine' course choices, while ignoring the conditions women working in 'masculine' occupations face, such as lack of childcare provision, sexual harassment and employer prejudices. Such liberal publica-tions as those from the Equal Opportunities Commission make no mention of race or class: girls are simply girls.

Although some commentators (for example, Weiner, 1985a) stress the incompatibilities between such positions, it is easy to overemphasize their differences. Radical and socialist feminists *do* work within education to improve the quality of girls' experiences, whatever their theories say about structures. And some liberals advance strategies of 'positive action', by which they mean giving special attention to girls (Robarts, 1981). Gearhart (1983) makes a case for alliances between radical and liberal feminists based on the fact that the *goals* of liberal feminists (for example, getting women into educational management to advance their own careers) may be the same as the *strategies* of radical feminists (getting women into educational management in order to introduce anti-sexist initiatives). And, as Janie Whyld (1983a) writes, 'Working within the system does not mean giving up the fight to change it' (p. 297). Feminists of all persuasions seem to use 'equal opportunities' rhetoric with equal abandon, some in its limited meaning, some as a strategic and expedient choice of words. Nevertheless, some feminists do deliberately speak of anti-sexism instead, in order to signal a more radical stance.

Who Promotes Feminist Educational Reform?

How is feminism to influence educational policy formation? There are many groups, legitimized and nonlegitimized (Kogan, 1975), with a potential or actual interest in issues of gender and education. Legitimized groups are those with statutory or conventional rights to be consulted on matters affecting them. There are no legitimized pressure groups with an interest solely in women and education. But many groups with a more general brief on education such as the Further Education Unit, the teachers' and lecturers' unions and subject associations have demonstrated some concern. Other groups more generally involved with 'rights' in general or specifically with women's rights, like the NCCL and the WNC have produced statements on the education of women and girls. A major initiative to establish a contact network and an information resource base on efforts to reduce sex differentiation in schools was taken under the auspices of the Schools Council (Millman and Weiner, 1985).

The Equal Opportunities Commission pays considerable attention to education, although the educational provisions of the Sex Discrimination Act seem particularly weak. The EOC's legislative powers under the sections of the Act relating to equal treatment in access to educational establishments and the facilities within them remain untested in the courts (Carr, 1984), although several cases relating to the employment of teachers have been successfully resolved. Most educational complaints are dealt with by informal means, for example by informing an LEA that its practices contravene the law. Extensive distribution of pamphlets and guidelines is intended to spread information and to promote good practice.

The EOC has also given financial support for conferences and research projects and has commented on government documents. It sponsored WISE (Women into Science and Engineering), a series of projects and publications, in 1984. Less well known are EOC Formal Investigation Reports, some of which make illuminating reading on such practices in schools and colleges as lack of clear criteria for internal promotions, which subtly disadvantage women and girls.

In the 'non-legitimized' arena are the many diverse groups and individuals who have something to say or a case to make, but to whom the government has no obligation to listen. An interesting example is the educational press, which regularly features reports on gender issues. There is also activity from researchers, sometimes on projects like GIST (Girls into Science and Technology) or GATE (Girls and Technology Education), and from other writers and lecturers whose efforts range from quiet reform within their classrooms to the writing of best-sellers. Bookshops contain a range of books on gender and education unthinkable not long ago. There are women and education groups in various cities, some with newsletters, and several library resources such as the Feminist Library and Information Centre, the Fawcett Library, and the Women's Educational Resource Centre, all in London.

The 'grassroots' activities of teachers, parents and others are more difficult to make widely visible, and their influence on policy hard to assess. Orr (1984) estimates that only twenty secondary and twenty primary schools in the country have extended experience of 'whole school' equal opportunity policies, few of which could claim striking success. Nevertheless small-scale initiatives appear to be fairly common. A survey of anti-sexist initiatives in London (ILEA, 1983) reported some sort of action occurring in 85 per cent of mixed secondary schools, a figure that must be breathtaking to teachers in some other regions of the country. Increasingly there are attempts to collect together and distribute results of anti-sexist projects, examples of which can be found in Millman and Weiner, 1985; Spender and Sarah, 1980; Weiner, 1985b and Whyld, 1983b.

The Government Response

Central Government

The government has so far been reluctant to show much commitment beyond a vague support for equal opportunities and a recognition of the need to recruit talented people of both sexes into science and industry. There has been no committee of enquiry set up to look into the education of girls and women. Expressions of educational policy have a curious now-you-see-it, now-you-don't character with regard to gender issues. Certainly one can find expressions of concern about the access of girls to science and mathematics, a notable example being Sir Keith Joseph's speech to the Girls' Schools Association in November 1983 where he argued that girls' lesser participation in such fields hampers their earnings and represents a failure to reach their potential. Teachers' attention to boys, differential treatment of the sexes, peer group pressures and even the lack of women in senior teaching posts were all mentioned, though mostly in the context of encouraging girls into science (Times Educational Supplement, 18 November 1983, p. 6).

In contrast, *Better Schools* (DES, 1985), a review of recent government policies and described in the press as a blueprint for the next century, has only minimal references to the issue. In a chapter on the curriculum, there are two places where sex equality is mentioned. One is when agreement on objectives and content of the curriculum is said to promote a range of desirable outcomes, including helping to remove 'preconceptions based on pupils' sex or ethnic origin' (p. 9). The other is a statement that the curriculum should be broad for every pupil, leaving no room for sex discrimination (p. 14). Unless statements about 'all pupils' are taken to refer implicitly to sex equality, those are the only references in ninety-one pages of text. There is no mention of possible changes in teacher training to promote equal opportunities and no hint of positive action.

Finch (1984) and others point out that educational policy is more likely to be based on a diagnosis of state needs than on considerations of justice. Thus, participation of girls in science is encouraged, whilst other feminist arguments are largely ignored.

It should also be recognized that government policies that are 'sex-blind' may still have major effects on women's lives. Within educational policy there are numerous examples, among them the 1970s cuts in teacher training and adult education, both traditional sites of female participation. In the 1980s, we have the 'swing to science' being enforced by selective cuts within higher education. These cuts may have disproportionately damaging effects on women lecturers, students and would-be-students, traditionally concentrated in the arts (Acker and Warren Piper, 1984).

Local Government

It is difficult to be sure exactly how many initiatives have taken place at this level or how extensive they are. As of September 1984, Orr (1984) reported that about 20 per cent of LEAs had issued policy statements on equal opportunities. In a 'small number' equal opportunities is a major commitment, but most provide relatively little practical support for school reform or in-service training. They tend to see the issue as one of many competitors for dwindling resources rather than a priority (*ibid*).

Two papers presented at the 1984 Girl-Friendly Schooling Conference provide an interesting contrast. One (Taylor, 1984) describes highly successful initiatives in the London borough of Brent, where there is an equal opportunities adviser, extensive in-service training, and school-based research, supported by extra finance and staff. The other (Wells, 1984) discusses attempts in Humberside by a County Working Party to write and distribute guidelines on equal opportunities to schools. This effort attracted tremendous opposition, in part politically motivated, and media ridicule. In the schools, the guidelines were seen as a threat to teacher professionalism and autonomy. The two contrasting cases suggest one must consider local variation in any attempt to evaluate the impact of feminism. This is also evident in the Women's National Commission's (1983) figures on regional variation in the proportion of headships and senior posts in schools held by women. The political complexion of a local authority, the presence or absence of sympathetic individuals in high places, and local traditions all influence the reception given to feminist educational initiatives.

Prospects

For feminists interested or involved in education, reform is a vital and urgent concern. Yet as Lodge and Blackstone (1982) say, 'policies are pre-eminently political choices between competing priorities' (p. 45). So feminists must make their case (or cases) competitively. Lukewarm government commitment and economic recession, plus severe under-representation of women in powerful decision-making positions, make progress difficult. Equal opportunity policy has frequently faltered on the need to redistribute limited resources by taking them away from the privileged and powerful (*op. cit.*), whilst those in favour of redistribution often see the universalistic traditions of welfare state provision as incompatible with special treatment for women.

Teachers tend to believe that individual achievements should determine rewards, not that a particular group should receive them as a matter of definition (as in 'positive action'). They also tend to advocate political neutrality in school, which may take the form of hesitating to interfere in matters that appear to be decided by parents' or employers' preferences or girls' natural proclivities (Pratt *et al.*, 1984). Moreover, they are understandably suspicious of arguments that appear to attack their professionalism and integrity. The extent of coverage of gender issues in teacher training varies greatly and depends on the commitment and presence of interested lecturers. And although there are plans to put management training within reach of all headteachers, there are as yet no requirements that the implementation of equal opportunity policies forms part of that training.

Can feminism counter all that? Some argue that the movement itself is too divided and too loath to participate in conventional politics to promise much success. The image of feminism — largely inaccurate — propounded by the media makes large numbers of people, including women, unsympathetic to what they believe its aims to be (Richards, 1982). Nevertheless, feminism survives even in these difficult times, and Randall (1982) says 'There is little doubt of the achievements or of the continuing vitality of the contemporary women's movement' (p. 159). The grassroots character of feminism promotes creativity and means that innovations can continue to appear without the need of massive bureaucratic planning and coordination. The combination of top-down 'liberal' initiatives (EOC, LEAs) with the incredible commitment of feminist teachers has a power unmatched by other reform movements. Whilst the special group argument alienates some, the special group in question *is* half the population and, moreover, the ideologies of teachers should also lead them to question any kind of stereotyped treatment of a group made without reference to individual needs. The whole rationale for teaching is to promote change in learners. Interrupting a process whereby pupils' pre-existing gender identities become transformed into male advantage and female disadvantage in the classroom (Kelly, 1985) is surely a legitimate educational intervention. To say this is not to attack the teaching profession; it is to challenge it.

Whatever the difficulties encountered in introducing and sustaining feminist activities in education, the efforts of committed teachers and parents are likely to continue and spread as long as feminism survives. It is a paradox that although education provides the conditions under which people are channelled into limited futures, it is also the primary means for liberation and transformation. Feminists will continue to use it in a liberating spirit, in and out of school. The efforts of each feminist teacher and parent will be reflected in the generations to follow.

Acknowledgements

I am grateful to Madeleine Arnot, Miriam David and Geoff Millerson for comments and suggestions about this chapter.

References

ACKER, S. (1982) 'Women and education', in HARTNETT, A. (Ed.) *The Social Sciences in Educational Studies*, London, Heinemann, pp. 144–52.

ACKER, S., MEGARRY, J., NISBET, S. and HOYLE, E. (Eds) (1984) *World Yearbook of Education 1984: Women and Education*, London, Kogan Page.

ACKER, S. and WARREN PIPER, D. (Eds) (1984) *Is Higher Education Fair to Women?*, Guildford, SRHE and NFER/Nelson.

ARNOT, M. (1985) 'Current developments in the sociology of women's education', *British Journal of Sociology of Education*, 6, 1, pp. 123–30.

CARR, L. (1984) 'Legislation and mediation: To what extent has the Sex Discrimination Act changed girls' schooling?', paper presented at the Girl-Friendly Schooling Conference, Manchester, 11–13 September.

DAVID, M. (1984) 'Women, family and education', in ACKER, S. *et al.* (Eds) *World Yearbook of Education 1984: Women and Education*, London, Kogan Page, pp. 191–201.

DEEM, R. (1981) 'State policy and ideology in the education of women, 1944–1980', *British Journal of Sociology of Education*, 2, 2, pp. 131–43.

DEPARTMENT OF EDUCATION AND SCIENCE (1985) *Better Schools* (Cmnd 9469), London, HMSO.

EISENSTEIN, H. (1984) *Contemporary Feminist Thought*, London, Unwin.

EQUAL OPPORTUNITIES COMMISSION (1985), *Ninth Annual Report 1984*, London, HMSO.

FINCH, J. (1984) *Education as Social Policy*, London, Longman.

FULLER, M. (1984) *Inequality: Gender, Race and Class*, Open University E205, Block 6, Unit 27, Milton Keynes, Open University Press.

GEARHART, S.M. (1983) 'If the mortarboard fits ... radical feminism in academia', in BUNCH, C. and POLLACK, S. (Eds) *Learning Our Way:*

Essays in Feminist Education, Trumansburg, NY, The Crossing Press, pp. 2–18.

INNER LONDON EDUCATION AUTHORITY (1983) *Anti-sexist Initiatives in ILEA Schools*, London, ILEA.

KELLY, A. (1985) 'The construction of masculine science', *British Journal of Sociology of Education*, 6, 2, pp. 133–54.

KOGAN, M. (1975) *Educational Policy-Making*, London, George Allen and Unwin.

LODGE, P. and BLACKSTONE, T. (1982) *Educational Policy and Educational Inequality*, Oxford, Martin Robertson.

MACDONALD, M. (1980) 'Socio-cultural reproduction and women's education', in DEEM, R. (Ed), *Schooling for Women's Work*, London, Routledge and Kegan Paul, pp. 13–25.

MCFADDEN, M. (1984) 'Anatomy of difference: Toward a classification of feminist theory', *Women's Studies International Forum*, 7, 8, pp. 495–504.

MIDGLEY, M. and HUGHES, J. (1983) *Women's Choices: Philosophical Problems Facing Feminism*, London, Weidenfeld and Nicolson.

MILLMAN, V. and WEINER, G. (1985) *Sex Differentiation in Schooling: Is There Really a Problem?* Final Report of the Schools Council Project on Reducing Sex Differentiation in Schools, York, Longman Resources Unit.

ORR, P. (1984) 'Sex differentiation in schools: The current situation', paper presented at the Girl-Friendly Schooling Conference, Manchester, 11–13 September.

PRATT, J., BLOOMFIELD, J. and SEALE, C. (1984) *Option Choice: A Question of Equal Opportunity*, Windsor, NFER/Nelson.

RANDALL, V. (1982) *Women and Politics*, London, Macmillan.

RICHARDS, J.R. (1982) *The Sceptical Feminist*, Harmondsworth, Penguin.

ROBARTS, S. (1981) *Positive Action for Women: The Next Step*, London, National Council for Civil Liberties.

ROGERS, B. (1983) *52%: Getting Women's Power Into Politics*, London, The Women's Press.

SPENDER, D. and SARAH, E. (Eds) (1980) *Learning to Lose: Sexism and Education*, London, The Women's Press.

TAYLOR, H. (1984) 'INSET for equal opportunities in the London borough of Brent', paper presented at the Girl-Friendly Schooling Conference, Manchester, 11–13 September.

WALKER, S. and BARTON, L. (Eds) (1983) *Gender, Class and Education*, Lewes, Falmer Press.

WEINER, G. (1985a) 'Equal opportunities, feminism and girls' education: Introduction', in WEINER, G. (Ed.) *Just a Bunch of Girls*, Milton Keynes, Open University Press, pp. 1–13.

WEINER, G. (Ed.) (1985b) *Just a Bunch of Girls*, Milton Keynes, Open University Press.

WELLS, J.H. (1984) '"Humberside goes neuter": Issues raised by LEA intervention and related anti-sexist initiatives', paper presented at the Girl-Friendly Schooling Conference, Manchester, 11–13 September.

WHYLD, J. (1983a) 'More than one way forward', in WHYLD, J. (Ed.),

Sexism in the Secondary Curriculum, London, Harper and Row, pp. 295–313.

WHYLD, J. (Ed.) (1983b) *Sexism in the Secondary Curriculum*, London, Harper and Row.

WHYTE, J., DEEM, R., KANT, L. and CRUIKSHANK, M. (Eds) (1985) *Girl Friendly Schooling*, London, Methuen contains revised versions of CARR (1984); ORR (1984); TAYLOR (1984) and WELLS (1984).

WOMEN'S NATIONAL COMMISSION (1983) *Report on Secondary Education*, London, Cabinet Office.

Public Schools

Roger Bullock

Introduction

Public schools have long been a focus of interest. Their style and philosophy have produced both imitation and counter-reaction elsewhere in the education system. They are also seen as socially divisive. They educate a small number of privileged children, their leavers move into top positions in society, they separate their pupils from other social groups and, until recently, from the opposite sex. What is more, they are said to form 'attitudes, assumptions and aspects of personality in their pupils by maintaining an ethos which in some chief respects is unlike that of state schools or ordinary life outside'.[1] The validity of these criticisms scarcely matters. For while opinions about public schools will certainly be heartfelt, they are more likely to reflect political zeal rather than scientific truth.

Yet, despite these criticisms and attempted reforms spanning several centuries, the top public schools continue to flourish. Why is this? Why do they continue to be so significant for the wider educational system, and indeed British society as a whole, given that only a few thousand pupils attend them? It is these questions that the following discussion seeks to explore.

Problems of Definition

One subtlety of the public school system is that while its products are distinctive, its boundaries are nebulous. Public schools cannot easily be identified in terms of administrative status or educational approach. For example, while all public schools are independent and their headmasters members of the Headmasters' Conference (HMC), so are many other establishments. Most public schools are boarding but many have day pupils, and there are numerous day public schools. Similarly, their curriculum, like that of many state schools, is geared to national examinations. Yet in our perceptions of the public school philosophy, style and product, we are un-equivocal: we know a public school by its sights, sounds, smell and feel. It is this 'knowing' that engrains such perceptions so deeply into wider social attitudes, and makes imitation so difficult for the outsider.

Most of the concern about public schools is directed to some forty top schools which, at any one time, educate about 30,000 pupils, mostly boys. However, even among these there are special traditions, and houses within a particular school may afford dif-ferential status. The HMC, in contrast, is a much wider body, with over 200 members whose schools educate 140,000 pupils, again mostly boys. In addition, there are forty SCHMIS schools and over 100 self-styled public schools overseas. For girls, there are some 160 leading private schools with 80,000 pupils. Yet even all of these form only a small part of the total independent sector which is composed of some 2500 establishments, and educates about 600,000 or 6 per cent of children in the United Kingdom, a figure that rises to 8 per cent for those of secondary age. Some famous names, such as Atlan-tic College, Summerhill and Dartington Hall, along with many other independent schools, are not members of the associations previously mentioned.

Public schools vary in their function. It would be a misinter-pretation of British upper middle class society to confuse the role of schools which teach manners to embryonic earls with those that facilitate the social mobility sought by successful tycoons. Even among the top twenty public schools, there are subtle differences, particularly in the balance between the provision of status main-tenance and social mobility. The willingness of public schools to absorb those seeking upward social mobility has been one of the main reasons for their continuation, as has their much less publi-cized role of providing for middle-class casualties of family break-down or disruptions arising from occupational mobility.

There is a danger, therefore, that in seeking a precise definition of the public school, we rely too much on administrative classifica-tions rather than on those unique aspects that fascinate observers of British society. Fletcher, for example, identified as the distinguishing features: the existence of an endowment fund, a governing body who work with that fund in mind, and an HMC headmaster in charge.[2] Yet, even if we *know* but cannot specify what a public school is we still find it difficult to be any more conclusive than Sampson who speaks of 'the influence of an elite still based on a tiny group of fee-paying boarding schools beyond the range of most parents, whose influence on the country now appears greater than ever. And in the meantime, the alternative route to the top, via the grammar schools, has disappeared'.[3]

These difficulties of definition have served to protect public schools from externally imposed changes. The educational and political arguments simply do not fit neatly into categories normally used to analyze social issues. The public school question straddles the political left and right, radical and conservative educational theory, and the balance between individual liberty and centralised power. The argument that wealth should not purchase privilege is offset by one defending the freedom of parents to spend their money as they choose. Similarly, while the existence of an independent sector has hindered the establishment of comprehensive state education, free enterprise is prized in other contexts. There is also a pragmatic perspective, why destroy what is often excellent? It is hardly surprising, therefore, that the reforms suggested by assorted commissions over many years have been unsuccessful. The last serious attempt, the Public Schools Commission of 1968, was dismissed almost before it had reported, although its Chairman, David Donnison, clearly foresaw the implications of impasse for the establishment of a truly comprehensive state school system.

Equally noticeable is the lack of rigour in the debate. All kinds of rationalizations and non-sequiturs, which would be quite unacceptable elsewhere, are tolerated. For instance, 'freedom to choose' is espoused, but what of the impoverished parent who wants Eton for his children? Indeed, the headmaster of that venerable establishment has said, 'All public schools would welcome some links with the state system if they can keep their independence'.[4] John Rae, a distinguished spokesman on public school matters, offers the following proposition, 'The basic problem is social injustice — yet you need injustice to achieve long-term ends. The biggest damage we do is to perpetuate a class division. But it may be the price we have to pay for excellence'.[5] These hypotheses, one suspects, have escaped the scrutiny to which that alleged academic excellence should submit them.

Politicians have been no more conclusive than educators. In the 1960s, there was the shock caused by radicals who, after much public soul searching, sent their children to private schools. Shirley Williams, a former Secretary of State for Education and Science admitted, 'It is with reluctance that I for one conclude the freedom to send one's children to an independent school is bought at too high a price for the rest of society'.[6] Thus, proposals for reform of the public schools have always ended up as an unsatisfactory compromise. They range from Fletcher's unlikely recommendation that the public schools should be truly independent, in market competition with state provision, to schemes which seek 'integration' between the state and independent sectors, whether along the lines of the scholarships awarded by the charitable foundations, of the Fleming Report of 1944, of the Report of the Public School Commission of 1968 or, the most recent initiative, the Assisted Places Scheme.[7] This scheme seeks to place in independent schools some 5000 academically able children whose parents could not normally afford the fees.

Thus, today, we find that the major public schools are confident and secure. They have successfully resisted attacks from political and educational reformers. Most have also survived a period of high inflation. In addition, they have adapted to changes in the expectations of parents and pupils, and have maintained that congruence between the school, work and family life that has made them such a powerful force in British Society. Let us look at these processes in greater detail, first concentrating on the relationship between public schools and the wider society.

Public Schools and the Wider Society

Whilst few would dispute the socially divisive qualities of public schools in the past, to what extent can they be said, in 1987, to be serving an elite? In reaching a conclusion, much will stem from the definitions employed, for identifying elites is as difficult as delineating a public school. Historically, the links between public schools and social class are clear, whether in times of stability or of rapid social change. After the industrial revolution, for example, the landed aristocrats were joined by emerging commercial and professional classes but, as both Wilkinson and Cole have pointed out, the long standing elite not only embraced commercial opportunities but also allowed the *nouveaux riches* to join them, a feature that has had far reaching political consequences for British society.[8] Hence, the emergence of new economic elites led to reform and expansion of public schools in the nineteenth century where one of their functions was to mould new arrivals into 'gentlemen'. They provided a moral code, encouraged a life-style, and fostered qualities appropriate to those destined to govern.

But since those Victorian times, meritocracy has increasingly stressed the need for achievement rather than breeding. Such new elites have emerged as managers, intellectuals, bureaucrats and professionals and such new power locations have emerged as the mass media and the multi-national corporation. In addition, women are increasingly gaining access to enclaves previously exclusive to men, thus breaking down that other discriminating factor which accompanies social class in the public schools, namely sex. Criteria for entry to the top positions in society have widened, and even if a public school education is still an asset, an Oxbridge degree is now more likely to be an essential qualification. What does this mean for the modern public school?

One of the problems in charting these changes is the dearth of reliable evidence about individuals in esteemed positions. For example, research which charts the distribution of wealth in British society is hampered by the ways that families spread their assets among relatives, a practice occasionally revealed by the huge estates of deceased minors. Similarly, kinship networks, built up over centuries, may unite seemingly disparate members of different elite groups. Research studies of inter-generation social mobility are only able to confirm the most general patterns. For example, the Oxford Mobility Study of men born before 1947 showed that boys from privileged families reached high status occupations, but were only matching their fathers' achievements.[9] The successful boys from state schools did rise to a higher social class than their parents but only usually a small step up the social ladder. They failed to penetrate the avenues available to those from public schools.

A further problem is the familiar sociological issue of separating the influence of school from family or of discovering what public school pupils would have attained had they been educated elsewhere. Yet, however scant the evidence, it does seem that many elites continue to be dominated by those from privileged public school backgrounds. For example, the public schools still educate 60 or 70 per cent of top people in political, aristocratic, judicial and business circles. While this figure has fallen in recent years, the decline has been relatively small.

This picture was clear from an analysis of admissions in the late 1960s to one of the most distinguished Oxbridge colleges. This group of students is now entering top positions in British society.[10] Of the 102 admissions, thirty came from top boarding public schools which included many famous names and the 'Clarendon' nine, namely, Charterhouse, Eton, Harrow, Merchant Taylors', Rugby, St. Paul's, Shrewsbury, Westminster, and Winchester, which were the subject of the Clarendon Commission's investigations between 1861 and 1864. However, this did *not* mean that the other seventy-two came from state schools; in fact only thirty-one did. Of the remaining forty-one, twenty-seven came from independent day schools, eleven from direct grant establishments and three via other esteemed routes. Thus, 29 per cent of the college entrants had been to top boarding schools and as many as 67 per cent came from HMC establishments. The social, as well as academic, selectivity is beyond doubt and the public school contribution is clearly significant on all criteria.

Thus, all evidence available suggests that the public schools are still an important part of recruitment to and socialization into top groups in British society. While their influence has been challenged by other agencies, the system has benefited from the demise of the grammar and direct grant schools, some of which have themselves become independent. But this role has only been maintained by considerable adaptation to changed circumstances. Much of the ritual and structure portrayed in literature and films of twenty years ago have disappeared. Regimes have been relaxed, schools have broadened their curricula, especially in science and computing, and cultural horizons have been widened to seek excellence in the visual and performing arts. The academic emphasis has been increased at the expense of sport and concern with hierarchy and the schools are more geared to examination success, the qualities now so essential for entry into many desired occupations.

This style is quite different from the Billy Bunter or Stalky experiences which prevailed until very recently. But, as Salter and Tapper indicate, the changes have been a subtle adaptation which has important social implications.[11] While the schools have 'successfully transformed their educational practices to fulfil this task in today's world, they have retained the idea that their essential purpose is to educate the nation's future elites'. An increased academic emphasis helps young people enter elites, and legitimizes the schools' educational and social role but, at the same time, probably disguises their continuing contribution to the process of social reproduction.

The Public School Ethos

If the public schools are still significant in maintaining and moulding social elites, how do they do this?

The observation that the segregation of the privileged in separate institutions leads to a 'cloistered elite', as described by Wakeford, is a serious social and educational accusation against the public schools.[12] While class segregation among pupils has been noted as a common feature of state schools in that streams are often socially selective and children tend to mix with those from similar backgrounds, at least this occurs in a context where there is a greater variation in the cultural and class backgrounds of children and of staff. The public schools, on the other hand, are separate institutions which are socially and sometimes geographically isolated. They are also highly selective, and the values they espouse are those of the upper and upper middle classes. Thus, these values are more likely to go unquestioned. What is more, the 'hidden curriculum' of attitudes, lifestyles and social skills affords advantages to those setting out for the top. Indeed, many of these 'expressive' qualities, be they dinner table manners or cultural refinement, turn out to be extremely useful 'instrumentally' in later life.

It is not possible to understand this complex socialization without knowing something of the structure, lifestyle, child-rearing patterns and values of the upper middle-classes, without examining the preparatory schools which educate children from 6 to 13, and without considering the prestigious occupations to which the leading public schools are inextricably linked. Here, the ancient universities are extremely significant, for they provide staff for the public schools, shelter their most successful products and allocate people to elite professions and statuses. Equally important are certain regiments, private institutes and business houses.

If we appreciate this 'career', that is the sequence of events from the bosom of nanny (or from the slightly more accessible *au pair*), to the smell of *Lifebuoy* soap, changing rooms, Latin books and so on to the polished voice and assumptions, we begin to see the value implications of the sequence, its internal logic, echoed by the experiences of family and friends, all of which produce the public school 'effect'. Even if we forget that this is a 'career', the boys do not.

My family has been coming here since the seventeenth century, it was the best way to eradicate a frightful Scots accent.

We went down and looked at my father's study and my grandfather's. Dad found his name carved under the window-sill and that made his day.

Years ago my family brought their own tutors here as well, in the eighteenth century, it was a hell of a place. Today, if it gets any more permissive, we will be able to bring our mistresses.

This tradition, and the security and confidence that it gives, are important to public school boys. In spite of early separation from home and an emotional dependence on institutional life, features alleged to have detrimental consequences for ordinary children, public school products seem to thrive, at least in their public duties. Indeed, the qualities of public schools which satisfy the needs of adolescents for a sense of belonging, a perception of self-progress, and an ambience for excitement and intrigue have perhaps been underestimated in the more general concern with the deprivations and violations of communal life.

Public schools also set out to educate the 'whole man', a concept in which academic success ranks equal with moral and spiritual development and social skill. One Roman Catholic headmaster, for example, said that his aim was to prepare pupils for death — a perspective hardly shared by his boys who seemed to be living life to the full. Although, as was said earlier, the academic emphasis has increased in recent years, public schools still offer a range of other avenues for pupil achievement, be they sports, positions of responsibility or art, music and drama. In addition, there is a continued stress on the orthodox Christian faith, conventional morality and service to the wider community. While some of the more obvious manifestations of these have disappeared, there is no evidence to suggest that the underlying values have changed. The hope is that pupils' behaviour will reflect deep commitment to these values rather than a superficial conformity.

Commitment also means loyalty, narrow loyalties to your friends who share your values, to the house in which you live together, and to the school which negotiates with the outside world. This loyalty, which only rarely comes adrift in times of scandal, usually when friends turn out not to be gentlemen, help form the so called 'old boy network'. The master of a distinguished Oxbridge college once proudly advised his freshmen, 'Wherever you go in the world, you will find a college man'. This, of course, is not only true but also gives you rights and obligations — rights if he turns out to be an ambassador and obligations if he is destitute on a Moroccan beach. As one prefect pointed out, 'As all my friends and relatives will be successful, and, as I know enough to sack most of them, I have a formidable data bank at my fingertips.'

This ethos is reflected in all aspects of school life, its internal organization, the ends which it serves, the expectations, manners, customs and behaviour of boys and staff and the ways in which individuals judge one another. This is what makes public school pupils differ from the majority of other children. It also confers on them skills which can be deployed in a variety of other complex organizations, especially those imbued with the same values such as the top professions, the civil service and business world. Public schools might differ in size, religious denomination and tradition, as do state schools, but they are unified by this common ethos. Here, in the values and assumptions which they display, there is much less variation.

Management skills are inculcated early by the division of schools into a plethora of small units, each with their own hierarchies and authority. Boys work their way to the top twice over, once at their prep school and later in their public school. On each occasion, there is continuous scrutiny and evaluation by staff and by older peers of the boys' performance, most of which is given in public. It is not difficult, therefore, to see how those reared in such establishments do well later in bureaucracies. For the public schoolboy, bureaucracies liberate and extend their power, they provide a home for abstract intelligence, they require recruits trained for status rather than for specific skills, and concern themselves with role performance rather than content. All of these features are expressions of the public school ethos. Indeed, there is a spiritual connection between the first-former forced to do his unseen when he would rather be playing cricket and the adult administrator pouring over official memoranda, longing for the week-end to arrive.

Finally, the emotional climate of public schools is also conducive to later bureaucratic success. Although public school homosexuality is declining as young people have more freedom and girls are introduced into sixth forms, public school life puts a premium on 'affective neutrality'. Identification with those under one's command is discouraged, emotional feelings of all kinds are repressed, except in the case of a few close friends, and extreme opinions are disapproved. 'When I listen to Rachmaninov, it makes me feel embarrassed', confessed one music teacher. Thus, the public self which is so confident, unruffled and brimming with managerial skills flourishes, while the private self atrophies. This 'affective neutrality' or stiff upper lip is the most commonly noted feature of public school products. It was, in fact, once thought by foreigners to be a characteristic of all British people, until the stereotype was rudely shattered by travellers from other classes.

The continuing importance of public schools rests, therefore, on two features. First is their ability to confer status on pupils, an attribute which seems undiminished and which still brings leavers success in later life. Secondly, the education offered not only meets academic requirements but also promotes values which are congruent with other life experiences, whether early on in prep school and in the family or in what happens subsequently. Until there is a variety of routes to top positions in society, schooling for the academically and socially aspirant is likely to ape the public schools rather than challenge them.

Public Schools and the Future

How significant are public schools likely to be in the future? While the prediction of social changes must always be hazardous, certain trends in British society will have some bearing on the future role of public schools. First, there is the fall in the secondary school population. But while the market may be declining, there are few indications that this will affect the leading public schools, although pressure may be felt by smaller, geographically isolated establishments, especially those for girls.

Secondly, there is likely to be growing competition from the state sector which offers much that is excellent free of charge. However, as with falling rolls, this is unlikely to trouble the more distinguished independent establishments, and if it does, it will be at the age extremes, at preparatory or sixth form level.

Thirdly, the increasing stress on meritocracy in all levels of society means that school allegiancies may no longer be sufficient to guarantee success. Again, this will most certainly affect the power of lesser establishments but the 'hidden curriculum' of the public school still appears to give leavers advantages over those with equal qualifications. In meritocracies, personal attributes are important and often form part of the criteria by which 'merit' is assessed. In organizations where commitment and loyalty are cherished, the public school factor seems likely to remain influential.

Fourthly, the economic and social assets gained by new entrants to meritocracies are largely based on income, increases in which are reduced by inflation. It requires many generations in top positions to establish wealth based on land or property, which is easy to pass on and is less subject to economic fluctuation, or to build up that wide kinship network which gives access to distinguished people in all walks of life. The growth of meritocracy, therefore, is likely to take considerable time before it challenges well established elite structures and the entries and exits available to public school boys.

Lastly, it may be that the relevance of the values embodied in the public school ethos will decline. Certainly, the areas of public school influence may contract as directors from multi-national corporations take over British businesses or public figures are exposed to impolite media. Yet, as before, while there may be change, it is likely to be superficial simply because the sub-structure of values, social networks and avenues seems so stable. The greatest threat to the public school system, therefore, is perhaps not so much extinction but fossilization. As national influence declines, pageants are enacted in an increasingly parochial ambience.

Conclusions

In this chapter the discussion has sought to explore the continuing significance of public schools for education and society. The available evidence suggests that they continue to be socially divisive in that their social class composition is narrow, the life chances which they confer on pupils are enhanced and their isolation from mainstream state education is severe. In addition, their ethos is distinctive and is manifest in the blinkered cultural perspectives conferred by the organizational structures and values, both formal and informal, that operate within them. Yet, while the public schools are so closely tied into social structures, they can and do adapt to wider social change. Hence, the power of the top few schools highlighted at the beginning of this chapter has been preserved.

Given a particular political ideology, even these weaknesses can be seen as strengths. Unlike many advanced industrial societies, Britain has an intelligent, relatively uncorruptable administrative class, which is motivated by a deep sense of service, whatever we may think of the values they espouse. Equally the public schools, by taking the heat out of arguments about blocked aspirations for the emerging middle classes and by providing avenues for social mobility, have contributed to a relatively stable society. However, it is a society that is probably suffocatingly conservative. On the debit side, the system directs the able to unproductive jobs, it divides the managers from the ruled, and continues to maintain deep divisions in social class and status, not just by upholding privilege but by virtue of its ethos.

Notes

1 LAMBERT, R., HIPKIN, J. and STAGG, S. (1969) *New Wine in Old Bottles*, London, Bell. See also LAMBERT, R. and MILLHAM, S. (1968) *The Hothouse Society*, London, Weidenfeld and Nicolson; LAMBERT, R., MILLHAM, S. and BULLOCK, R. (1975) *The Chance of a Lifetime?*, London, Weidenfeld and Nicolson. All quotations from individuals used in the chapter are taken from this research.
2 FLETCHER, R. (1984) 'The public schools controversy', in *Education in Society: the Promethean Fire*, Harmondsworth, Penguin, pp. 220–48.
3 SAMPSON, A. (1982) *The Changing Anatomy of Britain*, London, Hodder and Stoughton, p. 135.
4 Quoted in SAMPSON, A. (1982) *ibid*, p. 144.
5 Quoted in SAMPSON, A. (1982) *ibid*, p. 141.
6 WILLIAMS, S. (1981) *Politics is for People*, Harmondsworth, Penguin, p. 158.
7 HMSO (1944) *Committee on Public Schools*, London, HMSO; HMSO (1968) *First Report of the Public Schools Commission*, London, HMSO.
8 WILKINSON, R. (1964) *The Prefects*, Oxford, Oxford University Press; COLE, G.D.H. (1955) *Studies in Class Structure*, London, Routledge and Kegan Paul; GATHORNE-HARDY, J. (1977) *The Public School Phenomenon*, London, Hodder; OTLEY, C.B. (1966) 'Public schools and the army', *New Society*, 17 November.
9 HEATH, A. (1981) 'What difference does the old school tie make now?', *New Society*, 18 June, pp. 472–4; STANWORTH, P. and GIDDENS, A. (Eds) (1974) *Elites and Power in British Society*, Cambridge, Cambridge University Press; LUPTON, T. and WILSON, C.S. 'The social background and connections of top decision makers' in URRY, J. and WAKEFORD, J. (Eds) (1973) *Power in Britain: Sociological Readings*, London, Heinemann.
10 Unpublished paper (1968), Centre for Boarding Education Research, Cambridge.
11 SALTER, B. and TAPPER, T. (1981) *Education, Politics and the State*, London, Grant McIntre; WALFORD, G. (1986) *Life in Public Schools*, London, Methuen.
12 WAKEFORD, J. (1969) *The Cloistered Elite*, London, MacMillan.

Structure and Ideology in Upper Secondary Education

Bill Reid and Maurice Holt

Introduction

The use of the phrase 'upper secondary education' in the title of this chapter reflects the basic dilemma which it addresses: there is, in England today, no satisfactory way of referring to the education of students who have completed the basic secondary curriculum but are not yet old enough to enter higher education or trades and professions demanding qualifications beyond those obtainable at the age of 16. The difficulty is not merely one of terminology. Where this level of education is associated with coherent curricula and institutions, as in the senior high schools of the USA or in the gymnasia of Scandinavia, there can be critical debate about the nature and content of the education on offer. In England, such debates are about the nature and content of a host of separate and poorly articulated programmes, all belonging within the general area for which 'upper secondary' serves, however unhappily, as a label. The argument of this chapter is that we should not be misled by this plethora of offerings into believing that the structures of curriculum and organization observed at the upper secondary level are the result of unguided and contradictory initiatives, but that, on the contrary, they reflect the working out of a consistent ideology which has dominated state secondary education since the 1902 Act. We further argue that improvement of upper secondary education, and indeed education as a whole, can come about only through recovery and development of traditions which have been stifled by this dominant ideology. But before embarking on the substance of our chapter, we need to clarify what is meant by the terms 'improvement', 'ideology' and 'tradition'.

'Improvement' must be defined in relation to espoused goals or purposes. Our position is that, in modern societies, the education that young people experience is importantly related to how they come to see themselves as citizens of those societies. Does that education encourage them to behave as full members of the polity, entitled not only to choose leaders but to act as leaders? Not only to express opinions but to have those opinions taken into account? We believe that education directed to these ends is beneficial both to the individual who is given a wider sense of powers and responsibilities, and also to the society in whose service such powers and responsibilities will be exercised. It is not possible to describe here in detail the kind of education that would achieve this. However, a number of points need to be made.

First, it will be an education that extends beyond the age of 16. Even in the nineteenth century, those classes who were clear that they could exercise leadership in society were also clear that their children should be in school to the age of 18 or 19. Secondly, it will be an education the success of which depends as much on membership of an institution as on experience of a curriculum. The upper classes of the last century also understood that the sense of capacity as a member of society derived from contact with an institutional tradition as well as from mastery of subject matter. Thirdly, it will be education that is, to use Ringer's[1] terminology, more inclusive, more progressive, and less segmented. By 'more inclusive' we mean that it would enrol larger numbers of students. The goal would be to have as large a proportion of the age cohort as possible voluntarily continuing in education to the age of 18 or 19. However, in the foreseeable future, attendance would not be universal, and, through the period when it fell short of this target, we would be concerned that it should be progressive in the specific sense that the shortfall in attendance should not be disproportionately accounted for by the absence of lower middle and lower class students. Finally, we are opposed to the tactic of increasing enrolment simply by raising the level of segmentation in the system — that is, by creating parallel and distinct forms of curriculum and institution so that, while an appearance of progressiveness is created, lower class students can be relegated to membership in low prestige or stigmatized curricula.[2] Movements towards inclusiveness and progressiveness and away from segmentation constitute improvements in 16–19 education connected in fairly obvious ways with the general goals we have stated. How these movements could actually occur is a matter for debate.

Our use of the words 'ideology' and 'tradition' also stands in need of clarification. Whether we talk about schools or subjects or curricula, meaning is given to the contents and practices of education by the traditions in which they stand. We can see this by considering what would happen if the contents and practices of one educational system were suddenly transplanted to another. For example, the American high school system of units, grades and graduation would have no meaning to students and teachers reared within the very different tradition of the English sixth form. But in the USA there is a tradition of high school education which embraces knowledge of how to administer such a structure, how it relates to social and educational goals, and how it intersects with the lives and careers of students and teachers. Such traditions can be 'living', in the sense that they are open to reinterpretation and critical appraisal as society, culture and technology change, or they can become 'frozen' and incapable of responding to change other than by tactics which have as their main purpose to maintain intact the assumptions and practices of the tradition. We here refer to the 'frozen' tradition as an 'ideology'. Our distinction is similar to the one that Popper makes between first- and second-order traditions. A first-order tradition is 'a definite story', complete and conclusive in its claims, while a second-order tradition is equally a story, but with the important extra provision that it is passed on to others with the injunction that they critically discuss and modify it.[3] (An example of reinterpretation of a tradition would be the shift that took place in the USA in the 1950s and 1960s in the conception of how educational practices related to the goal of equality when the idea was abandoned that separate facilities for blacks and whites could be 'equal'.[4])

We suggest that education cannot be adaptive to circumstance yet guided by principle unless its traditions are second-order traditions or, as MacIntyre puts it, traditions 'in good order' since they are 'partially constituted by an argument about the goods the pursuit of which gives them their particular point and purpose'.[5] In the case of English upper secondary education, we are seeing the creation of structures which reflect a first-order tradition or, as we shall now revert to calling it, 'ideology' which excludes any critical discussion of 'goods'.

The Segmentation of Upper Secondary Education

The persistence of this ideology is most prominently shown in the way in which increased inclusiveness in education beyond the school leaving age is being accompanied by greater segmentation. Whereas the trend in many comparable countries is towards simplification of the range of courses and options on offer, combined with a search for ways in which common curriculum components can be shared within inclusive institutions, in the UK we have seen in recent years a proliferation of new curricula, each largely self-contained, springing up alongside existing elements which retain their own identity. Thus, the Technical and Vocational Education Initiative (TVEI), which is intended to span the 14–18 age range, the Certificate of Pre-Vocational Education (CPVE), and the Youth Training Scheme (YTS) have been added to the existing stock of academic and technical courses so that, even if a common institution were proposed to house all these offerings, it would still be hard to raise questions about the aims of education for the age group as a whole, while these sub-groups continued to follow distinctive curricula representing competing rather than complementary versions of what education should be about.

History shows, of course, that in all countries education beyond the elementary level was, by origin, segmented in character. At the lower end, secondary provision overlapped with elementary classes. (It was not until the Act of 1944 that the principle was established in England that secondary education was a 'stage' rather than a 'kind' of education.) In the middle ranges, secondary provision was divided between academic and technical programmes, while at the upper end students might find themselves in college preparatory establishments, finishing schools or vocational courses. The history of secondary education has been the history of the processes by which these varied curricula and institutions have been moulded into a common system. In some places change has gone faster or further; in others, movement has been slow or has been halted by obstacles. In practically all Western countries, education before the age of 16 is now provided within a common system offering a broadly similar curriculum to all students. In England, the development of comprehensive education 11–16, which began in the 1960s has recently slowed down so that institutional reorganization, though widespread, is not complete, while on the curricular front, some segmentation remains from the age of 13 or so. Beyond 16, the inclusiveness with little segmentation which characterizes the education system of North America and much of Europe has not been echoed in England, where traditional 'A' level courses have kept their specialized academic nature, and enrol only 20 per cent of the age cohort, while other students pursue tracks inside or outside the school system offering few or no overlapping elements.

As we consider the different structures of upper secondary education in various countries, three related factors can be discerned which affect the extent to which they are characterized by segmentation. One of these is the nature of the political and administrative arrangements through which education is provided. Where there is strong central control, there is a greater likelihood that the system will be relatively uniform. This is especially the case where, as in Sweden, those groups which have an interest in the promotion of a common system are able to have direct political influence on educational policy at the highest level. Under these conditions, central control not only increases the possibility of instituting a uniform structure of school organization and curriculum, but also emphasizes the character of schooling as an enterprise reflecting national aspirations for the equalizing of opportunity and the spread of responsible citizenship across the social classes. A second factor to be considered is the nature of the system of examination or assessment. Here, on the contrary, it would appear that a strong emphasis on uniform national standards may operate to increase segmentation, although the extent of this effect will naturally depend on the diversity of a country's population in terms of wealth, local affiliation or ethnic origin. Sweden, as a country of fairly undifferentiated population, can afford to implement a centralized assessment system without damage to goals of equality, but the USA, with its immensely varied racial groups and uneven distribution of wealth, can pursue such goals only by allowing standards of graduation to be set at the local level, so that, as Ringer remarks, 'Differences of academic and social standing in secondary and higher education have not been reinforced by curricular distinctions'.[6]

But the third and most pervasive factor which underlies the other two is that of tradition or ideology. To consider political and administrative arrangements in isolation as determinative of the character of education systems is to suggest that they are shaped solely by objective decisions about how the ends of education should be settled (for example by local or national, or lay or professional groups) and how the means to those ends should be chosen (for example through uniform or differentiated curricula, or through local or national assessment). However, the chosen ends and means are an expression of conceptions of schooling as part of the wider drama of national life. The structures of decision and implementation reflect such conceptions and, in turn, become instruments for reinforcing them. Where they are reinterpreted in the face of social and cultural change, we may speak of the existence of a tradition 'in good order'. In America at the turn of the century and in Scandinavia in the post-Second World War period, the tradition of secondary education, which until then had an essentially college-preparatory character, underwent substantial modification to adjust it to an approaching era when extended secondary education would be a universal prerequisite of full citizenship. Reinterpretation of the tradition brought modifications of structure to enable schools to become more inclusive and progressive in their enrolments and less segmented in their structures. American high schools moved to a unit-based curriculum with equivalence between subjects, and in Scandinavia an integrated common curriculum was adopted. However, the advent of state-provided secondary education in England after the Education Act of 1902 produced only minimal adjustment in the tradition which had animated the independent boarding schools of the late nineteenth century. Here the tradition was already assuming the character of an ideology which allows for no reinterpretation to take place either in the matter of the goods to which it aspires or the connection it postulates between those goods and the means of securing them. This ideology persists and accounts for the manner in which increasing enrolments in upper secondary education are being accompanied by more, rather than less segmentation of curricula. To understand how this is so, we need first to examine how the ideology came into being.

From Tradition to Ideology

In common with that of other countries, the English tradition of upper secondary education was originally shaped to support forms of education intended for the preparation of a small minority of the population. By the middle of the nineteenth century, the idiosyncratic experiences offered in a handful of boys' boarding schools had developed into an institution — the sixth form — which had a life and an informing rhetoric of its own and gave commonly understood meanings to the education of those who stayed in school to the age of 18 or so with a view to entering the universities or the professions.[7] Their numbers were small. At the time of the

Clarendon Report of 1864 the nine leading public schools mustered just over 300 sixth formers, and the addition of other public, proprietary and endowed secondary schools would bring the figure only into the low thousands. But the importance of the 'sixth' as an institution was great, not simply because of its connection through the universities with such national institutions as Parliament and the Civil Service, but also because of the conception of education by which it was shaped and to which it gave expression.

The tradition had not developed in isolation. It paralleled and reflected fundamental changes in society which took place in the late eighteenth and early nineteenth centuries: the movement from a local to a national focus in politics, commerce and administration; the growth of new cadres of professionals and civil servants; the spread of the new industrial economy; the movement away from autocratic and towards democratic forms of government. The tradition evolved to emphasize cosmopolitan attitudes, professional values and the incorporation of the upper middle classes into the business of government and administration. Central to this process was the question of how democracy was to be understood and how notions of democracy were to be related to conceptions of education. Of the many ways in which conceptions of democracy and education might have been developed, the most influential was that represented by Matthew Arnold, of whom it has been said that his *Culture and Anarchy* 'was the prime social text of the new English ruling class of the later nineteenth century, for it provided more persuasively than anything else the intellectual basis upon which the aristocracy and the bourgeoisie could adopt a common lifestyle'.[8] Arnold followed Burke in believing that extension of political power beyond the aristocracy could take place independently of any reconceptualization of how the exercise of power was to claim legitimacy. In Burke's case this apparent paradox was summed up in his notion of 'virtual representation': democratically elected representatives were not to be implementers of the wishes of an electorate — they were to act as the electorate *would have acted* if they had had the same endowment of 'true judgment' as their leaders. Arnold thought in terms of 'right reason' rather than 'true judgment' and considered that its possession depended on a particular view of the nature of knowledge — a view encapsulated in his well-known phrase 'sweetness and light'. This metaphor he drew from Swift's satire *The Battle of the Books* in which the author depicts a fight between protagonists of the 'ancient' knowledge — classical writers such as Homer, Euclid and Plato — and defenders of the 'modern' —

Milton, Descartes or Hobbes. Arnold favours the 'ancients' whom Swift represents as bees, 'which, by an universal Range, with long Search, much Study, true Judgment and Distinction of things' bring home honey and wax from which we obtain (or did in the seventeenth century) 'sweetness and light'. Since the ancients are the only true source of 'right reason', it follows that the condition of the extension of the leadership role of the aristocracy to other social classes is that the latter submit to a curriculum which, on the one hand, represents the knowledge worth having as firmly and indubitably established and, on the other, provides for induction into this knowledge through imitation of initiates.

Arnold's analysis of democracy, knowledge and education can be seen less as a proposal than as a legitimation of what was already on offer in the sixth forms of the new public schools for which Rugby was the model. There the curriculum was squarely based on classical texts (with occasional attention to 'moderns' such as Goethe) which a small group of selected middle class students studied under the personal tuition of the headmaster. And the connection between knowledge and power was made explicit in the giving to the sixth form of authority over boys in the lower school. The conception was essentially Platonic: the truth is known and is fixed. Anyone's ascent towards it is conditional on respecting and obeying those who are ahead on the path of initiation.[9] Such an idea was a powerful device for assimilating to the sixth form, within the context of the public schools, the new understandings of the national character and destiny which grew up in the last half of the nineteenth century. The growth of Empire both stimulated the expansion of public and private bureaucracy and emphasized the physical and military aspects of leadership. The sixth forms of the late nineteenth century made concessions to their expanded clientele in admitting to the curriculum 'modern' studies such as history and foreign languages, though these were alternative to and not added to the classical curriculum. At the same time the 'manliness' of earlier times, with its overtones of Christian moral responsibility, was supplanted by the 'manliness' of the sports field: 'honour, loyalty, skill at games, and a certain stoical acceptance of pain, injustice and malign circumstances'.[10] Hierarchy was celebrated in gradations of rank and status made visible by blazers, caps, ties and badges. School and curriculum were rationalized through class teaching, disciplinary procedures and the integration of boarding houses and games playing into the managed areas of student life. The inculcation of 'right reason' and the demonstration of its connection with power had been honed to an art of machine-like efficiency.

Thus, a potent model of upper secondary education was, in the latter decades of the nineteenth century, thrust upon the consciousness of the nation. Leaders internalized its values through having personally experienced it; followers absorbed its mores through school stories and boys magazines. Whereas other countries had, by now, mobilized varied interests into legal frameworks for secondary provision, English secondary schools experienced no such intervention. Thus, for example, science which was in most European countries a fixed part of the curriculum was here an alternative and less attractive option to the classics and was, in the leading schools, taught in a perfunctory fashion. An alternative model of secondary education, however, was to be found in the upper levels of the elementary system which was already under public control. Higher grade schools were developed in the larger cities which carried on the work of the elementary school for older students, offering them an integrated curriculum containing a variety of academic, scientific and practical studies without the trappings of chapels, boarding houses and games fields. When the government finally decided that there should be a publicly supported and controlled secondary education system, the question was whether it should follow the public school or the higher grade model.

The Act of 1902 did not make it inevitable that the public school model would be adopted and that secondary education would be cast as a 'kind' rather than a 'stage', but it made it probable, and the grant regulations which followed from 1904 onwards reinforced those aspects of the legislation which worked against any extension of the higher grade example. Control of education had been taken from school boards and put in the hands of local authorities. Now the grant regulations ensured the influence over secondary school organization of heads and governors many of whom would be imbued with public school values. They also decreed that 'the course of education must be complete' and that it could not be considered complete if it was not 'so planned as to carry on the scholars to such a point as they may reasonably be expected to reach at the age of 16'.[11] Since virtually the only scholars who did stay on to 16 were in the public schools or the endowed schools which copied them, their achievements, founded on experience from the age of 8 or so of a text-based literary curriculum, provided the exemplars for determining what should be learned in secondary schools by 11-year-olds who might stay there for two or three years.[12] Thus was the ideology of 'sweetness and light' carried forward into the state system, both in terms of the content of the curriculum and of the principle that what was done at the base of the pyramid should be settled by what happened, or was supposed to happen, at its apex. And the subsequent history of the secondary curriculum showed that, as the base was strengthened, the apex receded. By 1951 the problem of early leaving was largely solved in the grammar schools and most students were completing a five-year course to the age of 16. But in that year the Ministry of Education's pamphlet *The Road to the Sixth Form* announced that

> It is simply not possible for an academic education to reach any great measure of completeness by the age of 16, and to pretend otherwise would be doing no service to the many who do leave at that age. They are likely to get far more profit from travelling for some distance along an exacting but generous course of work which points at the future, than from a course which provides the illusion of a completed education.[13]

Preservation of the commanding heights of the curriculum demanded that they be from time to time moved: what had once been a 'complete course of education' was now an 'illusion of a completed education'.

Other countries, with the notable exception of the USA, were also slow to develop post-16 education as part of the common provision. But at least their curricula were framed in such a way that they lent themselves to adaptation and could be modified to cater for an expanded enrolment. Not so in England. The Crowther Report of 1959 called for a massive increase in enrolments in the 15–18 age range, but also urged maintenance and strengthening of the specialist curriculum of the sixth form so that the only respectable form of upper secondary education remained closed to all but a minority of students. The Crowther Committee's advocacy of the traditional curriculum was backed up by a range of arguments reflecting in their tone and content the ethos of the nineteenth century public school sixth form. Phrases such as 'The good and keen sixth former ... has looked forward to being a science specialist, or a classic, or a historian: his mind has been set that way by inclination ... specialization is a mark of the sixth form, and "subject-mindedness" of the sixth former',[14] could as well have been written in 1859 as 1959 (apart from the reference to science). What in the earlier period had been an informing tradition, capable of guiding the creation of new institutions to deal with changing social and political circumstances, had become a static ideology disconnected from the march of events and capable only of producing apologies for hallowed practice and old remedies for new problems. Arnold's attitude to democracy was still alive. Education was seen as the key to the preservation of the superiority of the governors and the subservience of the governed.

Immediately after publication of the Crowther Report, questions were raised about the appropriateness of the traditional forms of curriculum for the expanding sixth form, and the next twenty years saw a series of working papers, proposals and reports on the subject. Yet the even more massive expansion of enrolments in post-16 education and training that we are experiencing in the 1980s still assumes the sanctity of the Arnoldian curriculum. Pressures from beneath in favour of less segmentation are reduced by preservation of GCE and CSE under the cloak of a unified 16+ examination, while 'profiling' is instituted for the lower achievers. At the same time the specialist curriculum of sixth form scholars is reinforced from above by intensifying the competition for places in higher education and preserving Oxford and Cambridge as 'super' universities. It cannot be said that the grip of the ideology has lessened to any great extent.

The Uses of Vocationalism

At first sight it might appear contradictory that, on the one hand, Keith Joseph and other like-minded politicians extol the virtues of a 'work-oriented' curriculum with emphasis on 'useful knowledge' and 'transferable skills' while, on the other, they are assiduously preserving the apparatus of specialist 'A' level courses and restricted entry to higher education which ensures that the type of curriculum they seem to favour will rarely be attractive to the ambitious student. It may also seem contradictory that they bemoan the fate of the 40 per cent whom the schools 'have failed' while maintaining a course and syllabus structure which shapes the secondary curriculum according to the needs and interests of the top 20 per cent. But it is of the nature of ideologues that they not only tolerate contradictions but actively exploit them in conditions where the inheritors of a critical tradition might see contradiction as a sign of something needing to be put right. If it is the preservation of the ideology that is in question, then it makes sense for them to attack the education system for its failure to engage the interest of lower achieving students and for its neglect of industry and commerce while at the same time giving both overt and covert support to curricula designed for an academic elite. In this way they ensure that the elite remains small by directing other students to the inferior options of vocational programmes and preparation for work. It is ironic that the schools which have always done most to prepare students for work — the new comprehensives and ex-secondary moderns — are the target of the sharpest criticism for 'lack of relevance' in their curricula, while the public schools, which have done least, incur no such disapproval; and that while conservative pamphleteers, proclaiming the virtues of selective education, target on the public examination record of the few remaining grammar schools, the success of the maintained system as a whole in raising the level of examination performance is no obstacle to claims from the same sources that the system has 'failed'. But none of this should surprise us. More important to ideologues than questions of consistency is the propagation of slogans in forms of words which stifle reasoned debate. Nothing must be done to undermine activities that represent 'excellence', yet schools must prepare children for the 'world of work'. Indeed, who can proffer a platform of opposition to excellence or assert that schools should not educate for employment? Critics stand condemned before they have a chance to point out that the case for current policies rests on false premises; that, much as an influential section of the Conservative Party may yearn for a return to 'Victorian values', the world where leaders led and workers worked is gone. If the resources of society are to be unlocked by education, it has to be a different kind of education: one which acknowledges on the one hand the collapse of work and on the other the impotence of selected elites.

Our analysis shows that if such issues are to be joined and serious questions asked about what constitutes a worthwhile education, the crucial ground to be contested is that of the upper secondary curriculum. As long as segmentation is enforced in this part of the education system, the way is open for assaults on the progress which has been made towards a common curriculum for 11–16 year-olds in comprehensive schools. Divisive schemes which proclaim '14–18' as a span of curriculum to be thought of in a unified way (for lower achieving students, of course) can be readily pressed through the breaches already made by option systems geared to the demands of 'A' level courses. On the other hand, it is the existence of this same 'A' level system which enables universities to sustain a restrictive model of higher education. (It is noticeable that, if the mechanism of supply and demand is upset, university departments can, in spite of their rhetoric of 'standards', show themselves remarkably adaptable. When schools ceased to teach 'A' level Russian, admissions tutors who had been in the habit of demanding high grades in the language discovered that it could be taught to students who had never studied it before and that they could still go out after three years with an honours degree). Thus, 16–19 education is a key area for the preservation of the ideology, and it is one where its dominance has not been seriously challenged. The regular secondary curriculum, at least on the face of things, became a lost cause to the ideological purist with the introduction of almost universal comprehensive education, while higher education was symbolically, if not in reality, subverted with acceptance of the Robbins doctrine of expanding supply to meet demand. No similar retreat has been sounded in respect of the 'A' level curriculum, in spite of years of patient argument and research by Schools Council working parties.

Preserving the Ideology

The greatest challenge to orthodoxy at the 16–19 level has come about not in terms of curriculum policy, over which central authorities have control through the public examination system, but in the matter of organization which is the province of agencies of local government. The Exeter Education Committee decided in 1970 that resources could be more efficiently used by concentrating all sixth form 'A' level work in its new FE college, thus launching the idea of a 'tertiary college', an institution which could embody and carry forward in a unified way the tradition of upper secondary education. By the late 1970s enough of these colleges had been set up to suggest that the economic arguments for separate 16–19 institutions were winning support across the political spectrum, thus allowing the scope for links between the 'A' level curriculum and FE courses to be explored. It was a Labour Secretary of State (Mrs. Shirley Williams) who in 1979 took two decisions which tended to the preservation of the *status quo*. One was to reject the Schools Council's N and F scheme, which had been put forward as an alternative to 'A' levels, in so conclusive a fashion as to make it easy for the incoming Conservative administration to put a stop to all work on such innovations. The other was to publish a DES consultative paper which affirmed that the chaotic state of 16–19 provision, and the diversity of conceptions of what education in that age range should achieve were positive virtues: 'The loosely knit framework of departments and agencies is a source of great strength in enabling advances to be made'.[15] This endorsement of the agreeable segmentation entailed by the established sixth form gave the incoming Conservative government a useful opportunity to mobilize opposition to the threat to the ideology posed by the tertiary colleges and to amend the conclusions of the 1980 'MacFarlane Report'[16] which in their original form had been favourable to 16–19 colleges. The Secretary of State thus benefited from a textual basis on which to reject or amend reorganization schemes put forward by local authorities.[17]

But to secure the position, more was needed than simple opposition to the rising tide of potentially prestigious and innovating colleges. Grounds for a new offensive against trends towards a unified curriculum of schooling were found in a resurrection of the old controversy over the rival merits of 'education' and 'training' as guiding conceptions for the school curriculum — a move made ironically more plausible by the upsurge in unemployment over which the government was presiding. Concern for 'training' bolstered the role of the FEU in further education, and gave the signal for a massive injection of MSC influence over the upper secondary curriculum with the launch of YOP and YTS schemes. This soon spread to the curriculum of compulsory education with the distribution in 1983 of a document under the title of *Implementing the 14–18 Curriculum*.[18] This *vade mecum* of neo-vocationalist terminology links 'reform and innovation' in the curriculum to experience-based learning, problem-solving and project work, a negotiated curriculum, profiling, graded assessment, learning from the workplace, and community education — all this with an acknowledgement that this 'style of curriculum ... may be seen by many to be appropriate only for the 70 per cent of pupils ... who hitherto have gone on to no form of full-time further education'.[19]

For such an initiative to be taken seriously it has to be wrapped in some plausible terminology. Otherwise even supporters of Conservative policies might be provoked to question the worthwhileness of an exercise which seems to be aimed at training the non-academic for non-existent jobs. 'Pre-vocationalism' is one slogan that fulfils this role. What has the appearance of 'the vocational' is not really that because it is a *preparation* for vocational training. Another slogan is 'transferable skill'. This was promoted by the Institute of

Manpower Studies (IMS), based at the University of Sussex. The 1983 IMS Report *Training for Skill Ownership*[20] postulates eleven 'occupational training families', a notion which takes its place along-side 'pre-vocationalism' as a device for legitimating new curricula which are clearly not 'academic' but which at the same time can plausibly resist the accusation that they produce specific job-related skills which will in a short time be obsolete. Unfortunately, there is to be found in the IMS report no logical or empirical basis for the existence of these 'families' which, for example, attribute common transferable skills to wigmakers, nannies and fishmongers on the grounds that they are all in 'personal services and sales occupations'.

Rejection by the DES of proposals for new courses which built on the CSE tradition in favour of these 14+ FEU/MSC inspired initiatives has set up a context for the development of comprehensive school courses that look forward to the vocational and training segments of the 16–19 sector, just as the reformed 'O' level/CSE courses will be guided in style and content by the academic segments. Thus, for example, the RSA Education for Capability scheme which is beginning to make its appearance in comprehensive schools bases itself on the proposition that: 'There exists in its own right a culture which is concerned with doing, making and organizing ... (and) emphasizes the day-to-day management of affairs ...' and that, therefore, the curriculum should be given a purely instrumental end — to prepare 'people ... for a life outside the education system'.[21] The argument is not, of course, about whether schools should prepare for life — clearly they should — but about what kind of life this should be. The 'day-to-day manager' is not seen to be someone concerned with the meaning of life, still less the destiny of the nation.

Meanwhile, on the higher education front, we find pressures being put on universities to cut back provision in spite of the greater numbers of qualified students coming forward from schools. Moreover, the cuts are being applied differentially across the universities so that those of the highest ideological significance — Oxford and Cambridge — are leniently treated, while those at the other end of the 'sweetness and light' spectrum, such as Aston and Salford, are the subject of savage reductions in grants — this in spite of the fact that they are the ones which can least afford to lose support *and* in spite of their record of success in supplying highly employable technologists to industry. And further confirmation of the wish of those directing the education system to maintain a higher education sector which sits easily with a segmented 16–19 curriculum comes from the continuation and strengthening of the bipartite system which treats universities differently from polytechnics, colleges of higher education and other institutions providing degree courses.

Conclusion

Are we then faced with a 'conspiracy' to defend an outdated ideology of education through the creation and maintenance of a segmented structure of upper secondary education which ensures that 'real education' remains the province of the few? Such thoughts are hard to suppress in the face of an apparently concerted collection of policies and proposals which, though logically contradictory in terms of the justifications put forward for them, all accord fully with a programme of 'innovation without change'. They are made even more plausible by the action of the Secretary of State in deliberately handing over to the MSC functions which should properly — perhaps even legally, if the case were tested — be undertaken by the DES. However, the point we wish to make is that if current developments are seen as manifestations of the relationship between ideology and structure, no such conspiracy need be postulated. Present policies on 16–19 education are not simply the outcome of the neo-Conservative initiatives of Thatcher, Joseph and Tebbit — important as the contribution of this 'inner cabinet' has been. We also find administrators at the DES acting in ways consonant with the ideology. Labour politicians too have made their contribution in the spirit of Harold Wilson's defence of the grammar schools. Teachers and headteachers within the system have lent their support to the continuation and strengthening of the divided curriculum. The higher education sector, too, has combined innovatory postures with a refusal to see as problematic what the ideology declares to be fixed and immutable. As we reflect on this, what we have to remember is that most of those who have power and influence in the education system have themselves been 'touched' by it in a special way. Usually, they are the ones who have experienced the high status curriculum and, therefore, have the special view of it which the insider gets. They have absorbed the ideology through contact with structures of curriculum and organization that the ideology itself has shaped. Tradition-as-ideology propagates itself not only through words and opinions. It intersects with and moulds the institutions which are its carriers. Thus, for example, if teachers

support the specialist curriculum of 'A' levels, this is not just because they live within a milieu where specialization is a norm, but
more importantly because the very landscape of that world through
which they make their way takes its form from past contact with the
ideology. The resources given to schools are distributed through
subject departments; teacher careers are related to status in subject
teaching; allocation of space and time in school reflects the role of
subjects; future student placements depend on performance in subjects, and so on. All of these facts about the system can be traced to
historical events and processes which saw the translation of the
ideology into administrative arrangements, curriculum structures
and patterns of resource allocation.

How does a tradition shake itself free of such encrustations and
become again a tradition 'in good order', capable of confronting
new demands by fresh consideration of goods to be pursued and
rational policies for pursuing them? This is a question that cannot be
addressed within the scope of this chapter. But we can conclude by
giving an example of an education system which has a similar
inheritance to the English one and which faces much the same
problems, but which sees the question of upper secondary education
in a very different light.

The Australian State of Victoria has recently completed a ministerial review of 'post-compulsory schooling' and produced a discussion paper putting forward a number of proposals. Just as in
England, a major impetus for concern about education at this level
has been the upsurge in youth unemployment. The discussion paper
notes that 'Although a significant proportion of 16 to 19-year-olds
remains in full time education, unemployment is and is likely to
remain a serious social problem, a destructive experience for those
affected and, for some, a long term tragedy'.[22] It also agrees that
'continued prosperity will in future depend on the development of
human resource skills' but, significantly, combines this with the
observation that 'technological advance could equally well result in
the deskilling of a majority of the workforce and the concentration
of high skills and power in a minority of highly educated
workers'.[23]

Thus, the consequences drawn from the facts of unemployment
and technological advance are different from those embodied in
proposals for upper secondary education in this country. They are
different because the problem is seen as a whole and not as a
collection of separate parts to be individually considered:

A new curricular rationale for (this stage of education) is central. Without some view of what the stage should do for students and the society, it is not possible to resolve the undoubted tensions which exist between tertiary selection and mass education at this level or to consider what structures might better enable a changed perspective to be translated into practice.[24]

And again: 'the endless proliferation of narrowly focussed, alternative offerings forms an inadequate base for curricular policies at the post-compulsory level'.[25] How then should the overall question of provision be seen in the context of unemployment and technological advance? The discussion paper makes different connections from those which can be inferred from English policy documents:

It can be said with confidence that early occupationally specific training is inadvisable on all counts ... Amidst uncertainty, the safest course for a society which wishes to expand cooperative control of work situations and to share available work equitably is to ensure that all have a high basis of initial general education. This is undoubtedly the best preparation for the inevitable occupational shifts which lie ahead of any individual worker.[26]

This statement is the guide to the kind of renewal that is needed:

it becomes evident that the ways in which education called 'general' have been defined in the past themselves require radical overhaul. These definitions have, particularly at post-compulsory levels, excluded and denigrated the practical and the applied and the history, experience and cultural expressions of major sections of the population. The social exclusiveness of much education called 'general' contributes to the idea that there is no continuity or connection between the ordinary business of life and a 'high' culture available only to a minority.[27]

Thus, within the broad and inclusive context for debate which the document sets up, claims for a general or liberal education can be advanced without its advocates appearing to defend the abstract and irrelevant as the basis of a curriculum for those about to join the unemployed. This becomes possible because an argument about liberal education which embraces the whole age cohort implies drastic revision in the curriculum of those following high status courses. Renewal of the tradition can take place only if we transcend the idea of a segmented curriculum which allows the elite status of the few to be bought at the cost of a narrowly instrumental training for the majority. To do so, we must see how the collapse of work and the eclipse of elites reared in the Arnoldian ethic can provide positive grounds for a reformulation of democratic ideals and a reconceptualization of their capability for informing the structures of education.

Notes

1 RINGER, F.K. (1979) *Education and Society in Modern Europe*, Bloomington, Ind., Indiana University Press.

2 RINGER (1979) explains that 'A *segmented* or *tracked* system of education ... is one in which parallel courses of study are separated by institutional or curricular barriers, as well as by differences in the social origins of their students' (*ibid*, p. 29). Thus, a sixth form that was divided as between an 'arts' group and a 'science' group would not be segmented, since it is unlikely that the social class composition of the groups would be different. However, where the choice is between for example, 'A' levels and CPVE there would, on the evidence of many studies of the relationship between social class and educational enrolments, be notable biases in course membership. RINGER also uses 'segmentation' to describe the divide between those enrolled in the education system and those outside it, and therefore concludes that 'it is best to regard any decisive extension of an education system as a movement away from segmentation' (*ibid*, p. 30). In the instance discussed in this chapter, whatever cause there may be for welcoming the addition of more young people to the school population is nullified, firstly, by the fact that school/non-school segmentation is being enhanced by the introduction of YTS-type schemes and, secondly, by the fact that policies are being pursued, as in the case of TVEI, that have the effect of increasing the amount of segmentation already present in the 11–16 school.

3 POPPER, K.R. (1963) *Conjectures and Refutations: The Growth of Scientific Knowledge*, London, Routledge and Regan Paul, p. 126ff.

4 For an extended study of the evolution of the concept of equality in the USA, see POLE, J.R. (1978) *The Pursuit of Equality in American History*, Berkeley, CA, University of California Press.

5 MacINTYRE, A. (1981) *After Virtue: A Study in Moral Theory*, London, Duckworth, p. 206.

6 RINGER, F.K. (1979) *op. cit.*, p. 258.

7 See REID, W.A. and FILBY, J.L. (1982) *The Sixth: An Essay in Education and Democracy*, Lewes, Falmer Press.

8 SHANNON, R. (1974) *The Crisis of Imperialism 1865–1915*, London, Hart-Davis, MacGibbon, p. 34.

9 ARNOLD himself required the 'authority' of the ancients for what he

wrote. 'Whereas Shelley invented boldly, Arnold nervously admitted, "Where driven to invent ... I could not satisfy myself until I discovered in Pausanias a tradition which I took for my basis ..."', JENKYNS, R. (1980) *The Victorians and Ancient Greece*, Oxford, Blackwell, p. 102.

10 WORSLEY, T.C. (1940) *Barbarians and Philistines*, London, Robert Hale, p. 98.

11 Board of Education, (1904–5) *Regulations for Secondary Schools*, London, Board of Education, pp. 7–8.

12 By 1921, the average school life of a pupil in a maintained secondary school was only three years and one month.

13 Ministry of Education (1951) Pamphlet No. 19, *The Road to the Sixth Form*, London, HMSO.

14 Central Advisory Council for Education (England) (1959) *15 to 18* (Crowther Report), London, HMSO, p. 223.

15 Department of Education and Science (1979) *16–18: Education and Training for 16–18 Year Olds. A Consultative Paper*, London, HMSO, para. 4.

16 Department of Education and Science (1980) *Education for 16–19 Year Olds*, London, DES/CLEA.

17 REID, W.A. and FILBY, J.L. (1982) *op. cit.*, chapter 11.

18 BROCKINGTON, D., WHITE, R. and PRING, R. (1983) *Implementing the 14–18 Curriculum: New Approaches*, Schools Council for the Bristol Social Education Project.

19 *Ibid.*, p. 7.

20 Institute of Manpower Studies (1983) *Training for Skill Ownership*, Falmer, Institute of Manpower Studies, University of Sussex.

21 Royal Society of Arts (1983) 'Education for Capability', advertisement in *The Guardian*, 18 February.

22 Victoria Ministry of Education (1984), *Ministerial Review of Post-Compulsory Schooling: Discussion Paper*, Melbourne, Victoria Ministry of Education, p. 5.

23 *Ibid.*, p. 6.

24 *Ibid.*, p. 24.

25 *Ibid.*, p. 39.

26 *Ibid.*, p. 6.

27 *Ibid.*, p. 6.

From Theoretical Critique to Alternative Policy

Frank Coffield

I'm sick with everybody ... sick with govvy schemes. They just stop people getting proper jobs. Firms are getting work done for nothing. I blame the government for these schemes. They'll not be able to stop the schemes now ... now that local firms know they can get labour for nothing. There's no chance of labouring jobs now ... 'cos they're all done by people on schemes ... The scheme I'm on now ... no chance of a real job ... it's a scheme for the supervisors as well! (Pete, aged 19)

Young people do not need to be told what is wrong with Manpower Services Commission schemes. For the majority of young people in the North East, Youth Training Scheme and the Community Programme lead straight back to the dole queue. In 1983, for example, only about 29 per cent of young people leaving MSC schemes in the northern region found jobs (NECCA, 1984, p. 17); and only 10 per cent of the 125,600 adults eligible for placements on the Community Programme were provided with places. In County Durham, moreover, only 40 per cent of the first year of trainees on YTS obtained jobs: the corresponding figure for the whole of the country has been claimed to be by ministers 70 per cent, but was no more than 59 per cent, according to a careful MSC postal survey of a 15 per cent representative sample (MSC, 1985).

There are, in other words, deep seated regional differences which need to be taken into account in national decision-making. There may soon come a point in the North-East when there may not be sufficient industry or commerce to provide every 16-year-old 'trainee' with experience of the world of work.

Given the anxieties about, and at times the hostility to, MSC schemes by most recipients in the North-East, and given the trenchant analyses of the ideology behind such programmes by Ruth Jonathan and others in this volume, I want to ask a question, which I have rephrased from a recent article of Philip Cohen's (1984, p. 105): why has opposition to MSC programmes and to the policy initiatives of the DES been so divided and ineffectual? Cohen's answer to his own question cites 'force of economic circumstance' and 'lack of political strength', but mainly blames 'a failure to contest the *ideological* background'.

There is much, as usual, in his argument but I think it is incomplete. There is now a burgeoning literature which challenges the ideology and the faulty diagnosis behind the new vocationalism, a literature of which both the volume *Schooling for the Dole?* which contains Cohen's article and the present text are prime examples. The first, vital task is to present a critical analysis which exposes the inadequacies and inconsistencies in official thinking and practice, both of which are subject to constant change. Too often, however, the analyses which have been completed tend not to go far enough: they remain at the level of theoretical critique with the occasional pointer for action included in the final section. The slow, painful process of constructing alternative policies has tended to go by the board.

Philip Cohen is himself an honourable exception to this general rule in that he has explained (1984, p. 139) in some detail an alternative *practice* to life and social skills, but even here there is little or nothing on alternative *policy*. There is a clear and urgent need for well grounded alternatives to be developed by the critics before the new structures begin to set as firm as concrete.

Before presenting my own set of suggestions, I want to suggest two further reasons for the lack of an alternative policy to the dominating influence of current official ideology: the language in which that opposition is so often couched and the ignorance of most commentators (including myself) about social policy. My own favourite example of the former comes from a best-selling and much praised book on the transition from school to work. Notice the random sprinkling of inverted commas which is presumably meant to convey an awareness of the imprecision and complexity of language, but tends rather to convey — to me at least — a lack of concern for communication. But back to the quotation: 'Although the "lads" somehow "penetrate" the opacity of their "objective" domination within the social relations and relations of production of capitalism, they are inevitably drawn back into collusion in their own subordination by their valorisation of manual labour.' What an irony that a discussion of penetrations itself becomes impenetrable!

The second reason why I think alternative policies are rarely proposed is the continuing failure of most psychology and education departments to introduce their students to social policy. There is all too often a measurable gap between the reports of academic researchers and the concerns of administrators: too often the conclusions of the former are not sufficiently fleshed out in policy terms to begin to interest the latter. A typical example comes from an interesting comparison of the daily life of unemployed men in Belfast and Brighton which ends by arguing '. . . as with most social research the present study was not designed to give straight answers to questions about practical problems' (Trew and Kilpatrick, 1984, p. 132). It does not take the driest of dry Thatcherites to ask: is it acceptable for work on such a subject, which has been supported from public funds, to refuse to give *any* answers, straight or crooked?

One final introductory matter. It needs to be admitted that the MSC initiatives and the present government's concentration on 'the bottom 40 per cent' have brought national attention and resources to a large minority of young people who have been woefully neglected by educationalists, employers and politicians in the past. Both the government and the MSC deserve to be congratulated on finding the political will and the resources to lay the foundations in this country of a *system* of vocational training. But neither the government nor the MSC has a monopoly of concern in this area: we are all united in our desire to see Britain succeed economically, be socially harmonious and to see young people play a prominent and creative part in those processes. The argument is with the quality of thinking which has given rise to the particular means being employed to achieve the goals which are not in dispute.

That thinking is seriously deficient in a number of ways, only two of which I have space to enlarge on. First, we are being asked to believe that the supply of skilled workers *by itself* creates jobs: a new economic law is being promulgated to the effect that it is mainly skill shortages which cause unemployment. Who believes that more than 180 collieries in the North-East have been closed since 1947 because of skill shortages? Are there silent and empty shipyards on the Tyne and Wear because of a lack of skilled manpower? Was the Consett steel works closed for lack of skilled workmen? Hudson (1985) has clearly demonstrated that the

Northern region has suffered disproportionately as a result of the policies of *nationalized* industries such as the British Steel Corporation and the National Coal Board; the policies were adopted to solve national and international economic problems such as overcapacity in the steel industry and had little, if anything, to do with skill shortages or even the profitability of particular works such as Consett.

There is, on the other hand, no denying that there are skill shortages in Britain, and that some of these are serious in specific areas such as systems engineers, real time programmers, and process and design engineers. My argument is rather that, compared with the total numbers of young people in YTS (354,000) or of young people under 25 years who have been unemployed for over a year (332,000 in April 1984), the shortages are strictly limited. The MSC, in its evidence to the House of Lords Select Committee on Science and Technology (MSC, March 1984a, p. 4), estimated that 'there will be a shortage by 1988 of between 7000 and 10,000 technologists and 30,000 technicians with the skills to develop and exploit new technology'. Even if all 40,000 were to be trained and employed in time, there would still be more than 3,000,000 people unemployed. And how many top level technicians will be produced by a one, two or even three year YTS? The Director General of the CBI in April 1985 commented upon the findings of a special survey of more than 1300 firms: 'the survey shows that skill shortages are not great ... Six per cent of firms expected shortages of highly skilled labour to hold back investment over the next twelve months.' (CBI News Release).

The second deficiency in official thinking is that it totally disregards the main criterion used to assess MSC schemes by both the fifty young people we[1] have studied for three years in the North-East and by thousands of young people in answer to official questionnaires. Young people have been remarkably consistent and unswervingly realistic in continuing to judge YTS by their chances of landing a job as a result. However laudable the MSC's current emphasis on improving the *quality* of the training on YTS, young people make clear in a number of ways that they would prefer a job — almost any job — than become the most highly skilled members of the dole queue.

In answer to our questions about their views on the causes of unemployment, the sample of fifty answered laconically: 'Nae jobs'. At first I was dismissive of this reply as a mere tautology, but further discussion revealed that they understood all too well the general predicament of young people in the North-East, even if they had no knowledge of the detailed figures. The latter show that in Newcastle upon Tyne between the years 1974 and 1983 the number of jobs available to school-leavers fell from 2767 to 443 (Careers Officer, Newcastle upon Tyne). Since 1979 more than 200,000 jobs (or 16.5 per cent of the total) have been lost in the Northern region, including almost 30 per cent of the region's manufacturing base (NECCA, 1984, p. 11). Is it any wonder that in such circumstances the Job Centre is known as the Joke Shop?

There is a remarkable consistency in the declared intentions and behaviour of young people whether studied intensively in a small scale project like ours or surveyed nationally by the MSC itself. The detailed postal survey of 15 per cent of young people who left the YTS in 1984 is based on almost 18,800 respondents (a response rate of 66 per cent). One *leitmotiv* runs through this report: the single-minded concentration of young people on jobs. For instance, the most popular reason for joining YTS was: 'You thought it would help to get a job' (52 per cent). Of the 15 per cent who left their YTS within thirteen weeks of starting, by far the most significant reason they gave for leaving was to take a full-time (49 per cent) or a part-time (3 per cent) job. In comparison, only 1 per cent left YTS to return to school. Work experience was thought by 65 per cent of the sample to be 'very useful', while only 28 per cent considered that off-the-job training was as useful. With a sample as large as 18,800 some wider spread of opinions could have been expected, but the message seems unambiguous. If we do not listen to what young people are saying and if we do not draw the appropriate conclusions from their actions, then vast sums of public money may be misspent.

Nor should young people's sharp focus on jobs be dismissed as narrow and instrumental as long as British remains a 'society in which paid employment is the most important source of identity, status and income' (Watts, 1983, p. 83). 'It was not easy to find a man who had studied for three years without aiming at pay', according to Confucius (as quoted in the Robbins Report, 1963, p. 6) and the remark is as true now of all sections of the community as it ever was.

To provide training for all when only a steadily declining percentage will obtain paid employment is an immoral trick played on the young; and yet, for all the criticism of the *Youth Task Group Report* which began by claiming that it 'is about providing a per-manent bridge between school and work', both the MSC's Annual

Frank Coffield

Report for 1983/84 and the Corporate Plan for 1983–87, insist on entitling their chapters on YTS 'Preparing Young People for Work'. Both documents continue to talk of providing 'young people with a bridge between school and work'. The permanence of the bridge has apparently begun to be doubted but neither its structure nor its efficiency. Actual expenditure on the first year of YTS was £136 million less than planned because there were fewer than expected entrants and because 35 per cent of those who did join left before completing the full year; and these are the elder sisters and brothers, cousins, friends and neighbours of those still at school who are likely to be encouraged to join a two year YTS.

Alternative Policies

Are there realistic alternatives to the all-party and trade union consensus, displayed at the time of the Budget in 1985, on introducing a two-year YTS and an extended Community Programme? I have space to outline only four tentative ideas and I am aware that what follows is a starter for discussion rather than a complete programme for action.

Link Training to Jobs and Jobs to Training, Wherever Possible

Before extending YTS and the Community Programme, would it not make more sense to ensure that all those who completed an MSC scheme obtained a job and used their newly acquired skills rather than returned to the unemployment register? The following table (adapted from MSC, 1985, table 3.1) describes the destinations of those leaving YTS in 1984:

	Activity	%
1	In full-time work	59
2	Unemployed	28
3	On another YTS	5
4	Back at school	1
5	Full-time FE	4
6	Doing something else	3
		100

The present proposal would create jobs for those 28 per cent who became unemployed and would ensure that there were opportunities for day release and further education for them and for all those who went straight into employment. Such a proposal is more likely to provide the bridge from school to work which the MSC are anxious to build and it would also check on the quality of the jobs and training in industry and commerce. It is acknowledged that there may be a small percentage who, for a number of reasons, may be difficult to place in paid employment, but the fact that the vast majority of each age group would be obtaining jobs is likely to have a powerful impact on the motivation of young people. The time to start extending YTS to two years would be when young people, after successfully completing a one-year YTS, were flowing regularly into jobs and *not* when almost one third of them leave only to become unemployed.

A Comprehensive System of Education, Training and Employment post-16

Present provision deserves to be called the most confusing, inadequate and hierarchical sector in the world of education and training. The MSC are attempting to unravel the confusions by setting up a review of vocational qualifications under George Tolley, but introducing greater equality and flexibility will prove more difficult. A start could be made by accepting Tony Edwards' suggestion (p. 131) of providing common status and common benefits for all those aged 16 to 18. The Labour Party's *Charter for Young People* (1985) is, however, in favour of a clear differential between a minimum allowance of £36 per week for trainees on YTS and an educational maintenance award of £27 per week to encourage young people to stay in on full-time education: the argument to justify the difference is that someone with a job or on a scheme should be paid more than someone on a full-time course. A unified, comprehensive system post-16 is only likely to offer a wide range of options to young people if they are able to move easily round that system without incurring financial penalties. The provision of all forms of education and training in one building, called the tertiary college, might also help to break down the deep divisions between academic and vocational streams.

Introduce a Strong Regional Dimension into all Aspects of Government Policy

The particular economic structure, which sets the parameters within which young people in the North live out their lives, has been transformed in recent decades into a 'global outpost' (Williamson and Quayle, 1983, p. 29). Local companies tend to be branch plants without centres of research and development; and the North's stake in the new technologies is not an impressive one.

Put briefly, the Northern region neither has sufficient resources nor political clout to solve its own problems. There is also no-one to speak for the region in Whitehall, Brussels or beyond in the way that the Secretaries of State for Scotland and Wales represent their areas. Is it significant, for example, that the Consett steel works were closed but Ravenscraig in Scotland and Llanwern and Port Talbot in Wales have so far avoided closure because such a move is considered politically unacceptable? This suggests that the assisted regions in England require a minister of Cabinet rank to protect their interests.

A campaign has been mounting steadily to obtain a fairer deal for the North ever since the first strategic plan for the area was drawn up in 1977 and the first annual state of the region report was published in 1979 (see NECCA). Others have since entered the debate (see Holliday, 1982; Robinson, 1982; and Chapman, 1985) and have presented more detailed criticisms and proposals than is possible here. So far the present government's response has been to announce in November 1984 cuts in regional aid of £300 million. The decision was made after the EEC had calculated that Britain already had ten out of the Community's fifteen most disadvantaged regions. The EEC analysis, based on unemployment and productivity, showed that, in the words of the latest NECCA report (1984, p. 1): 'Northumberland, Tyne and Wear, Durham and Cleveland are in the bottom twelve out of 131 regions in Europe. They are accompanied by the recognized "poor men of Europe", such as Calabria, Sardinia, Sicily and Northern Ireland'.

To this needs to be added Hudson's (1985, p. 77) telling point which was referred to earlier: not only are state policies for the region uncoordinated and chaotic, but they themselves are 'the major proximate cause of employment decline' because of the policies adopted by nationalised industries.

Whatever new structures are introduced, they need to play to the strengths of the region. The guiding principle, suggested by reading Papert (1980), would be that the regeneration of communities is most likely to succeed if it springs from the roots of local culture and is most likely to fail if the plans are imposed by distant bureaucrats. What are the strengths of the North? There is still a strong sense of community, a rich network of supportive families, a long history of skilled work and pride in craft, and a deeply felt loyalty to the area. Its distinct geographical boundaries have helped to give northerners an historical, regional and cultural identity and this collective self-respect could help to launch an economic revival. But for how long can any region survive the increasing emigration of the most talented of its young people in the search for jobs?

Change the Model of Learning at the Heart of the New Initiatives by the MSC and DES

A series of comparisons have recently been made between education and economic performance in such countries as Germany, France, the United States and Japan (NEDC/MSC, 1984; and Worswick, 1985); these comparisons have all tended to be highly unfavourable to this country.

Visits to the Federal Republic's *Berufsschulen* and dual system of training made a deep impression on me, partly because the Germans have a long established *system* of vocational training and partly because the level of up-to-date equipment was so lavish. These advantages gave an urgency to my thinking which was missing before, but further reflection and visits have suggested that the much praised dual system may have weaknesses in those very areas where British education is (or could be) strong.

Interestingly, the international comparisons referred to above have much to say about 'inputs' and 'outputs' of vocational education, but are silent about the processes at the heart of all learning: the quality of relationships between teacher and taught, and the model of learning adopted. Allowing for some predictable variation in the German system with almost 2,500,000 pupils in vocational schools in 1982, the general ethos of such institutions may be characterized as formal, teacher-centred, rule governed, traditional, highly systematized and, at times, even authoritarian. As a consequence, the social distance between teacher and taught tends to be considerable, thus reducing the prospects of producing creative, flexible and self-motivating learners. In addition, a behavioural objectives model of learning has been enthroned at the heart of the

German system and pupils (who do not have the status of students) work their way through hundreds of small, specific behavioural objectives every year.

There may well be parts of our own educational system which could be described in similarly unflattering terms. Indeed, some of our further education colleges appear to have become temples to the same behavioural objectives approach to learning which prevents students seeing connections, learning generic ideas and going beyond the information given (Bruner, 1974). On the whole, however, smaller classes enable teachers in Britain to be closer to their students and to take a more personal interest in them than happens in France or Germany. Our more open and relaxed teaching relationships could with advantage be married to a more powerful model of learning, based on the work of Piaget, Bruner, Donaldson and Papert, whose influential book *Mindstorms* is based on the dictum: 'The best learning takes place when the learner takes charge'. (p. 214). Ruth Jonathan (pp. 135–45) has explored an alternative model further than is possible here.

A third ingredient could be added to improve the quality of learning. Throughout Great Britain, universities and local industry are developing closer links through the creation of science parks. Local variations in the North include Cleveland's CADCAM centre, Durham University's Centre for Materials Science and Technology and Newcastle's Technology Centre. What is missing from all of these initiatives is an educational dimension. If local schools, polytechnics and colleges of further education are left out of the plans, the cultural gap which already exists between the latest research and the curriculum of schools may widen still further. It is not enough to produce new knowledge and processes: each new generation (and not just an elite sub-group) needs to be challenged by that new knowledge and their initiation can no longer be left to chance: it needs to be planned.

Elsewhere (Coffield, 1983), I have detailed a proposal to bring together universities, local industry and schools to form a new body from which all the partners would benefit. TVEI needs to be built into some such system if it is to survive and remain up to date when MSC support comes to an end.

The standard riposte to any set of alternative proposals is that the expense alone would prevent implementation. Sinfield and Fraser (1985) calculated for the BBC North East what they called 'the real cost of unemployment': not just the direct exchequer costs, but the lost taxes (both income and direct), the lost national insurance contributions and local authority costs (for example, initiatives to help the unemployed like Durham County Council's Youth Employment Premium to employers). They conclude that it would be reasonable to work with an estimate of £7000 as the annual cost to the Exchequer of an unemployed person. NECCA (1984, p. 18) has particularized the argument for the Northern region, using the House of Lords lower estimate of £5000, calculated in 1982: 'If this figure is applied to unemployed claimants in the North, the total cost becomes a staggering £1125 million per year'. Seen in this light, the financial implications of alternative programmes including job creation seem less forbidding. These calculations have, moreover, omitted any wider social or individual costs such as the effects of unemployment on health, family tensions or personal suffering. The effects of long-term unemployment on the young is a new factor in Britain and we have to turn for a parallel to the black ghettoes of the United States, where the wealthy are retreating into estates which are privately patrolled. If the economic argument does not on its own open up a debate on alternatives, then perhaps self-interest may in time prevail.

Note

1   For a fuller account of the arguments in this article, see COFFIELD, F., BORRILL, C. and MARSHALL, S. (1986), *Growing up at the Margins*, Milton Keynes, Open University Press.

References

BRUNER, J.S. (1974) *Beyond the Information Given*, London, Allen and Unwin.

CHAPMAN, R.A. (Ed.) (1985) *Public Policy Studies: The North East of England*, Edinburgh University Press for the University of Durham.

COFFIELD, F. (1983) 'Learning to live with unemployment: What future for education in a world without Jobs?' in COFFIELD, F. and GOODINGS, R., (Eds), *Sacred Cows in Education*, Edinburgh University Press for the University of Durham.

COHEN, P. (1984) 'Against the new vocationalism' in BATES, I., *et al* (Eds), *Schooling for the Dole? The New Vocationalism*, Basingstoke, Macmillan.

HOLLIDAY, F.G.T. (1982) 'The lands between: Some thoughts on regions, resources and representation', Durham City Sword Address by Vice-Chancellor of Durham University.

Frank Coffield

HUDSON, R. (1985) 'The paradoxes of state intervention' in CHAPMAN, R.A. (Ed.), *Public Policy Studies: The North East of England*, Edinburgh University Press for the University of Durham.
LABOUR PARTY (1985) *Charter for Young People*, London, The Labour Party.
MANPOWER SERVICES COMMISSION (1983) *Corporate Plan 1983–1987*, Moorfoot, Sheffield, MSC.
MANPOWER SERVICES COMMISSION (1984a) *New Technologies*, Written Evidence to the House of Lords Select Committee on Science and Technology, Moorfoot, Sheffield, MSC.
MANPOWER SERVICES COMMISSION (1984b) *Annual Report 1983–84*, Moorfoot, Sheffield, MSC.
MANPOWER SERVICES COMMISSION (1985) *Leavers in July — September 1984: 15% Follow-up*, Moorfoot, Sheffield, Youth Training Board.
MINISTRY OF EDUCATION (1963) *Higher Education*, (Cmnd 2154) (Robbins Report) London, HMSO.
NATIONAL ECONOMIC DEVELOPMENT COUNCIL/MANPOWER SERVICES COMMISSION (1984) *Competence and Competition: Training and Education in the Federal Republic of Germany, the United States and Japan*, London, National Economic Development Office.
NORTH OF ENGLAND COUNTY COUNCIL ASSOCIATION (NECCA), (1984) *The State of the Region Report: 1984*, NECCA.
PAPERT, S. (1980) *Mindstorms: Children, Computers and Powerful Ideas*, Brighton, Harvester Press.
ROBINSON, F. (1982) *Economic Prospects for the North*, Newcastle, Centre for Urban and Regional Development Studies, University of Newcastle upon Tyne.
SINFIELD, A. and FRASER, N. (1985) *The Real Cost of Unemployment*, BBC North East.
TREW, K. and KILPATRICK, R., (1984) *The Daily Life of the Unemployed: Social and Psychological Dimensions*, Belfast Photographic Units, Queen's University of Belfast.
WATTS, A.G. (1983) *Education, Unemployment and the Future of Work*, Milton Keynes, Open University Press.
WILLIAMSON, W. and QUAYLE, B. (1983) 'Work technology and culture in the North East of England' in *North East Local Studies, Technology and Change in the North East*, Durham, University of Durham.
WORSWICK, G.D.N. (Ed.) (1985) *Education and Economic Performance*, Aldershot, Gower.

Education and Training 16–19: Rhetoric, Policy and Practice

Tony Edwards

Introduction

In remarkably short time, post-compulsory schooling is being transformed in its organization, content and scope. The rapid creation of a far-reaching 'tertiary' stage has been less a late conversion to 'continuing education for all' than a series of hectic responses to unprecedented problems. These problems extend to Britain's industrial decline, for which successive governments have chosen to find a main explanation in the failure of the education system to meet the needs and demands of employers, and a steep rise in youth unemployment which Mrs. Thatcher's government, especially, has found it expedient to attribute largely to school leavers' frequent lack of employable skills. My purpose in this chapter is to consider how the proposed 'failure' of the schools (and colleges) has been used to justify looking outside the education system for more adequate, relevant forms of education and training and so to justify the dominant role given to the Manpower Services Commission in initiating or providing them. The rhetoric of criticism has been powerful. It has highlighted features of post-16 provision which are hard to defend, and drawn strength from other policy priorities of the Thatcher government. In particular, the confidence with which remedies have been announced contrasts sharply with the perplexity of those unable to believe that complex problems can ever have such simple solutions. My own expression of doubts and uncertainties is, therefore, likely to be dismissed by the advocates of so many new training initiatives as yet another example of academic pre-occupation with analysis when what is needed is action.

The immediate causes of crisis in post-compulsory education and training are clear enough. Within the education sector, perennially difficult questions about viability of provision have been further complicated by severe pressures to cut public expenditure, and by the reduction of a third in the 16–19 age group between the early 1980s and the mid-1990s. Local authorities certainly needed no urging from the MacFarlane Committee (1981) to 'reconsider the institutional basis' of what they provided when falling rolls were already concentrating their attention on how to combine greater diversity of courses with less cost. More and more unfilled places, while actual sixth formers were scattered in so many schools, often caused enough concern to dominate their entire planning of secondary education (Fiske 1982: Ruffett and Chreseson, 1984, chapter 5). Whether they are following the logistics of rationalization or the 'logical conclusion of comprehensive reorganization', many LEAs have been led to override long established boundaries between secondary and further education, and so between pupils, students and trainees. Around the education sector, and increasingly intruding into it, have grown the training initiatives of central government, forced to intervene as never before in the transitions from school to work, to direct preparation for work, or to the lengthening search for work. It has thereby created, in a country previously distinguished by its failure to provide any further education at all for half its young school leavers, 'a nationalized youth training industry without counterpart in any non-communist country' (Roberts, 1984, p. 10: Edwards, 1983a). It has done so through the agency of the Manpower Services Commission, created in 1974 to coordinate the various services offered by the Department of Employment, and then forced by rapidly worsening *un*employment to give priority to 'youth opportunities' and youth training. Its responsibilities extended to one in eight minimum-age school leavers in 1978, to one in four by 1981. With the implementation of the National Youth Training Scheme in September 1983, it had to guarantee a year's work experience and related training to all those who were neither in full-time education nor yet in work (Department of Employment, 1981). As was widely expected even before the Budget announcement of March 1985, that Scheme is now to be extended to two years, immediately adding an additional £125 million a year to an already soaring expenditure. In this extraordinary extension of education and training, the MSC has 'led the field, set the agendas, dominated the debate, and bought out the institutions' (Green, 1983, p. 60). It is not surprising, then, that it is widely regarded from within the education sector as a brash, un-cultivated but undoubtedly forceful neighbour might be viewed by impoverished gentry whose orchards he threatens to take over. Certainly the Department of Education and Science (if not its Secretary of State) has limped behind, insisting on the 'important contributions' to be made from within the 'education system' while acknowledging at least implicitly that it is following 'a largely employment-based approach' which it has done little to shape (DES 1982).

The Validity of the Diagnosis: Inadequacies of Scale and Irrelevance of Content

The scale of educational provision post-16 has certainly been well below that in comparable countries (MSC, 1982; Labour Party, 1982, pp. 15–16: Cassels, 1985). Criticism of some MSC initiatives has therefore been muffled, or made ambivalent, by the recognition that they have occurred not in 'educational' territory, but in territory which had hardly been colonized at all. From various perspectives, they have therefore been interpreted as a long-delayed effort to treat the years from 16–19 as being *primarily* a time for learning, or as a formidable late challenge to the long preoccupation with an academic minority, or even as a 'context of opportunity for egalitarian policy' in so far as they reduce the gulf between those who continue to benefit from heavy investment in their continued education and those who had previously received no provision at all (Lodge and Blackstone, 1982, pp. 187–216).

When those initiatives were beginning to gather force in the late 1970s, there was already enough variety of courses and qualifications to require signposts and guidebooks for those accustomed to a smaller, well-cultivated terrain (Dean *et al*, 1979: FEU, 1980). The former 'clarity of provision', which Dean and her colleagues noted was rapidly being lost, had been achieved by concentrating on the sixth forms, and beyond them on another minority judged to need and be capable of further education or training. As the Crowther Committee argued, 'the education of our brightest children' had been what the English system did best, or at least with most conviction; what was needed now, in order to build a proper educational base for an advanced industrial society, was the provision of continuing education for all to the age of 18. Yet, twenty years later, the proportion of young people treated as being ready for work at 16 had hardly been reduced. As the then Director of Special Services for the MSC complained, those locked in argument over the future of the sixth form often ignored the facts that the majority of that age-group were already in employment, and that most of that majority lost all contact with formal education as soon as the law allowed them to do so (Holland, 1979). And although the MacFarlane Committee (1981) was more enthusiastic about the rationalization than about expansion, it had to record its concern that the highest ratio of 'actual' to 'potential' provision was still in traditional forms of preparation for higher education, while the lowest was among those who continued to enter employment at 16 without any of that continuing general and vocational training which Crowther had demanded. Neither from an economic nor an egalitarian position was there significant progress to report. Indeed, one long-established form of training was in steep decline. Apprenticeship was under attack from many sides — as time-serving, unnecessarily prolonged by vested craft interests, as tied to rigidly specified and often obsolete skills, as heavily biased against girls and ethnic minorities, and as excessively concentrated in a few industries. The 40,000 places available in 1983 compared with 100,000 only ten years earlier (and with 620,000 completing apprenticeship in West Germany in 1982), and in manufacturing industry there had been a drop of 24 per cent in the previous three years alone (Secretaries of State, 1984). From what direction, then, were new forms of preparation for the world of work to come, given the now conventional complaint that this country had 'one of the least trained work-forces in the industrial world (MSC, 1982, p. 2)?

Despite frequent claims to the contrary, the driving force for a 'nationalized youth training industry' has not been a culpable lack of training for employment, but a growing lack of employment itself. For all the well-publicized anxiety about school leavers being unprepared for the world of work, there is no firm evidence that they, or their employers, had found the transition especially troubling as long as the jobs were there for them to enter (Clarke, 1980; Roberts, 1984). The age of 16 had been a crossroads at which a minority chose to continue their education full-time, another minority began some form of work-with training (or training with work-experience), and a majority began work on the assumption made by themselves (*and* by their employers) that what they did not know already they would pick up as they went along. Lack of qualifications, employable skills and appropriate habits of work do not appear to have been the severe handicaps they appear to be now (Makeham 1980). The present high vulnerability of school leavers to unemployment, with rates for 16–18 olds already twice the national average by 1983, is not evidence of declining quality in the labour they supply, but of a severe slump in *demand* especially in such traditionally heavy employers of young workers as the building and manufacturing industries. Opportunities to try out a series of short-term jobs, something which had long been a favoured (and apparently quite effective) method of entry to 'working life', have dwindled rapidly. With so many fewer jobs to offer, employers are likely to favour 'tried' and 'steadier' recruits even for unskilled employment, unless subsidised from public funds to do otherwise. Among the 400,000 unemployed school leavers in 1983, a figure which has to be compared with 4000 in 1974, were very large numbers (including many with 'respectable qualifications') who would have been considered evidently employable even a few years before. It trivializes their problems to claim otherwise. The startling pace of deterioration is more vividly illustrated on a smaller scale. In 1977, only eight of the 225 pupils leaving a Jarrow comprehensive school failed to find employment; five years later, 134 of their 168 successors failed to do so (Secondary Heads Association, 1982, p. 17). A West Midlands survey, which followed the fortunes of 1979 and 1981 minimum-age school leavers, found sharp contrasts in their early careers. Two years after leaving school, 21 per cent of the 1979 cohort were unemployed, 7 per cent had spent less than six months at work, and only 3 per cent had not worked at all. For the 1981 cohort, the equivalent figures were 49 per cent, 35 per cent and 26 per cent. The only comparative increase was in the involvement of 65 per cent of the later cohort, and 19 per cent of the earlier, in youth opportunity programmes (Jones, 1984; see also Raffe, 1984).

It has been the depth of economic recession which has forced governments in all industrial countries to intervene energetically and rather similarly in the management of entry to work and in the provision of alternatives to work. Common characteristics in their response, despite marked differences in the initial scope of their training programmes, are strong reasons in themselves for questioning over-simplified causal connections between vocational preparation and employment (Rees and Atkinson, 1982; William-son, 1983; Watts, 1984). If youth training schemes in this country have become unusually extensive, the explanation may lie partly in the limited scope of what was previously available and a lack of confidence that existing institutions would respond swiftly enough to the crisis. But the method of intervention has made it expedient for central government to stress both the failures of the education sector, and the contribution that improved training may make eventually to the amount of work available. It would have been difficult anyway to have given large additional funds to an already 'discredited' education service, even without the slow pace of change likely to come from LEAs forced to consult with, and then balance, competing local, regional and national interests. It has certainly proved much more congenial to a Conservative Government, strongly centralist in intention, unimpressed by the financial autonomy traditionally conceded to the LEAs and highly impressed (when it chooses) by the beneficial consequences of market forces, to channel emergency funds through an agency of the Department of Employment which has been quite open about its 'employment-oriented approach' and its willingness to buy appropriate forms of vocational training wherever they could be found. The most bitterly contested expression of its preferences was the announcement in the 1984 White Paper *Training for Jobs* that one-quarter of the government's funding of non-advanced further education would be reallocated in 1986–87 from the LEAs to the MSC. This reallocation was justified by already well-practised arguments — training leads to jobs, and those who provide the jobs should largely decide what forms the relevant training should take. The 'needs' and 'demands' of employers were therefore to be given, at last, their proper priority.

The force of those arguments depends on the validity of the criticisms made of existing provision. Even before the crisis of youth unemployment, schools were on the defensive against charges that they transmitted an often outmoded curriculum and were too insulated from the 'real world'. Applied to post-compulsory schooling, criticism focussed on an excessively academic bias which diverted too many able students from more applied studies and denied vocational alternatives the space in which to develop. A general failure to reconstruct the curriculum of secondary schools along with their comprehensive reorganization is seen as being exemplified in the long-continued failure to cater for growing numbers of 'non-traditional' sixth formers described as being 'without academic aspirations', for whom the prestige of A-level presented 'a seductive but demoralizing target' because there was so little else at which to aim (MacFarlane, 1981, p 8; Schools Council, 1980, p 13). These criticisms have to be qualified. Aloofness from the 'world of work' is not apparent among students, whose strongly calculative view of the benefits of staying on has been reported in every major survey of sixth form and college opinion (for example, Dean *et al*, 1979). Nor can their calculations be dismissed as merely (and unrealistically) reflecting those 'academic' values which their teachers supposedly hold dear. The NFER survey certainly recorded complaints from sixth formers about being treated as second-class citizens if they were not involved (in effect) in pre-vocational preparation for those occupations which required higher education (*ibid*, pp. 252–62). But while the main use of 'A' level and 'O' level remains that of providing entry to further qualifications, their more general uses in at least the first-phase of occupational selection ensures that they will be sought by many for whom they were not designed, that many 'non-traditional' sixth formers will continue to *have* traditional 'academic aspirations', and that more 'vocationally relevant' qualifications will often be sought as a side route to the academic mainstream by those who 'failed' in it earlier or who have been initially denied the opportunity to float upwards on its current (Drake and Edwards, 1979; Atkins, 1984).

The attribution of irrelevance to academic courses and credentials, therefore, ignores the extent to which sixth forms (and their FE equivalents) have functioned as a preparatory stage for the more prestigious professional and managerial occupations. In so far as they have been over-academic, this is not in defiance of employers' demands at this level of recruitment; employers have not consistently asked for anything more 'relevant'. Indeed, in the 1982 DES proposals for an explicitly vocational qualification at 17, the acceptability of a 'real' alternative to 'O' and 'A' level is seen as being dependent on employers' willingness to look beyond the familiar academic passports on which they have relied so heavily. Yet a Brunel University survey of graduate recruitment by a large number of companies again revealed a highly conservative regard for 'good 'A' levels and degrees in traditional subjects from traditional universities, and a relatively low regard for more obviously work-related, polytechnic-based courses' (*The Guardian*, 3 September 1984). Critics of excessive academic bias within the education sector rarely admit how pervasive that bias is, and so how realistic it may often be to follow it. For example, the chairman of the body now responsible for implementing the new Certificate of Pre-Vocational Education (and also of IBM-UK) repeats the familiar complaint that 'too much of our best intellect went into the perpetuation of the 'O' level, 'A' level, university degree route' at the expense of industry, as though their choice displayed ignorance of their real interests rather than a clear awareness of how many of the best occupational chances (including many in business and industry) were *only* accessible from along that route.

The government itself has not been single-minded in its support for direct vocational relevance in post-16 education. Its rejection in 1980 of the Schools Council's N and F proposals was accompanied by a clear statement of intent to preserve 'A' level in its present form. Plans for a broader, though still academic, intermediate-level examination in five subjects as a 'genuine alternative' were so unrealistic in their disregard of many similar attempts as to deserve thoroughly their almost immediate oblivion (DES, 1980). Subsequent proposals for an advanced-supplementary ('AS') level have not pretended to offer an alternative, but are presented as a broadening influence on students for whom 'A' level will remain the main target. The high value placed on traditional sixth forms by some members of the government deterred the MacFarlane Committee from recommending the solution of tertiary colleges (or at least a tertiary stage) to problems of viability, and has led to several rejections of local plans for tertiary or even sixth-form colleges where they are seen as removing sixth forms from schools 'of proven excellence'. Most strikingly, the Assisted Places Scheme, introduced in 1981 to subsidize the fees of able children in independent schools who could not otherwise afford the special academic opportunities they were assumed to offer, has been restricted to schools selected explicitly in terms of such conventional criteria as the proportion staying on into the sixth form, the range of academic subjects available to them, and the numbers going on to higher education. Nowhere in this selective government sponsorship of able pupils is there any reference to vocational relevance, applied knowledge or new technology. Traditional versions of the appropriate 'training' of a necessarily limited elite have, therefore, been powerfully sustained (Reid and Filby, 1982), while reform has concentrated on what should be done for the rest.

The Validity of the Remedies: Some Dubious Conclusions

Despite the preservation alongside it of the 'old academicism', the 'new vocationalism' has risen spectacularly. Contrasts between old and new were strikingly illustrated in 1984 in the almost simultaneous proposals for an 'AS' level at 18, and a CPVE at 17. The first is intended to mitigate excessive specialization by adding more subjects to the present narrow range. The second is for students needing courses which are 'neither conventionally academic nor purely vocational', but which provide skills and knowledge relevant to groups of occupations on a broad base of common studies (DES, 1984; Joint Board, 1984). Reading both documents together requires considerable switching between educational codes. 'AS' level is presented as a broadening of study in depth with complementary and contrasting studies in ways which will not dilute academic standards. These are key terms in a debate going back more than fifty years (Edwards, 1983b). The frame of reference for CPVE included relevance, motivation, vocational focus, integrated programmes, skills, profiles, and performance-based assessment. As the Joint Board comments, much of this language 'may not be familiar yet to those chiefly concerned with subject-teaching to norm-referenced external examinations' — that is, who are engaged in traditional sixth form work. Yet, the new Certificate is to be offered in schools and colleges. A single coordinated system of academic *and* vocational qualifications (with two-way progression between them) is promised to replace the present separation and confusion, although there is growing alarm within the education sector at the prospect of even more bewildering vocational and pre-vocational alternatives being offered to those aged 16–17, under very different auspices (traditional examination boards, CPVE, TVEI, and YTS).

Questioning the predominance of the MSC among all these initiatives is often dismissed as the grudging response of those unable to think beyond traditional, and traditionally restricted, forms of education and training. Yet much of the rhetoric used to justify the scale of MSC activity is itself open to challenge. Blanket condemnation of its definitions of how best to prepare for the 'real world of work' ignores the diversity of local schemes. It also attributes to the MSC more consistency of purpose, and more competence in implementation, than it has so far merited. It is, nonetheless, unfortunate that the defensiveness of the education sector in relation to a post-16 stage deficient in scope and unclear in purpose has allowed the MSC, and especially its most dogmatic advocates in the government, to act so extensively without having to defend in depth the assumptions from which they operate.

The most questionable of these is the unqualified assertion that 'with skills young people can get jobs' (Young, 1984 and 1985). A government often disposed to admire American practices has certainly not taken account of a considerable loss of confidence in vocational education at school and junior college level in the USA.

Evidence of the kind to which I have referred already indicates that specific vocational preparation rarely leads to employment in the occupations to which it is directed, does not reliably enhance general 'employability', and may be less useful in that respect than continued 'general' education (Hurn, 1983). In this country too, employers continue to defer to 'academic' qualifications, at least at the 'higher' levels of occupational recruitment. This may partly be 'in the absence of any more reliable guide' (Young, 1985), certainly with anything approaching the prestige and national currency-value of 'A' level and 'O' level. But they are often using them as 'proxy measures' — as indirect evidence of ambition or persistence or social background rather than as direct indicators of specifically relevant skills and knowledge. At lower levels of recruitment, the 'unqualified' *are* much more at risk of being unemployed, and of being so for long periods, but it is less obvious that it is their lack of specifically relevant attributes and skills which explains their vulnerability. In so far as it is known or believed that those with certain qualifications are likely to come from more favourable social backgrounds, then those without them may be rejected as unsuitable for much more general and implicit reasons (Ashton *et al*, 1982). At a time of increasing competition for jobs, qualifications are likely to be heavily used as a convenient, and apparently fair, means of reducing the number of applicants to manageable proportions so that the real selection can begin. More fundamentally still, the argument that 'training leads to jobs' is fatally confused if it fails to distinguish between the 'competitive edge' which individual participants may obtain (provided that the supposed benefits are not spread so widely that they blunt the edge of any advantage), and the overall increase in employment through greater productivity and competitiveness which *may* come from having a 'better skilled and better motivated' labour force (Raffe, 1983). Even the YTS itself was initially presented as being 'first and last' a *training* scheme rather than a direct means of reducing youth unemployment (DoE, 1981, p. 9; MSC, 1982, p. 1). And while the majority of trainees may still go on to jobs — the proportion who do so being a matter of dispute, but certainly declining — it seems to be those who are best qualified *at entry* who are more likely to be successful.

Outright critics of that Scheme have identified among its functions those of muffling the full force of unemployment figures, delaying entry to real jobs in the interests of controlling a troublesome age-group more effectively, and providing employers with publicly subsidised labour and with opportunities to screen potential recruits (Finn, 1983; Coffield, 1984; Bates *et al*, 1984). They are also strongly inclined to locate it in the long series of politically expedient attempts to blame the schools for, and then find educational remedies for, problems which are much deeper and more intractable (Grubb and Lazerson, 1981). It may of course be all these things, and yet provide many trainees with experiences intrinsically preferable to the loneliness and boredom of unemployment (Jones, 1984). More broadly, the sheer scope of present provision, especially when YTS becomes a two-year scheme, not only challenges the prolonged neglect of 'half our future' from the age of 16, but has led such otherwise unlikely allies as the Labour Party (1982), the Secondary Heads Association (1982) and the British Institute of Management to argue for a common status of 'trainee' for all those aged 16–18 reinforced by common allowances. Any significant movement in that direction might conceivably blur the deeply-entrenched and hierarchical boundaries between the academic and the vocational, and between students and trainees (the market for 'workers' 16–17 having withered away). It will certainly not do so in present conditions. The strong protection being given to traditional academic standards in a small, selective sector of the education system while the tides of pre-vocational and vocational courses and certification wash over the rest is more likely to widen the gulf between the minority being sponsored for 'education' and the majority being prepared 'directly' for work. There are also many signs of that preparation being defined too narrowly in terms of specific employability, and of repertoires of 'skills' divorced from content and from understanding (Jonathan, 1983). Thirty years earlier than Ruth Jonathan's critical analysis of the 'Manpower service model of education', the American, Robert Hutchings (1953), deplored his own country's pursuit of a curriculum relevant to its immediate needs, and crammed with the 'social and life skills' through which students could learn to adjust and fit-in 'with a minimum of discomfort to their society'. He did so in terms which retain much of their force. He saw the outcomes of serving economic demands too zealously as the production of 'poor mechanics without education', equipped with skills which were obsolete almost as soon as they were learned, and ill-equipped to be, as a good general education ought to make them, *badly*-adjusted to a society which was badly in need of change.

Tony Edwards

Acknowledgements

Several contributors to this book commented constructively on an earlier draft of this chapter. I am grateful to Frank Coffield, Maurice Holt, Ruth Jonathan, Michael Naish and Bill Reid for suggesting improvements (not all of which I have been able to make) or for indicating common ground. I am also grateful for the comments of two more local colleagues, Madeleine Atkins and Bruce Carrington.

References

ASHTON, D., MAGUIRE, M., and GARLAND, V. (1982) *Youth in the Labour Market*, London, Department of Employment (Research Paper No. 34).

ATKINS, M. (1984) 'Pre-vocational studies: tensions and strategies'. *Journal of Curriculum Studies* 16, 1, pp. 403–15.

BATES, I., CLARKE, J., COHEN, P., FINN, D., MOORE, R. and WILLIS, P. (1984) *Schooling for the Dole*, London, Macmillan.

CASSELS, J. (1985) 'Learning, work and the future'. *Royal Society of Arts Journal*, June, pp. 438–46.

CLARKE, L. (1980) *The Transition from School to Work: A Critical Review*, London, Department of Employment Careers Service Branch.

COFFIELD, F. (1984) 'Is there work after the MSC?', *New Society*, 24 January, pp. 128–30.

DEAN, J., BRADLEY H., CHOPPIN, B. and VINCENT, D. (1979) *The Sixth Form and its Alternatives*, Windsor, NFER.

DEPARTMENT OF EDUCATION AND SCIENCE. (1980) *Examinations 16–18: A Consultative Paper*, London, HMSO.

DEPARTMENT OF EDUCATION AND SCIENCE. (1982) *The Youth Training Scheme: Implications for the Education Service*, Circular 6/82, September.

DEPARTMENT OF EDUCATION AND SCIENCE. (1984) *AS Levels: Proposals by the Secretaries of State for a Broader Curriculum for A-Level Students*, London, DES, May.

DEPARTMENT OF EMPLOYMENT (1981), *A New Training Initiative: A Programme for Action*, (Cmnd 8455), London, HMSO.

DRAKE, K., and EDWARDS, A. (1979) 'Examinations at 18+: Innovation without Change', *Educational Studies* 5, 3, pp. 217–24.

EDWARDS, A. (1983a) 'The reconstruction of post-compulsory education and training in England and Wales', *European Journal of Education* 18, 1, pp. 7–20.

EDWARDS, A. (1983b) 'Specialization under constraint: The universities and the sixth form curriculum' in ANWEILER, O. and HEARNDEN, A. (Eds) *From Secondary to Higher Education*, Cologne, Bohlau Verlag, pp. 157–73.

FEU (1980) *Signposts: A Map of 16–19 Education Provision*, London, FEU.

FEU (1984) *Supporting YTS*, 2nd ed., London, FEU.

FINN, D. (1983) 'The YTS — a new deal?' *Youth and Policy* 1, 4, pp. 16–24.

FISKE, D. (1982) *The Reorganisation of Secondary Education in Manchester*, Bedford Way Papers No. 9, London, University of London Institute of Education.

GREEN, A. (1983) 'Education and training: Under new masters', in WOLPE, A. and DONALD, J. (Eds) *Is There Anyone Here From Education?*, London, Pluto Press, pp. 58–70.

GRUBB, W., and LAZERSON, M. (1981) 'Vocational solutions to youth problems: The persistent frustration of the American experience', *Educational Analysis* 3, 2, pp. 91–103.

HOLLAND, G. (1979) 'More than half our future: 16–19 year olds in employment', *Oxford Review of Education* 5, 2, pp. 147–56.

HURN, C. (1983) 'The vocationalisation of American education', *European Journal of Education* 18, 1, pp. 45–64.

HUTCHINGS, R. (1953) *The Conflict in Education in a Democratic Society*, New York, Harper and Row.

JOINT BOARD FOR PRE-VOCATIONAL EDUCATION (1984) *The Certificate of Pre-Vocational Education: A Consultative Document*, London, BTEC and CGLI.

JONATHAN, R. (1983) 'The manpower service model of education', *Cambridge Journal of Education* 13, 2, pp. 3–10.

JONES, P. (1984) *What Opportunities for Youth: Deteriorating Employment Prospects for School Leavers and the Role of Government Schemes*, Youthaid Occasional Papers No. 4.

LABOUR PARTY (1982) *16–19: Learning for Life*, London, Labour Party Discussion Document.

LODGE, P. and BLACKSTONE, T. (1982) *Educational Policy and Educational Inequality*, London, Martin Robertson.

MACFARLANE, N. (Chairman) (1981) *Education for 16–19 Year Olds*, (review undertaken for HM government and local authority associations), London, HMSO.

MAKEHAM, P. (1980) 'Youth unemployment: An examination of evidence using national statistics', London, Department of Employment (Research Papers No. 10).

MANPOWER SERVICES COMMISSION (1982) *Youth Task Group Report*, London, MSC.

RAFFE, D. (1983) 'Can there be an effective youth unemployment policy?' in FIDDY, R. (Ed.) *In Place of Work: Policy and Provision for the Young Unemployed*, Lewes, Falmer Press pp. 11–26.

RAFFE, D. (1984) 'The transition from school to work and the recession: Evidence from the Scottish Leavers Surveys 1977–83' *British Journal Sociology of Education*, 5, 3, pp. 247–65.

REES, T. and ATKINSON, P. (Eds) (1982) *Youth Unemployment and State Intervention*, London, Routledge and Kegan Paul.

REID, W. and FILBY, J. (1982) *The Sixth: An Essay in Education and Democracy*, Lewes, Falmer Press.

ROBERTS, K. (1984) *School Leavers and their Prospects* London, Oxford University Press.

Ruffett, F. and Chreseson, J. (1984) *Secondary Education: the Next Step*, London, Policy Studies Institute.

Schools Council (1980) *Examinations at 18+: Report on the N and F Debate*, London, Methuen (Working Paper No. 66).

Secondary Heads Association (1982) *Youth in Need: A Call to Action*, London, Secondary Heads Association.

Secretaries of State for Employment, Education and Science, Scotland and Wales (1984) *Training for Jobs*, London, HMSO.

Watts, A. (1984) *Education, Unemployment and the Future of Work* London, Routledge and Kegan Paul.

Williamson, B. (1983) 'The peripheralisation of Youth in the labour market' in Ahier, J. and Flude, M. (Eds) *Contemporary Education Policy*, London, Croom, Helm, pp. 139–63.

Young, D. (1984) 'Response to Coffield' *New Society* 7 February.

Young, D. (1985), 'A sense of vocation', opening address to the Education for an Industrial Society conference, 24 April.

Education and 'The Needs of Society'

Ruth Jonathan

Our society educates its young, at public expense, for a minimum of eleven and a maximum of nineteen years. From that expenditure of time, effort and resources it is reasonable to expect substantial return. Current demands for a redirection of emphasis at all levels in education, away from the academic and towards the vocationally relevant, result from the perception that our educational investment is failing to deliver the social goods.

Present proposals to bring the content and process of education more closely in line with 'the needs of society' invite one of three responses. The first is to recognize that all is not well with existing practice, and to endorse proposed reforms without further ado. The second is to reassert traditional aims and values and to defend the educational *status quo* against attacks seen as philistine. The third is to look more closely at the concept of 'the needs of society'; to ask what social benefits can realistically be sought through education, whether in the short or the long term; to examine how benefit to individuals relates to the increased welfare of the group, and only then to evaluate present proposals for a change of focus for educational effort. This last strategy is adopted here.

The first obvious difficulty with talk of the 'needs of society' lies in deciding what these might be. This is not simply the familiar problem, much discussed in the heyday of the progressive movement when individual needs were an educational vogue, that identifying needs involves more than a straightforward process of grasping the relevant facts. Beyond basic survival, our needs depend upon our goals and purposes: since these are partially grounded in judgments of value, the needs they generate will be contentious.

Today's talk of 'the needs of society' is doubly misleading in its apparent simplicity. For a further complication is that this slogan falsely presents 'society' as a homogeneous unit, such that benefit to all seems the sum of similar benefits to each. Unproblematic talk of the needs of society may be appropriate in a human group where deficits and goals are basic and universally shared. It has little meaning in a complex society which is pluralist in values and stratified in terms of social status, rewards and power.

The premise underlying this slogan is that one social need *is* indeed basic and universally shared: the collective requirement for internationally competitive economic performance to provide the means of funding differing aspirations. The impulse towards vocationalism in education further assumes that, in an industrial society, the needs of society are to be conflated with the needs of industry, and that, moreover, the needs of each individual are best served by preparing him/her to serve the needs of society, understood in economic terms. Both assumptions require further scrutiny, but it is sufficient at this point to note their inherent conservatism, entailing endorsement of the socio-economic status quo. However, in a hierarchically differentiated society like ours, where social roles are functionally interrelated but differentially rewarded, members of the collective clearly do not all have an equal interest in preserving our present institutions and arrangements. For example, educational reforms aimed at simultaneously securing 'benefits for employers and young people' disguise the fact that in a free market economy, the interests of capital and labour may not always coincide. An open society acknowledges that different interest groups may have conflicting aspirations and allows for their expression: to obscure a genuine clash of interests is necessarily to subvert the aspirations of one group so as to serve the purposes of another.

Moreover, because we do not live in the sort of homogeneous society which would allow us to talk unproblematically about its 'needs', the question is further complicated when we look to education to serve them. For each of us stands in a dual relation to the education service, as providers funding the service, and as both direct and indirect consumers of its benefits. Our expectations in these roles may well be conflicting. As providers and indirect consumers of mass education we expect collective benefit in terms of improved economic performance and social cohesion. But as direct consumers we seek personal emancipation and even individual advantage in a competitive context.

An historical thumbnail sketch throws the dilemma into relief.

At the time of the first industrial revolution, an elementary education, charitably provided for the masses, was designed to serve the interests of the providers by equipping their potential labour force with the basic skills of numeracy and literacy and the appropriate habits of hygiene, obedience and industry. Education privately provided by the wealthier members of society for its own group aimed to pass on a cultural inheritance and a system of values thought appropriate to individuals who would control their own, and others', lives. Limited patronage, private and public, allowed for the revitalization and enlargement of the providing group by exceptional talent from the pool of the poor, thus avoiding social stasis. Over the following 150 years a series of political and social changes were accompanied by cumulative educational reforms opening up access to a diluted liberal education for an ever-widening circle of the population. The creation of comprehensive schools can be seen as the logical conclusion of this historical trend, since a common programme of education seems required by justice when the providers of mass schooling are coextensive with its consumers.

Throughout that period, reforms focussed on questions of access, of distribution and of effective transmission, for the extension to a wider pool of talent of an education, historically associated both with the possession and production of economic and social advantage, seemed attractive from both the individual and the collective points of view. We are all familiar with the benefits envisaged for individuals: each child should be enabled to fulfil intellectual potential, to develop creative faculties, to develop, after critical reflection, a personal system of values — the qualities providers have always looked to foster in their own group. The most discussed collective social benefit was a hoped for increase in social equality and cohesion, although it was, of course, also assumed that the maximization of individual talent and opportunity would produce collective economic benefits. If the former collective benefit had come about, the latter would again have allowed the benefit of all to be retranslated into the similar benefit of each.

This ideal scenario could only materialize, even in the long term, if educational reforms could of themselves entrain structural social change — an assumption to be queried below. In any case, the economic recession of the early 1970s brought to the surface the underlying tension in educational policies which aimed to serve the dual purposes of individual emancipation and collective economic efficiency. When it becomes evident that the second of these goals is not achieved as a simple by-product of pursuing the first, they are easily conceived of as conflicting alternatives. Once that is accepted, it is a short step to the claim that economic efficiency must take precedence, since that is a prerequisite for funding individual development on a mass scale. These conclusions can be shown to be over-hasty.

However, if they are taken at face value, they prompt a radical change in the focus of educational reform, from broadening access to retooling content. Acquiring 'useful' skills and 'relevant' knowledge seems a much more down-to-earth aim than fulfilling intellectual potential, provided we avoid the contentious questions of useful to whom and relevant for what. Acquiring acceptable social attitudes seems more straightforward than building a personal system of values, provided we assume agreement on what is acceptable. Becoming responsive to economic and social realities is less airy-fairy than developing critical awareness, provided we take these realities as given and agree to interpret them from one perspective. However, to suggest that today's proposals to fit the content of education to the needs of society are far from the simple mixture of realism and common-sense that is claimed is not to deny that some kinds of change are required. Similarly, calls for a change of curricular emphasis cannot just be dismissed as a reassertion of control over the process of social reproduction by powerful interest groups.

It is tempting to see the new emphasis on skills, on (education and) training, on 'An Education for (Life and) Work', as a return to Victorian values, whereby the development of rational autonomy is seen as an unrealistic, wasteful and dangerous aim for the mass of the population, for whom education should be merely a means of acquiring whatever skills and attitudes are appropriate to their allotted social role. Although there is an element of this in the new vocationalism, that trend would be less powerful and more politically transient if it did not coincide with public disenchantment concerning the actual benefit to many individuals of existing educational provision. For attempts to broaden the distribution of once-high-status educational content have brought no greater gains in social and economic equality than in collective economic performance. Thus, while policy-makers berate the education system for not having increased the size of the collective cake, their complaints are echoed by large sections of the public who also recognize that their own experience of education has led to no relative increase in their individual shares of that cake.

For liberal educators to respond that these economic and social effects are anyway not the prime purpose of education cuts little ice, for the intrinsic value of education is an acquired taste: its promised exchange value is often what motivates individuals to acquire that taste, and is what persuades politicians to fund its development. It is also unhelpful simply to reiterate the priority of individual emancipation over social efficiency as the prime aim of education, for to do so further dichotomizes the two goals, leaving unquestioned the assumptions on which the dichotomy rests, and allowing an unequal power struggle to decide the predictable outcome.

Leaving aside moral arguments about their relative importance, it is undeniable that the beneficial social side effects of investment in mass liberal education were heavily oversold, in the now discredited belief that such investment would of itself bring social progress and economic expansion. This is not to say that educational programmes are not a potentially powerful source of social change, but only to note that they must be carefully and consciously dovetailed with structural social changes if they are to be effective in those terms. An inadequate understanding of social processes in a hierarchical society may explain why less privileged individuals welcomed meritocratic access to education, supposing it would make room for more at the top. But ignorance of economic mechanisms cannot similarly be used to excuse the present claims of policy makers that a new emphasis on vocational training will create markets for products and jobs to supply them. Our schooling practices may be a politically acceptable scapegoat for economic and social failings, for that implies that the public, as products of the system, have only themselves to blame. However, a false diagnosis implies misguided remedies which compound the problem.

If we have now learnt that it was a mistake to suppose that education alone would produce particular social and economic effects, then to attribute failure to produce them largely to deficiencies in education is irrational. To suppose that in the future it will produce them, provided content is changed, is to misdiagnose the source of the original error. Indeed, at the heart of the new vocationalism, there is a hopeless paradox. Not only does it falsely suppose that — given the right content — schooling can yet become a sufficient cause of social change; it simultaneously falsely denies education's necessary role in social development. Whereas, on the one hand, education is still seen as the prime cause and sufficient remedy for economic and social ills, conversely, this movement takes social circumstance as given and wishes to adapt educational programmes to serve circumstance, thus overlooking the essential function of education as *one* of society's instruments of change. For we are told that education should cease to offer a mandarin experience which few want and which collectively we cannot afford, and get on with the down to earth business of preparing children for the future.

Given that our best guess about the future in a period of rapid and accelerating technological and social change is that its demands may well surprise us, it is not obvious how this should be done. It is quite clear, however, that we will predetermine the future in the guise of preparing for it, if we circumscribe both individual and social possibilities to those which we currently forsee and endorse. Although it would be irresponsible to ignore inevitable future circumstance in educational programmes, and perverse to prepare young people for a vanishing world, the function of education cannot simply be to prepare children for the future, for they will comprise that future in social terms. Since determinism, whether social or technological, is a self-fulfilling prophecy only for those who believe in it, it is both illegitimate and shortsighted to impose on the young a future limited by present awareness. Had that been done in the past, the present would look very different.

In an open society which allows for social and political change, and which depends for its economic well-being on technological change, education must open up possibilities for learning which cannot be prespecified. To vocationalize schooling programmes, as currently advocated, implies short-term expedience and long-term stagnation, whether for individuals or for society as a whole. It is analoguous to abandoning basic research for research applications, whereby both the legacy of the past and the potential of the future are sacrificed for present gains. Without past encouragement to pursue disinterested enquiry, we would have had, not difficulty in exploiting new technology, but no new technology to exploit. Without educational programmes which promote understanding and critical questioning of past and present circumstance — cultural, social, political, scientific, technical, economic — the stagnation of society is assured. Of course, technical and economic progress could be bought at the price of social stasis if crude vocationalism were envisaged for only some of the young, but that is not what is overtly proposed. If we assume that, since we are all providers of mass education as well as its consumers, we would not find it collectively acceptable to divide the next generation up into those who will generate social and economic demand and those who will facilitate its supply, it is clear that attention only to the supply side of the equation is shortsighted. Even if we accepted that today's learning should be tailored to tomorrow's tasks, what those will be depends in part of what kind of society will be generating them. And that partially depends upon the education the young receive today.

It is, therefore, neither Luddism nor ivory-tower arrogance to suggest that the prescriptions of industrialists and technologists can never be more than a partial element in debates over curriculum reform. What should be taught is at bottom a matter for moral and political discussion, for it is a function of the kind of society we wish to live in. Of course, economics and technology place constraints upon our choices, making some more realistic than others, but just as, through education, individuals must be equipped to generate circumstance as well as to respond to it, so, for society as a whole, rational discussion of our goals should not be dominated by experts in some of the means of achieving those goals.

It is currently supposed, however, that the role we might expect rational discussion to play in educational decisions can be adequately discharged by the play of market forces on the system. After all, following socio-economic theories which suppose each individual to be equally free and rationally self-interested, these represent the most democratic means of reaching collectively beneficial decisions. Even if those dubious premises were accepted, to allow the market to dictate educational provision is to conflate worth with its public estimation and to decree that dominant values (whether dominant by force of numbers or of power) win the day. To do so is to legislate against minority interests, specialized pursuits and cultural diversity. Not only is it questionable whether a dominant group has the right to abrogate to itself those judgments of value which can only be made by the individual, it is further questionable whether any such group, even if it were an overwhelming majority, would welcome the social homogeneity and cultural decline which would ensue. Unless we believe that there is no connection between educational provision and eventual capacity for intellectual and aesthetic discrimination and the critical appraisal of values, or that these qualities in individuals are of no benefit to society as a whole, we have every reason to put great effort into fostering them, whatever their lack of immediate economic return or their lack of instant appeal to the market.

Appeal to the market lends an apparently democratic gloss to today's vocationalism, for the political acceptability of that change of educational direction depends upon its free endorsement by the public in a 'new mood of realism'. It is evident that what counts as realism is a function of present realities, and in a period of acute unemployment many parents and pupils cannot afford to take the longer view. However, whilst it may be rational for individuals in adverse circumstances to seek to minimize the worse outcome, it is incumbent on policy-makers to aim in their planning for maximization of the best outcome.

Clearly the market is not the most rational source of educational policy, since damage limitation as a principle for choice is optimal only in crisis management, and educating the next generation is a long-term affair. The strongest argument in favour of the voice of the market is that this is democratic: let the consumer decide. In much current policy debate, however, it is far from clear who the educational consumer is thought to be. At the start of Mr Callaghan's 'Great Debate', pupils, parents and the wider public were invited as consumers to appraise the education service. Five years later, by the time the New Training Initiative was launched, pupils were widely referred to in consultative and policy documents as 'products' of the system, with industrialists and employers referred to as 'consumers' of these products. A constructive response from educators is required when many products of the system are dissatisfied with their experience of it, but the complaints of consumers in this latter sense invite quite different questions. Here, consumer dissatisfaction with products of the system cannot serve as axiomatic justification for particular policy changes, unless we presume general and exclusive endorsement of the social and economic functions for which these products are claimed to be ill-prepared. The assumption that educational change should be consumer-led in *this* sense constitutes a proposal to regard the individual primarily as a cog in a given socio-economic machine, and the education system as merely a device for manpower supply. Thus to allow market forces a dominant role in educational policy is either an abrogation of responsibility by educators and policy makers or a covert decision to jettison personal emancipation as an educational goal in favour of collective economic efficiency.

None of this is to say that education should ignore the demands of working life. It is rather to query a defective interpretation of these demands and their implications for learning. Since the ability to support oneself and one's dependents is a precondition for adult autonomy, any process which prepares for life must pave the way for this. But current proposals that we understand preparation for life primarily as preparation for economic role are the matching converse mistake to the demands of the sixties that we educate for leisure. Both approaches are based on a rigid dichotomy between education and training and between work and leisure, presuming a divorce between the knowledge, capacities and attitudes which are required for fulfilment and creative productivity in the two areas of life. Both approaches also share an unimaginative conception of the technological future.

Education for leisure envisaged a world in which automation would free us from much of the burden of labour, leaving time on our hands for intellectual and aesthetic activity. Education for work envisages a world in which the displacement of people by machines requires us to foster skills and attitudes which will enable us to compete successfully (with each other) for a diminishing number of tasks. Each vision looks only at the supply side of the equation. The first forgets that work has a cultural as well as an economic function, with the quality of experience in each area partly dependent upon the other. The second similarly overlooks the point made here that a culturally impoverished or undiscriminating public will generate fewer and less varied tasks. On a wider conception both of working life and of our power to be masters rather than slaves of our technology, it is by no means obvious that the pre-conditions for economic autonomy are distinct from the precondi-tions for personal autonomy, to be developed through a general education, with content reappraised to that end.

This is even more pertinent in the case of individuals than in that of society as a whole. Although it is shortsighted to do so vocational preparation *can* be seen collectively as having solely economic importance; from the individual's standpoint it has economic *and* personal importance. For unless we envisage a society in which individuals are drafted, by circumstance if not by statute, into particular economic activities for the presumed good of the economic collective, the individual has choices to make in these matters. He/she requires a certain level of material reward, but also cares how this is gained. Unless the individual chooses from a range of occupations according to inclination and aptitude as well as opportunity, we not only deny the value of individuality and of personal freedom; we also make ineffective use of human resources. The prime tasks of education must be to promote diversity of capacity and interests in individuals (which cannot be prespecified or costed) and to foster the ability to make considered judgments about a worthwhile style of life. Equipping young people to *make* such choices must take priority over equipping them to carry them out, as a simple matter of logic. If we try to ignore or reverse this necessary order of priority in educational programmes, the individual becomes a victim of his/her own ignorance and irrationality: if, to escape this consequence, society makes choices for the individual, he/she becomes a victim of circumstance — a cog in a machine either of collective irrationality or of cynical vested interest.

It is therefore morally unacceptable, economically shortsighted and fatal to future social and technological development to suppose that through education we could achieve collective welfare by adapting the individual to envisaged circumstance, tailoring mass education to the 'needs of society'. For we must aim to prepare the young, not just to cope with life, but to understand and critically evaluate the circumstances they inherit. If they can merely cope, or passively adapt, they will not only lack the means to choose from among a range of options for their future individual lives: they will also have neither the moral nor intellectual nor technical capacity to modify and extend that range for those who come after them. Fashions in educational policy often lead to wasteful diversions, but this latest trend is a narrow cul-de-sac. All this is of course only one side of the issue. If we are to realize the twin goals of education which have evolved through successive reforms, namely personal emancipation and social progress (understood only partly in terms of economic well-being), then even the most careful reappraisal of what is taught must be accompanied by structural social changes which no educational reforms could bring about unaided.

References

BAILEY, C. (1984) *Beyond the Present and Particular: A Theory of Liberal Education*, London, Routledge and Kegan Paul.

BATES, I., CLARKE, J., COHEN, P., FINN, D., MOORE, R., and WILLIS, P. (1984) *Schooling for the Dole?*, London, Macmillan.

BECK, J. (1981) 'Education, industry and the needs of the economy', *Cambridge Journal of Education*, 11, 2, pp. 87–106.

ENTWISTLE, H., (1970), *Education, Work and Leisure*, London, Routledge and Kegan Paul.

HOLT, M. (1983) 'Vocationalism: The new threat to universal education', *Forum*, summer, pp. 84–6.

JONATHAN, R. (1983) 'The Manpower Service model of education', *Cambridge Journal of Education*, 13, 2, pp. 3–10.

JONES, K. (1983) *Beyond Progressive Education*, London, Macmillan.

O'CONNOR, D.J. (1982) 'Two concepts of education', *Journal of Philosophy of Education*, 16, 2, pp. 137–46. Reply by JONATHAN, R., pp. 147–54.

REEDER, D. (1979) 'A recurring debate — Education and industry', in

BERNBAUM, G. (Ed.), *Schooling in Decline*, London, Macmillan.
WHITE, J. (1982) *The Aims of Education Restated*, London, Routledge and Kegan Paul.
WILLIAMS, S. (1984), 'Getting our act together', *Times Educational Supplement*, 25 May, p. 20.

Comprehensive Schools

David H. Hargreaves

Two years ago, at a conference for headteachers and senior staff of comprehensive schools, I said that I feared that before long we would witness a serious attempt to restore grammar schools to the secondary education system of England and Wales. I had no special evidence on which to base this prediction: it was a guess grounded in my reading of the general political climate of the time and my sense of the growing divergence in views about the comprehensive school, with, at one extreme, a complacency that the battle for comprehensive education was securely won and, at the other extreme, a distinct nostalgia for the grammar schools in the light of dissatisfaction with the comprehensive school. A few months later one local education authority in England made the predicted attempt to restore grammar schools. That attempt failed, largely because the majority of parents in the area concerned, who doubtless supported a whole range of political parties, were firmly opposed. But the attitude and philosophy which led to that failed attempt still remains strong. 1985 was a difficult year for the comprehensive school. The failure to provide adequate salaries for teachers dealt a terrible blow to the morale and commitment of comprehensive school teachers. It seems likely that some of the traditional goodwill shown by teachers to their schools and to their pupils will have vanished forever. In July 1985 the announcement of the government's acceptance of the review of 'top' salaries came as an end-of-term blow for teachers. They could hardly fail to notice that the Permanent Secretary at the DES was to get a 32 per cent increase — without any strings attached. The leader in *The Times* described it all as 'unrestrained irresponsibility'. In the same week the press was reporting concern about the retention and recruitment of teachers in some shortage subjects such as mathematics, physics, computer studies and craft, design and technology, even though there is a growing acceptance that these subjects must be available for all pupils within the comprehensive school.

Nor was this the end of the story. In the same week there was a further significant announcement in the press. The Prime Minister told the nation that she was thinking about plans to create new direct grant schools. The effect of the abolition of the old direct grant schools by the Labour government of a decade earlier was, of course, to create a significant increase in the private sector of secondary education. New direct grant schools would simply increase the private sector still further. Within a few days a junior minister of education said that he wished 'to set education free, to set the people free'. His aspiration was to 'denationalize' the school system and create a system of separate and independent schools responsive to market mechanisms.

When the Prime Minister and her ministers speak in this way, there is likely to be a significant national discussion of their views. Within this debate it must be recognized that the future of the comprehensive school as we have come to know it is now at stake. We can no longer be complacent. We can no longer assume that the comprehensive school is the dominant form of secondary schooling for the nation's young people, apart from a relatively small private sector. The shift in public opinion from the tripartite system to the comprehensive school was engineered by capitalizing upon parents' dissatisfaction with secondary modern schools. It was Harold Wilson who, somewhat misleadingly, proclaimed that the comprehensive schools would be 'grammar schools for all'. Will it now become possible, by trading upon parental dissatisfaction with some comprehensive schools, to change public opinion yet again? Is this but the first stage of a return to what would in effect be a new bipartite system of secondary education: private schools, essentially grammar schools, for the rich (and a few 'bright' working class pupils) and under-resourced comprehensive schools for the rest?

Without question there are some excellent comprehensive schools. But not all of them are as good as we would wish. I am convinced that there has been substantial progress in the quality of secondary education during the last ten years, and one effect of this has been that parental and public expectations of secondary schools have been steadily rising. That is surely highly desirable, but it creates a pressure upon the comprehensive school for continuing improvement. Their evolution is far from complete. The comprehensive school will in coming years need to be defended, but the best defence is their continuing improvement and, therefore, growing public satisfaction with them. The major concern of this chapter is the means by which that can be achieved. And the theme which unites all my suggestions is that of partnership and collaboration. I shall offer ten forms that this partnership should take as the most urgent ways in which the comprehensive school can be improved and defended.

Schools, Local Education Authorities and Central Government

In most matters of detail, our system assigns most powers to the individual school, its headteacher and governors — and rightly so, since in matters of detail the best decisions will be made at the local level. Most commentators have detected a recent trend to centralization in the field of education. But it is important to remember that this has characterized both Labour and Conservative policies. Circular 10/65, which was the major formal step towards the establishment of comprehensive education, and which is now mainly seen as a positive step, was a bold act of centralization much resented in some quarters at that time. Action taken in the field of education during Mrs Thatcher's Conservative administration after 1979 simply carries forward the agenda established by 10/65 and James Callaghan's famous Ruskin speech. Circulars 6/81 and 8/83 on the school curriculum are in the same tradition as 10/65. Indeed it can justly be said that 6/81 and 8/83 did much to ensure that comprehensive schools made the necessary change of focus from organizational to curricular issues. Moreover all this aroused local education authorities to their curricular responsibilities, for the majority did not have an adequate authority policy on the curriculum prior to this. In this sense, central action made a positive contribution to the evolution and improvement of the comprehensive school. I confess to having little patience with those who denounced this central action, for they have no alternative strategy for developing the curriculum of the comprehensive school. At the same time the balance of power between schools, local education authorities and central government, obscure though it is, is both precious and precarious. It should not be a battleground between these three great partners as each tries to wrest power from the other two. The relationship should and could be characterized by partnership and collaboration in the best interests of schools and their pupils. Unless we learn to respect this balance of power and work in collaboration, it is likely that damage will be done to the education system. I believe this matter to be of fundamental significance to the future both of our education and of our society, and although I do not have space in which to elaborate upon the theme, I believe we neglect the issue at our peril.

Partnership between Teachers and Parents

Secondary school teachers in general remain somewhat distant from parents and are inclined to be a little afraid of them: 'good' parents are supportive of teachers but remain firmly at arm's length, unless they are invited into the school on the teachers' terms. Some real improvement in recent years should be acknowledged. Much effort has been expended to improve written communication between school and home and this is but one example of a new sensitivity to parents. But in most schools there is an urgent need to make a movement from a concern to improve *liaison* between school and home to a new conception of a *partnership* between teachers and parents. Partnership is a richer and much more demanding notion than mere liaison. Partnership recognizes that parents do not hand over their children to the teachers for their education, but that education is a joint enterprise between parents and teachers for the simple reason that education takes place not only in school but also in the home and in the community. Partnership, if it is to be effective, requires a sharing of agreed goals and means for reaching those goals; it requires both mutual support and mutual accountability between the partners. Most secondary school teachers feel rather threatened by such a conception. This is hardly surprising. The comprehensive school has helped to move teachers away from a conception of teaching as a highly autonomous process conducted by individual teachers in the privacy of their classroom. One of the comprehensive school's great successes has been the development of the whole school approach to policy development and implementation. But if secondary school teachers are beginning, slowly but surely, to collaborate with their colleagues, most have much to learn about collaborating with parents. I continue to be amazed by secondary teachers' defensiveness towards parents, since the evidence shows overwhelmingly that a more overt collaboration with parents both enhances the quality of pupil achievement and increases support for, and understanding of, the teacher's work. If we are to improve the comprehensive school and persuade parents to defend it, then collaboration between teachers and parents must assume a much higher priority than is currently accorded to it.

Partnership between Teachers

I have already noted that the comprehensive school has contributed to this development. Co-teaching — teachers working together in a variety of ways with a group of pupils — is certainly becoming more common. This allows teachers to share their skills and to complement one another. But whilst teachers are learning to collaborate, schools themselves remain remarkably insular and isolated. Very few teachers have any detailed knowledge of what is happening in another comprehensive school a mile or two away; neighbouring schools are more likely to see one another as rivals and competitors rather than as collaborators, especially in areas which are badly affected by falling rolls. This is understandable, but it cannot be in the interests of comprehensive schools as a whole. The comprehensive school will evolve rapidly only if different comprehensive schools are prepared to share both in the problems they experience and in the solutions, or 'good practice', they devise. I think it unreasonable to expect individual comprehensive schools to attend to this matter themselves: this is surely a responsibility for each local education authority. In the Inner London Education Authority we are launching a scheme, to be known as INDEX (namely, the innovation and development exchange), through which teachers experiencing a common problem and searching for a solution can be put in touch with one another. It is hoped that it will allow teachers using the exchange to meet and to visit one another. It is potentially a powerful mechanism for the improvement of the comprehensive school since its main function is to facilitate collaboration between talented and committed teachers. I have more faith in this approach than some of the traditional methods, so beloved by inspectors and teacher educators, through which teachers are simply *told*, by discredited didacticism, about either theoretical or actual 'good practice'. For too long we have failed to trust in the creative capacities of teachers to find solutions to their problems. Schools do not become better by being *instructed* to improve themselves but by facilitating self-improvement.

David Hargreaves

Partnership between Teachers and Pupils

When, as an inspector, I visit either a primary school or a college of further education, I find my presence far less intrusive and disturbing than when I visit a comprehensive school. In the primary school or the college I can quickly merge into the various activities, and talk with teachers or pupils/students with very little disturbance. More often than not, my entry into the comprehensive school classroom has a somewhat disruptive effect. The explanation is quite simple: in both primary schools and colleges the pupils/students are much more likely to be engaged in group work or practical work or individualized study than in the secondary school, where teaching of the whole class by chalk-and-talk methods remains surprisingly common. In comprehensive schools, the learner is more likely to be cast into a passive role of boredom. In the research undertaken for the report *Improving Secondary Schools* (ILEA, 1984) 48 per cent of the fifth year pupils agreed with the view that 'on the whole this year at school has been boring' and no fewer than 77 per cent said that 'at school there is too much book learning and not enough practical work'. These are surely very alarming figures. Some of the best ideas about the necessary reform for the comprehensive school have come not from the schools themselves but from further education, especially the work of the FEU. Concepts such as 'the negotiated curriculum' have been developed in FE precisely because it was these colleges which had to undo the damage wrought on their students by the comprehensive schools. It is frequently said by secondary school teachers that concepts such as 'the negotiated curriculum' are irrelevant to them, because the secondary school system is dominated by the predetermined syllabuses of the examination bodies. This is for the most part a feeble excuse as well as a failure to recognize the meaning of 'the negotiated curriculum'. It is true that much of the syllabus may be predetermined by an examination board. But is it not possible to share with pupils the different courses offered both within and between examination boards? Is it inevitable that the teacher should decide this unilaterally? Even within a particular course there is often room for choice. In most literature courses, for example, there is a choice of set books. Why cannot the selection of set books be a joint enterprise of teacher and pupil? Moreover the negotiation covers more than content: it can be applied even more powerfully to methods of teaching and learning and to assessment. In the comprehensive school, teachers rarely give pupils control over methods of learning. Yet most pupils of 14 to 16 are perfectly capable of making choices — and of changing their mind — over the most effective methods of teaching and learning. In the same way the assessment of progress need not lie exclusively with the teacher. Pupil self-evaluation is essential, not least because it is through self-evaluation that pupils can come to diagnose their own strengths and weaknesses and so to conjure up the internal motivation which is necessary to progress. If I had to select the single most important factor to explain the under-achievement of pupils between the ages of fourteen and sixteen I would without hesitation point to this lack of a collaborative partnership between teacher and learner over what is to be learnt, over how it is to be learnt and over how it is to be assessed. Of course there are schools and classrooms where this approach is being adopted. In the ILEA it is hoped that the proposed system of units and unit credits in the fourth and fifth year, as recommended in *Improving Secondary Schools*, will promote this new collaborative relationship between teacher and pupil.

Partnership between Pupil and Pupil

Most adults today have few memories from their own school days of collaborative experiences with other pupils. Almost all classroom work as well as homework had to be done by oneself: to work with another pupil acquired an aura of cheating. Collaborative experiences were confined largely to the sports field (and even then within a competitive framework) or extra-curricular activities. No doubt this encouraged independence in learners, but was it really sensible to put education in cooperation so clearly at the margins? In adult life, whether at work or in the home, so much of our success rests upon our capacity to cooperate successfully with others.

Those of us who were involved in the ILEA enquiry into under-achievement in secondary schools soon discovered that we had available to us no explicit definition or philosophy of achievement appropriate to the comprehensive school. At the beginning of *Improving Secondary Schools* we attempted, in a rather primitive way, to write such a philosophy of achievement. We call them the four aspects of achievement, recognizing that although each was analytically distinct from the other, in practice the four constantly interpenetrate. Aspect III is concerned with a range of personal and social skills. Certainly we included self-reliance and the ability to work alone. But we also felt it essential to include the ability to cooperate with others in the interests of the group as well as of the individual, and the skills of leadership. This was not merely because the capacity to cooperate and collaborate is so essential to adult life, and therefore something which the secondary school cannot afford to ignore. We also bore in mind the simple fact that cooperation and collaboration with others provide one of life's greatest pleasures. A failure which is shared becomes much more tolerable; a success that is shared is no less rewarding than a success gained by oneself. Every teacher who has organized a school play or a musical event knows this well. Such collaborative extra-curricular activities are amongst the most treasured memories of our school days. Is there any good reason why the power of such collaborative experiences should not be made part of the normal work of classrooms? Well organized collaborative work between pupils takes much of the pressure off the teacher. It allows pupils to be more actively engaged with their work; it allows pupils to talk through their ideas and difficulties; it encourages them to try out ideas and use their creativity; it frequently motivates a pupil who in other contexts becomes easily bored. Naturally it requires considerable teacher skill to organize such experiences, but they seem to me to be one of the most important ways at which we can improve the comprehensive school.

Partnership betweens Institutions of Teacher Education and Schools/Local Education Authorities

It is now widely recognized that comprehensive school teachers need regular opportunities to acquire the new skills to meet the new challenges which they face. This requires frequent opportunities for in-service education and training. Much of the relevant INSET is provided by institutions of teacher education, which run courses of varying length, from a few hours to a whole year. The content of the majority of these courses, especially those which lead to an advanced qualification or a higher degree, are provided by the lecturing staff. The content is often selected on two grounds. The first is that it meets what is considered appropriate to an 'academic' award. The second is that it matches the existing expertise, interests and preferences of the lecturers concerned. It is very rare for a course to be planned because it is known to meet the existing needs of teachers or a local authority. Indeed, colleges and universities usually question their courses only when they find it difficult to recruit students. The staff are thus rarely under any kind of pressure to question existing courses and they often believe their own rhetoric that the content of the course does not matter, because the secondment offers the practising teacher an opportunity to think and study. There is, of course, some truth in this: teachers do indeed need time to think and study. But the content matters. Teachers and their schools have need of particular kinds of knowledge and skill. But the practising teachers are in a weak position. Very rarely are they in a position to negotiate with an institution of teacher education about the content of their course of study. More typically, they have to select, from whatever courses are currently on offer, that which best approximates to what they need. This is a most unsatisfactory situation so far as teachers and their schools are concerned.

But do teachers really know what they want? It has to be admitted that for the most part their schools certainly do not. Most comprehensive schools have not undertaken the important task of defining what the school needs for its improvement and then relating this diagnosis to the needs, both personal and professional, of the teaching staff. The vast majority of comprehensive schools have no overall staff development policy into which the INSET needs of individual teachers can be placed coherently. Of course most comprehensive schools now have a much better policy for the induction of new teachers, but this rarely extends beyond the first few years of a teacher's professional life. There can be no effective use of INSET and secondment until every comprehensive school has a proper plan for its own development over, say, a five-year period and the INSET needs of individual teachers are fitted into that overall plan. In the ILEA we are moving to a position where a teacher will not be seconded unless two conditions are met: first, that a teacher who applies for secondment should be seen to be meeting an institutional as well as a personal need; second, that the school has an effective plan to make use of the new skills the teacher is expected to acquire on his or her return to the school in the interests of the improvement of the school as a whole. These are seen to be no more than the first steps of a better approach to staff development. The next steps involve much more detailed negotiations between the local education authority and each institution providing courses for experienced teachers. In the absence of a much more effective partnership between local education authorities and institutions of teacher education we shall continue in our failure to deploy INSET resources towards the improvement of the comprehensive school.

Partnership between Schools and Outside Agencies

During the last decade we have witnessed a dramatic growth in the partnership between education and industry and commerce. This notable success story is too complex either to describe or to explain here. Attitudes on both sides, which a few years ago were simplistic, suspicious or even hostile, have changed dramatically. There is still a long way to go but there is no lack of commitment to make the rest of the journey.

There remain many other agencies external to the school with which teachers could and should forge a partnership. Let me take one example. Thankfully it is now recognized that all comprehensive school pupils between the ages of 14 and 16 should be pursuing courses in the expressive and creative arts as part of the core curriculum. Now it is true that most schools send a party of pupils on the occasional trip to a museum or gallery, or perhaps to see a play, especially if it is a set work for a public examination. That is far too little. Art galleries, museums, cinemas, concert halls, opera houses and theatres are significant centres of culture from the present to the distant past. Making use of them is a habit and for many pupils, especially of working-class origin, the habit should begin at school. Visits to them must be a regular part of the curriculum, not the occasional treat or break from routine. There is plenty of scope for the more imaginative use of such visits: as Rod Taylor has shown in Wigan, visits to an art gallery can be occasions for making art as well as observing it. On their side the arts' organizations, if I may so call them collectively, are reaching out to the schools, for many of them are now employing their own education officers. Standing in the way of further development is the curious prejudice, still surprisingly common, that children are not really learning unless they are in school.

There are many community organizations which have much to offer the school if only the school will reach out to them. So often the premises of a comprehensive school are under-used in the evening, when for very little cost they could be offered to a variety of community organizations. Such use of the school by the community could be the beginning of a much richer interpenetration between school and community, and therefore between young people and adults. It is to me one of the great mysteries of contemporary life that the school serves to shield young people from adults — and then we become surprised that young people are seen to be 'a problem'. If we want young people to behave in a more adult way and to take more responsibility, then the best way is to let them mix more frequently with adults. This is known to be one of the important benefits of work experience, but we have failed to apply this lesson more widely.

Partnership between the Comprehensive School and the Primary School

The institutional break which for most of our children occurs at the age of 11 persists for what are now entirely irrelevant historical reasons. The evidence, especially that from the University of Leicester, shows quite clearly that the root of much under-achievement in the secondary school is to be found in the first few weeks and months of a pupil's life in the secondary school. There is a desperate need to create greater curricular and pedagogic continuity between the primary and the secondary school. This will not be easily achieved, largely because of the substantial barriers between the two phases of education. Primary and secondary school teachers share the compulsory period of education for each individual child, yet they do not act as partners in that enterprise. Most of the fault lies with the comprehensive schools, which too often persist in making a fresh start with each 11-year-old; and the frequent description of the first two years of secondary education as 'the foundation years' is a profound insult to primary colleagues. Some fault must also be attributed to primary teachers, who have paid too little attention to the need for some agreed curriculum for top juniors and to the need for better recording of pupils' achievements which can be carried on into the secondary school. I believe this is being increasingly understood on both sides and in the last year or two I have seen signs of much improved partnership between primary and secondary school teachers. When that partnership is fully in action we shall, I am convinced, see a definite improvement in the achievement of pupils at the comprehensive school.

David Hargreaves

Partnership between the Comprehensive School and Further and Higher Education

At present we are in a confused state over what arrangements should apply to those in education beyond the age of 16. The explanation is quite simple: the structures we have inherited presuppose that the majority of pupils will leave full-time education at 16; a small minority will continue with an academic education in the sixth form; and a few will continue with vocational education in the colleges of further education. Massive unemployment amongst young people as well as rising educational aspirations in the population have demonstrated the weakness of those structures. There is also a growing recognition that the fundamental principles of comprehensive education need to be applied to the 16–19 age range. There may well be a variety of solutions to this problem, though the tertiary college has evident attractions to those local education authorities who are not badly hampered by past arrangements. In deciding on the new arrangements we must bear in mind that from now on we can assume that the vast majority of young people will be taking some form of education or training beyond 16: 16 is no longer an end-point, but merely another point of transition. Has the comprehensive school considered carefully enough the educational destinations of all their fifth-formers? And have they, in consequence, forged new partnerships with all those agencies which represent this wide variety of destinations?

Partnership between the Comprehensive School and the Media

Education is news: as far as the media are concerned, bad news about comprehensive schools makes even better news. There are certain sections of the press which make a consistent and determined effort to show comprehensive schools, and their teachers, in as bad a light as possible. This is unfair and very frustrating to teachers. Some sections of the press are willing to engage in partnership with the teaching profession. I know from experience that there are many education correspondents from newspapers as well as radio and television reporters, editors and producers who are very ready to engage in partnership with the teaching profession. Others are not. But our capacities to enter into partnership — our 'PR' skills if you like — are very feeble. Teachers learn nothing about this in their initial training or in their early years as a qualified teacher. But skills are suddenly needed when one becomes a headteacher. If we want the media to tell people about the many good things that happen in comprehensive schools, we shall have to collaborate with the media. I sometimes wonder if teachers, instead of simply inviting the media to their conferences, actually arranged a few conferences between themselves and people from the media, there would not be much to be gained on both sides.

These ten forms of partnership present a tall order for busy teachers. But then nobody, or at least nobody with any sense, ever entered teaching in a comprehensive school for an easy life. By forging these partnerships, I believe, we would not only provide a better education for young people, but would also create a powerful and varied force of people who would be very ready to defend the comprehensive school if and when it appears to be threatened. But it is more than that. We have all learned in recent years that some of the most powerful messages of schooling are transmitted not in the formal curriculum but in the so-called 'hidden curriculum'. By creating the partnerships I have described, teachers would be transmitting to pupils the important message that successful and rewarding achievements are created through collaboration. The *process* by which we make comprehensive schools better is perhaps the best guarantee that we shall create the right *product*, namely young people with the skills of collaboration on which the future of our society, and our planet, depends.

Reference

Inner London Education Authority (1984) *Improving Secondary Schools*, London, ILEA.

Curriculum Conflict in the United States

Michael W. Apple

If there are lingering doubts that the curriculum in American schools is a political battleground, these may be quickly dispelled by a few simple statistics. The National Council of Teachers of English (NCTE) and such organizations as the Association of American Publishers (AAP) estimate that approximately 30 per cent of the school districts throughout the country have recently found themselves embroiled in conflicts over books and curricula. Both the NCTE and the AAP, as well as such organizations as the American Library Association, argue that such conflicts, and the calls for censorship that usually accompany them, are becoming more widespread. At the same time, the proponents of curricular censorship are becoming more sophisticated both legally and politically. Given the history of McCarthyism in the United States, these movements are not something that should be taken lightly.

These kinds of conservative movements are not new, of course. One cannot fully grasp the history of the curriculum in American schools without seeing the many periods in which the form and content of the curriculum were very much political issues used, by a multitude of diverse groups to further anti-statist, 'pro-American', or other positions. One important instance can provide an example. This was the campaign mounted against one of the more progressive textbook series that were widely used in the United States during the 1930s, *Man and His Changing World* by Harold Rugg and his colleagues. The National Association of Manufacturers, American Legion, Advertising Federation of America, and other 'neutral' groups mounted a campaign against the series, charging that it was socialist, anti-American, anti-business, and so forth. They were

161

more than a little successful in forcing school districts to withdraw Rugg's series from classrooms and libraries — so successful in fact that sales fell from nearly 300,000 copies in 1938 to approximately 20,000 in 1944.[1] Thus, we should not underestimate the power of the Right, in concert with capital, to bring its case to our attention and make us feel its presence. As I shall demonstrate in this chapter, this is not only an historical phenomenon, but once again sits at the very center of the influences on curriculum and teaching today in the United States.

At the same time that censorship of all kinds of books and materials for classroom use seems to be growing, so, too, are two other movements. The first is the increase in the number of Christian fundamentalist schools throughout the country. As publicly funded schools have declined in enrollment, the increase in children attending church supported schools of this kind, with their own conservative class, gender, and race ideologies, has been rather dramatic. The second concerns something that is less popular but has significance beyond its numbers. This is that group of parents scattered throughout many sections of the United States who, for political, religious, and ideological reasons, have decided to teach their children at home rather than to send them to state supported schools.[2]

All of these tendencies indicate something of considerable import. The state itself is losing legitimacy. Large groups of people simply no longer trust either the institutions of education or the teachers and administrators in them to make 'correct' decisions about what should be taught or how to teach it. The political Right in the United States has been very successful in mobilizing considerable numbers of people around a variety of seemingly anti-statist themes. In fact, one of its major victories has been to shift the blame for unemployment, for the supposed breakdown of 'traditional' values, and for tensions within the family *from* the economic, cultural, and social policies and effects of capital *to* the school and other public agencies. This has caused a near collapse of the consensus that stood behind most liberal educational reforms in the United States.

The fracturing of the previous consensus over education has had the effect of altering some of the major educational alliances that existed previously. Whereas before, minority groups, women, teachers, administrators, government officials, and legislators often acted together to propose social democratic policies for schools (for example, expanding educational opportunities, developing special programmes in bilingual and multicultural education, and for the handicapped, and so on), the new alliance in power combines Industry with the New Right. Its interests are less in redressing the imbalances in the life chances of women, people of color, or labor, and more in providing the educational conditions necessary both for capital accumulation and for a return to a romanticized past of the 'ideal' home, family, and school.

The power of this alliance can be seen in a number of educational policies and proposals: (i) proposals for voucher plans and tax credits to make schools more like the idealized free-market economy; (ii) the movement in state legislatures throughout the country to 'raise standards' and mandate both teacher and student 'competencies' and basic curricular goals and knowledge; (iii) the increasingly effective attacks on the school curriculum for its anti-family and anti-free enterprise bias, its 'secular humanism', and its lack of patriotism; and (iv) the growing pressure to make the needs of Business and Industry into the primary goals of the school.[3]

The effects of this reorientation of public discourse in education can be seen in a number of national polls. For example, one of the major samplings of public opinion recently found that the 'idea of a voucher system — a plan whereby the federal government allots a certain amount of money for the education of each child, regardless of whether the child attends a public, parochial, or independent school — is favored today by a majority, 51 per cent to 38 per cent.'[4] Other findings are equally significant in terms of the ideological shift.

> Promotion from grade to grade based on examinations rather than 'social' promotion is endorsed by a substantial majority (75 per cent), the same percentage of the survey respondents who also want to see students in the local schools given national tests so that their achievement can be compared with students in other communities. Two-thirds of the parents of children (and those without children) in the public schools agree that the workload given to students in both elementary and high schools is too light.[5]

At the same time, there is growing support for lengthening the school day by one hour and the school year by one month. This is coupled with a two to one margin in favor of merit pay plans for teachers, where teachers would, in essence, be paid by results.[6]

What are these 'solutions' responses to? By and large, the perceived lack of discipline in schools, the lowering of quality and standards, the poor quality of teachers, and declining moral and intellectual results, are among those most discussed.[7] It is actually unclear whether all of these conditions *are* getting significantly worse,[8] but it is very clear that the solutions — rationalizing, standardizing, gaining greater economic and ideological control of teaching and curricular — assume the worst.

These general tendencies do not have an effect on schools in the abstract. They are rapidly creating an environment in many sections of the country in which the working conditions of teachers and the kind of knowledge that is taught are under constant attack. Let me discuss these effects in greater detail by first focussing on the curriculum itself. As we shall see, the ability of the Right to mobilize and join forces with Business and Industry can have a profound impact on making their knowledge the most legitimate to teach on a national level, even though the United States has a long tradition of local authority in curriculum decision making.

Unlike some other countries, the curriculum in American schools is by and large the textbook. In fact, it would be an unusual classroom that did not have a standardized set of texts and worksheets in most of its subject areas. Teachers may at times alter what is in the text; they may go beyond it occasionally. But by and large, it is the standardized, grade-level specific text that provides the 'official' curriculum for most schools. (It is interesting to note that a number of large southern school districts have specifically asked teachers *not* to deviate from what is set down in the standardized text). Most activities in classrooms center around it. In fact, so large is its impact that it is estimated that 75 per cent of the time elementary and secondary school students are in classrooms and 90 per cent of their time spent on homework is spent with such standardized text materials.[9] To know the politics of the textbook, then, is to know a good deal about the emerging conflicts over the curriculum in the United States.

In order to understand the determination of curriculum here, it is important to gain a sense of what might best be called the 'political geography' of curriculum. If you envision a map of the United States with its forty-eight contiguous states, a large portion of the states that are located in what is popularly known as the 'sun belt' — the southern part of the east coast continuing around to the southwest to California — have some form of state textbook adoption policy. (These states tend to be the most conservative politically, economically, and ideologically.) There are variations on the basic state adoption models, but in nearly half of the total number of states in the United States, what textbooks are used in schools is determined at a statewide level. Thus, usually a politically appointed statewide committee will screen text materials in mathematics, social studies, science, reading and the language arts, and so forth and will establish which five or ten of the many texts published annually can be used by local school districts. Or in some states, a list of approved texts is centrally determined, but local schools and districts are free to choose any text available. However, the district will be reimbursed by the state for the majority of the cost of purchasing the textbooks but *only* for those texts that are on the approved list. Given the fiscal crisis in education, the freedom to choose text material from a wide universe of possibilities is actually a fiction. The cost of choosing anything not on the approved list is simply prohibitive.[10]

The economics of this can be even more powerful nationally. Over 20 per cent of all of the textbooks sold in the United States are purchased by only two states, Texas and California. An even larger proportion of the textbook market is covered by other large southern states who also mandate particular texts. In the highly competitive world of textbook publishing, this means that publishers *must* aim all of their text publishing efforts at those populous states that have guaranteed sales. Not to get one's books on a state approved list can be, and is, financially disastrous for textbook publishers. Because of this, the content that is considered to be 'legitimate knowledge' in the curriculum nationally is largely determined by what will sell in Texas, California, and the other primarily southern states with statewide textbook adoption policies. Given the risky nature of the business of publishing, it is too expensive for publishers to alter significantly the content of their volumes to produce different texts for different areas of the country under the conditions of a capitalist market. Hence, the curriculum of, say, Texas becomes the curriculum for the nation as a whole.[11]

Such state adoption policies are not guaranteed to be regressive culturally and politically and, in fact, were originally instituted partly to bring about a measure of public accountability and control over the rapaciousness of some text publishers in earlier periods of this century. However, in a time of reaction, they provide a highly visible forum for Rightist attacks on teachers and curricula, and an exceptional lever for changing the content of schooling.

Thus, although the political battles over the content of the curriculum have always been rather intense in the USA, they have recently grown particularly contentious. Whereas before, those groups who believed (correctly) that their knowledge, history, and culture were being disenfranchised by the school curriculum were primarily women, people of color, and to a lesser extent, labor, there has now been a marked shift. Instead, the political, religious, and ideological Right and powerful segments of the business community are resurgent. The school text provides an arena for this resurgence.

California and, especially, Texas have become the primary battlegrounds. For example, the Texas text adoption process mandates public hearings on all curricular materials that may be approved. However, while seemingly democratic, these hearings have had an odd stipulation. Only those individuals and groups who were *opposed* to entire books or sections of the material could speak. Thus, those people who are highly organized against material are at an advantage in the proceedings. The Right has been particularly successful here in forcing texts to give much greater emphasis to 'free market values' and the 'evils of communism', to patriotism and American nationalism, and to a return to traditional values. It has also waged a campaign, one that is gaining ground, against 'secular humanism', the 'overemphasis' on social criticism and values, the contributions of women and minorities (its position against feminist beliefs is very strong), and the teaching of 'anti-Christian' and 'pro-socialist' beliefs.

While movements have begun to be organized to counter these Rightist tendencies (for example, in the formation of a more liberal national group called 'People for the American Way' whose purpose is to defend books and schools that are more open to diversity), and both national teachers' organizations have been active in fighting against such Rightist attacks on the school and the content of its texts, there is no doubt about the growing influence of these right-wing tendencies at both the national, state, and local levels. The content of many texts has been 'sanitized' and homogenized. Controversial material is often systematically eliminated in many textbook series. And text publishers are increasingly cautious of including anything that will offend these well-funded and very active interest groups.[12]

While these groups are very prominent in raising serious questions about the school curriculum and in politicizing the issues surrounding it, what may be an even more powerful and long lasting set of pressures is coming from capital itself. In a less visible but no less effective way, many corporations and business groups have themselves established offices to lobby state legislatures and national

and state educational authorities to stress the benefits of free enterprise in schools, the importance of teaching work norms and discipline, and in general to create closer ties between Industry and the
formal institutions of education in the curriculum and teaching
practices in schools as well as in broader issues of educational policy
formation.[13] 'What is good for business and industry is good for
education' has become one of the dominant messages in the calculus
of values now being instituted by the new alliance. In a time of
severe economic problems and clear ideological crisis, many states
and local school districts have themselves actively sought to create
such ties. Work skill programs (even though there may be few jobs),
an emphasis on discipline, greater stress on standards and 'saleable'
knowledge, the utter 'puffery' of computers where it is assumed
(very wrongly) that they will solve all of our educational and
economic problems,[14] etc., all of these are the tangible results of
these pressures. When coupled with the resurgence in New Right
politics, this too has had a significant impact.

On the one hand, these tendencies are clearly negative. It is
very hard for local communities, minority groups, and sympathetic
educators to maintain the gains — and there *were* gains — made
over the past decades in teaching more honest and culturally relevant knowledge about class, race, and gender relations. It is also
very difficult for teachers to continue to teach well under such
threatening conditions. On the other hand, they do point out something that a number of scholars have argued for years — the
existence of a *selective tradition* in curriculum. Rather than seeing
official knowledge as that content which is neutral and deemed
worthy to pass on to all, the curriculum is and has always been a site
of struggle in which only a limited amount of identifiable groups'
culture is selected to be school knowledge.[15] The current politicization of the text and the curriculum brings to the forefront what had
been there all along — the deeply ideological nature of school
knowledge, and the possibility that the content and form of the
curriculum in schools is not as democratic as conventional wisdom
would have it. Although it uses slogans about the rights of the
'people' and of parents, the Rightist campaign to deal with this,
however, is not necessarily a democratic one. It is itself based on
what has been called an 'authoritarian populism' and can ultimately
serve to disenfranchise further those groups who historically have
not benefited from the dominant cultural, political, and economic
relations of this society.

These conflicts over the school curriculum are of no small

importance, since it is here that what counts as official knowledge is largely determined. We ignore them at our own peril. However, the ideological, political, and economic control of content that is increasing because of the political geography of the curriculum is not the only area where regressive changes are being made. Greater control of the people who populate the institutions of education — students and teachers — is increasing too.

For example, at this very time nearly forty of the fifty states have instituted some form of state-wide competency testing. In an attempt to 'raise standards', students are often required to pass a standardized test near the end of their secondary school experiences to demonstrate 'competency' in a number of basic subject areas. If they do poorly, they do not graduate and are supposed to be given remedial attention. However, in reality, this has usually become one more instance of blaming the victim. Since there have been widespread cuts in monetary support for education, and school systems are not usually being given enough resources to meet the needs of these students, the tests act to recycle students through existing educational programs that were unsuccessful in the first place. Furthermore, since the future employment situation of the students who most often do poorly in schools and in these competency tests (these are almost always poor and the youth of minority groups) is at best bleak even *with* a high school credential (unemployment among black and brown teenagers is regularly around 50 per cent, and is as high as 75 per cent in some urban areas), these tests redirect attention away from where much of the problem lies.[16] They do, though, partly perform a latent economic function, in that they tend to keep some students out of the declining labor market for an extra period of time.

Yet it is not just these students who are feeling the brunt of this rationalization and standardization. Many states, concerned about the supposedly low quality of teachers and pushed by Industry and by the Right, are establishing competency tests for teachers as well. The mistrust of teachers is especially evident in the increasing number of states that now have legislation to mandate such testing programs. As I have argued at length elsewhere, all of these are but instances of a considerably larger movement in which teachers are losing autonomy and in which their control of their skills and knowledge and of curricular and teaching policies and practices are being eviscerated.[17] In essence, we are witnessing the *deskilling* of teachers, as the conditions of their work become more and more similar to the tightly controlled and rationalized labor of so many workers in factories, stores and offices. Since two-thirds of the teaching force overall and

87 per cent of elementary school teachers are women, the ultimate effect is actually to continue the process of interfering with and rationalizing 'women's work' that has had such a long and unfortunate history in the United States.[18] The conscious attempts by the Right and capital to make unions less powerful in the United States have made it even more difficult for teachers to resist the loss of control over the curriculum and their own teaching actions. It is clear, then, that this is not a good time for those teachers, parents, or students who want a genuinely more democratic school system.

Conclusion

In this chapter, I have sought to show how the fracturing of old alliances and the building of new ones has had a major impact on schooling in America. The knowledge that is taught, the very way it is taught, the manner in which it is evaluated have all become subject to restructuring. However, while this new alliance between the New Right and capital is having no small measure of success, it is also clear that many groups who are not of this ideological persuasion have, at times, been successful in defending (and occasionally extending) the substance of a more democratic curriculum in schools. This, of course, has itself led to considerable conflict over teaching and curriculum at all levels of the school system. Such conflicts and such defense of the gains made by women, minority groups, labor, and others are critical at a time of conservative restoration. Just as war is too important an issue to be left to the generals, so is education too important to be left to the Right and capital. To lose the school to them is not only to lose control of teachers' jobs; it is also to make certain that so many of our children's futures will be bleaker in crucial ways. Can we afford to let this happen?

Notes

1   SCHIPPER, M.C. (1983), 'Textbook controversy: Past and present', *New York University Education Quarterly*, 14, spring/summer, pp. 31–6.
2   See ARONS, S. (1983), *Compelling Belief: The Culture of American Schooling*, New York, New Press and McGraw-Hill.
3   For an analysis of the current tendencies, see APPLE, M.W. (1982) *Education and Power*, Boston, MA, Routledge and Kegan Paul; and

APPLE, M.W. (in press) *Teachers and Texts*, Boston, MA, Routledge and Kegan Paul.

4   BUNZEL, J.H. (Ed.) (1985) *Challenge to American Schools*, New York, Oxford, p. 7. I have discussed the problems of such plans at greater length in APPLE, M.W. (1982) *op. cit.*, especially chapter 4.

5   BUNZEL, J.H. (Ed.) (1985) *op. cit.*, p. 7.

6   *Ibid*, p. 8.

7   *Ibid*, pp. 6–7.

8   See STEDMAN, L.C. and SMITH, M.S. (1983) 'Recent reform proposals for American education', *Contemporary Education Review*, 2, Fall, pp. 85–104.

9   GOLDSTEIN, P. (1978) *Changing the American Schoolbook*, Lexington, MA, D.C. Heath, p. 1.

10 See APPLE, M.W. (1982) *op. cit.*, especially chapter 5; and APPLE, M.W. (1985) 'The culture and commerce of the textbook', *Journal of Curriculum Studies*, 17, 2, pp. 147–62.

11 For further discussion of these issues, see APPLE, M.W. (1985) *op. cit.*

12 *Ibid*. The effect of such pressures on publishers is further detailed in APPLE, M.W. (in press) *Teachers and Texts*; Boston, MA, Routledge and Kegan Paul.

13 The impact this is having at the university level is also large. See DICKSON, D. (1984) *The New Politics of Science*, New York, Pantheon Books.

14 APPLE, M.W. (in press) *Teachers and Texts*, Boston, MA, Routledge and Kegan Paul.

15 For a summary of this work, see APPLE, M.W. (1979) *Ideology and Curriculum*, Boston, MA, Routledge and Kegan Paul.

16 An elaboration of these economic conditions can be found in CARNOY, M., SHEARER, D., and RUMBERGER, R. (1983) *A New Social Contract* New York, Harper and Row; and COHEN, J. and ROGERS, J. (1983) *On Democracy*, New York, Penguin Books.

17 See APPLE, M.W. (1982) *op. cit.*; APPLE, M.W. (in press) *Teachers and Texts*, Boston, MA, Routledge and Regan Paul and APPLE, M.W. and TEITELBAUM, K. (in press) 'Are teachers losing control of their skills and curriculum?', *Journal of Curriculum Studies*.

18 See APPLE, M.W. (1985) 'Teaching and "women's work": A comparative historical and ideological analysis', *Teachers College Record*, 86, Spring, pp. 455–73; and APPLE, M.W. (in press) *Teachers and Texts*, Boston, MA, Routledge and Kegan Paul.

Teachers as Political Activists: Three Perspectives

John White and Patricia White

I

According to what we shall call the 'purist' view of teaching, any political activities in which teachers may want to engage must take place outside the classroom and outside the school. On this view teachers are hired to teach French or physics or the basic skills of numeracy and literacy. They are expected to stick to these lasts. If they want to work for a political cause, they are at liberty to canvass, march, make speeches, lobby, attend meetings as much as they like in their own time; but they have no right to bring their political interests into school.

Is it an assumption of the purist view that politics and education belong to different and impermeable worlds? Not necessarily. Certainly *variants* of purism have held this to be true. One variant has held that education is essentially concerned with the pursuit of intellectual and perhaps also aesthetic values for their own sake: its role is not to prepare pupils for the *practical* tasks of social organization with which politics has to do. Another variant has seen education, less academically, as the liberation, or full-flowering, of the individual child. Whilst, if *pressed*, its proponents would, no doubt, allow that some children may find their self-realization in political activities, the whole setting for this kind of education tends to be apolitical. In the child-centred classroom, to judge by the files and ingenious displays of work, children's interests seem naturally to incline towards projects on trees, narrowboats, fruits or teeth, rather than explorations of the police force, the slave trade or investigations of income differences. Certainly even if some children do gravitate towards political/social topics, there can be no question, within this ideological framework, of the teacher's guiding others, who show no such predilection, along this path.

There are difficulties in the claim that education and politics belong to different worlds. Whatever education is taken to aim at must carry with it a certain conception of what society should be like: and this brings in politics. This is true even if one holds either the academic or the child-centred variant of purism just mentioned: the former brings with it a picture of a good society as one where either an elite or the mass of citizens engage in intellectual and aesthetic pursuits for their own sake; while the latter works with a social vision of universal self-expression.

If one *rejects* the belief that education and politics do not meet, one can still remain a purist. The difference between the two varieties of purism can be well brought out by looking at the recent changes in the control of school aims and curricula in England and Wales. Until recently the doctrine that education and politics belong to different worlds was enshrined in the *de facto* practice of letting schools determine their own aims and curricula, with no local or central government interference except in the matter of religious education. The doctrine is now seriously challenged; and with it, too, the practice of leaving the schools autonomous. Central government and local authorities have come out in the last few years with ever-increasing lists of what they expect the schools to be doing. These injunctions are of varying political complexions. Among them we find expressions of the purist view mentioned in our opening paragraph.

It is quite possible, on this view, to believe *both* that the content of education should not be self-contained but should reflect political ideas about what society should be like, *and* that teachers should keep their political activities outside the school gate. In one way, indeed, the rejection of the education-politics divide might well *reinforce* purism in some quarters: once responsibility for the broad content of education is firmly allocated to politicians rather than professionals, teachers can come to be classed more as civil servants or bureaucrats, each carrying out delimited executive functions within an overall political plan. It is thus quite understandable that a government, which wants to orientate the educational system towards helping to create a society of industrious workers whose training fits them for the jobs they undertake, should insist on teachers who are above all adequately prepared in the specialisms demanded by this economic aim. It will see no advantage in these teachers' bringing political interests into their work. It will find it better, for several reasons, to keep its teachers blinkered within their specialisms: if economic aims are to be paramount, workers will need have no wider horizons than their particular job, and blinkered teachers may be a good means of producing not only adequately equipped, but also blinkered workers; it will be difficult to shift a whole mass of such teachers, once in post, towards working for alternative educational goals if a different political party comes to power; and indoctrinating, as intentional steering towards a set of beliefs in such a way as to make it difficult for the believer to reflect on them, will become all the more effective because it will be hidden: classroom teachers, always a likely target for the charge of indoctrination, will plead 'not guilty' to the charge on the grounds that they are simply sticking to their job. The real indoctrinators, however, namely the political planners, will be well out of sight.

Purism, then, *can* go with the view that the aims and content of education are matters for political rather than professional decision. But it is difficult to hold the two positions in conjunction if one is to do full justice to ethical demands (as we explain more fully in section III.). Both teachers and, as they become capable of under-standing the issues involved, also pupils, have the moral right to know how a particular curriculum content — maths, say, or French — fits into the wider political plan, and the moral duty not blindly to accept this plan and its constituent parts, but to reflect on its moral acceptability. Insofar as teachers carry out their responsi-bilities towards their pupils in this respect, they are stepping outside their specialism into forms of political activity. Once the political nature of educational aims is conceded, it is difficult to deny that teachers have a political role within schools. To preserve a purist line, one will be tempted to tread the indoctrinator's path in trying to prevent both teachers and pupils from reflecting on what they are doing and why.

II

If purism is rejected and if it is accepted that, in some sense or other, teachers should be politically active in school, there is more than one way in which this political activity can be conceived.

There is, first, the Marxist approach. To talk of '*the* Marxist approach' ignores the many varieties of Marxism at work in the world of education and the account we are about to give may fail to meet all cases. It is, however, we believe, a view to which many Marxist teachers and teacher-educators would subscribe.

State institutions — the parliamentary system, the Civil Service, the judiciary and so on — are on a Marxist account said to subserve the interests of the dominant capitalist class. Schools in particular, as state institutions, have this function. They operate to maintain capitalism and to reinforce the oppression of those classes under its yoke. Their role is to shape the dispositions, beliefs and skills of their pupils so as to fit in with the disparate demands of a capitalist economy. This involves selection and differentiation, whether by different kinds of school, by streaming, by public examinations, or in other ways. It also involves keeping pupils in a state of false consciousness about the oppression to which they are subject, whether this draws on religion, on psychometrics (which can be used to convince pupils that they are not endowed with the intelligence necessary to 'get on'), on the encouragement of racist prejudice (which can serve to deflect the working class, black and white, from their real adversary), or on other things.

Teachers belong to this oppressive structure. However well-meaning they are, however much they see themselves as benefiting their pupils, their institutional role aligns them with the oppressors.

Purism, on this account, is itself an ideological tool in the hands of the dominant class. The more teachers can be made to believe that their work is self-contained, disconnected from a larger political reality, the more effective agents of capitalism will they become.

Marxist teachers must, therefore, reject purism. They must see it for what it is, an instrument of oppression. Their task within the school is to promote the revolutionary goal of the overthrow of capitalism. In this they will have to be careful, of course. If they are hired to teach maths and are discovered also to be teaching Marxist conceptions of society, the state and the educational system, they risk the sack. As one Marxist writer (Harris) has recently put it (1982), they have to see what they can 'get away with' (p. 153).

> Promote class consciousness wherever possible. Use what freedom and control you have over the curriculum to intro-duce the working class and the concept of class struggle into schooling. This can be done in a subtle manner in all subjects and at all levels. Don't dig out the 'hard core' material; it isn't necessary and it could get you into trouble. Kids don't

have to confronted with 'The Communist Manifesto': a *sensitive* reading of Dickens will do very well. (*ibid*, p. 151)

The same writer goes on to give several other 'immediate' revolutionary strategies which teachers can adopt within the school, including attacks on sexism and racism, encouraging a cooperative rather than competitive ethos, helping pupils to become more aware of the way authority structures and economic systems influence their lives, being as honest as conditions will allow about one's political views, etc. (*ibid*, p. 151–2).

How acceptable is the Marxist conception of the teacher as political activist? It has its merits, in our view. It helps to prevent the imprisonment of teachers within the limited conception of their role that purism would foist on them. And certainly *one* factor in shaping current conceptions of this role has been the long-standing desire of industrialists, conservative politicians and their supporters to make teachers into handmaidens of the economy. It is also true that some teachers and some pupils have been blinkered in their perceptions of social reality by religious doctrines which encourage an acceptance of the status quo, as well as by doctrines about the genetic basis of ceilings of intelligence, and by racism. These doctrines have been favoured by *some* of the conservative forces just mentioned, who have either encouraged the promotion of these ideologies within the educational system or at least discouraged reflection on them. It is wholly desirable, in our view, that both teachers and pupils should become more conscious of doctrines like these of which they may not be focally aware and which may restrict both their own and their pupils' autonomous agency.

Insofar as it encourages such reflectiveness, there is much to be said for the Marxist point of view. But there are features of it which point in a quite opposite direction. It holds that the central task of the teacher is to promote the revolutionary overthrow of capitalism. Marxist teachers can join with liberal reformers in opposing various forms of injustice — sexism and racism, for instance — or in supporting moves towards cooperative learning or the democratization of authority structures. But these moves are purely instrumental to the main revolutionary goal and have no intrinsic value.

The problem is: what grounds are there for thinking (a) that there should be one central goal directing teachers' efforts, and (b) that the one goal should be the overthrow of capitalism? Recent work in philosophical ethics has made a monistic view of ethical values difficult to accept (see, for example, Nagel, 1979; Williams, 1979). There is, it is suggested, an array of irreducible ethical considerations which can bear on our actions and decisions: utilitarian values to do with the amount of pleasure, happiness or desire-satisfaction which actions generate; demands of justice and universalizability; personal values to do with our commitments to our projects and life-plans; obligations which we have taken on; and no doubt others. Living ethically, on this view, is not a matter of sticking dogmatically to one value, but of taking account of the diversity of values, weighing them against each other, where relevant, in one's judgments of what to do.

This ethical pluralism is opposed to *any* monistic viewpoint which teachers might adopt, whether this be religious, political, utilitarian or deontological, or whatever. By contrast, insofar as Marxist teachers are successful in getting their pupils to accept a Marxist analysis and with it the paramount need to struggle to promote revolutionary ends, they are encouraging them to live by a monistic ethic, formally similar to a monistic religious ethic. Not only that: a particular aspect of Marxist monism is that it gives no prominence to the fact that people have one, unique, life to lead. It is important for teachers to realize exactly to what they are committed if they sincerely hold this view and carry out their teaching responsibilities within its framework. The revolutionary struggle must take precedence in this ethic and the value of the pupil's personal commitments and projects must be subordinated to the general well-being of a future generation.

And what of Marxist teachers' relations with their colleagues? They will almost invariably treat senior staff as 'the management', supporters of the status quo. Their treatment of other staff will be varied according to the latters' willingness to consider or oppose Marxist views. Those with some understanding of, and sympathy for, Marxist analyses of contemporary industrial society but who do not accept the whole framework, will be regarded more favourably than out-and-out opponents of Marxism. As time goes on, though, and they seem to be no nearer to the adoption of the whole theory, an increasing impatience with what is seen as a kind of weakness of character, perhaps an unwillingness to go further because of threats to self-interest, may well manifest itself.

For the committed Marxist, then, pupils must be led towards the truth of Marxism which will give a unitary direction to their lives and colleagues must be treated according to their positions on, and progress up, a developmental scale of Marxism. Sincere Marxist teachers have to realise that the onus is on them to justify this absolutist stance. Unless they are to be forced into a position similar to that of the adherents of some fundamentalist religion, they have to be able to justify their view of human good and the good society. What defence of their position as the unique bringers of illumination to a benighted world can they produce?

Many Marxist teachers will protest at this point. They will argue that they do not put over their views in this way. They *do* have regard for the one life children have to lead. They do not fail to represent liberal-democratic views to their students, although they think them misguided, and they leave pupils to make up their own minds. Neither do they have a patronizing attitude to colleagues as being in varying degrees of moral and political benightedness. They treat them as fellow professionals and value their contributions to the life of the institution.

Teachers like these certainly exist, in our experience, but where they do, they can only be at best *inconsistent* Marxists. Theirs is no longer a monistic theory, since their Marxist principles are held alongside others, to do, for instance, with the value of intellectual autonomy and the intrinsic value of persons, and are sometimes overridden by these. This, as we suggested above, may well be an ethically justifiable position, but it is one which only an inconsistent Marxist could hold. The implications are interesting. If pure Marxism is not a justifiable position for educators — and we have left it open for Marxists to produce a justification — perhaps inconsistent Marxism may be.

We are aware, finally, that many proponents of Marxism may not think of it as 'inconsistent' at all but as a multi-value system which they see as true Marxism, as opposed to other vulgar varieties. If that is so, we must leave them to give an account of that position, including an account of what the different values are and how judgments are made when these values conflict. We have simply been concerned to examine a monistic Marxism, to which both Marxist theoreticians and teachers are often attached, and which insistently raises a number of questions about the teacher's role in political education.

III

It seems likely, given our earlier comments about recent work in philosophical ethics, that Marxist teachers of the pure variety will face severe difficulties in attempting to justify their monistic position. Does it follow, then, that until such a justification is forthcoming or Marxism is shown to be a viable multi-value system, there can be no role for the teacher as a political activist? Not at all. In fact, given a conception of the teacher's task that would be widely acceptable and should raise no spectres of indoctrination, to argue that teachers should avoid political activity in schools could land one in severe logical difficulties.

Few would deny that every schoolteacher has some responsibility for moral education. There might be differences of opinion over what this should entail, but few would deny that teachers should try to promote in their pupils such virtues as truthfulness, fairness, tolerance and some concern for others' rights and interests. To the development of these other-directed virtues most people would also add the cultivation of a proper regard for one's own interests and projects and of independent-mindedness in one's conduct. Most people, too, would want teachers themselves to possess and exhibit just these same virtues that they are fostering in their pupils.

These desiderata are hardly unorthodox, but much more controversial conclusions about teachers' political activism seem to follow from them. Many people these days seem to feel, for instance, that ILEA's and other local authorities' attempts to get schools to formulate codes of practice on anti-racism and anti-sexism are illicit forms of politicization. But if one begins from the unexceptionable premise that every pupil should be seen, by staff and pupils alike, as equally worthy of respect and moral concern, then it would seem to follow that schools should try to remove whatever obstacles they can to the realization of this principle. If pupils who are members of certain ethnic groups or are of a certain gender tend to be treated, by other pupils, by individual members of staff, or by the school collectively, as less worthy of respect and concern than others, then schools have a duty to counteract this: hence antiracism and antisexism.

What is clear from this example is that boundaries cannot be set around a 'legitimate' area of moral education to demarcate it from the 'illicit' territory of political activism. Many other examples could be provided. Every teacher will want his or her pupils to be attentive to the needs of a handicapped child; many will see it as part of their role to encourage sympathy for victims of catastrophes like famine or a flood; but to talk with children about the sufferings of the ill-housed, those on low incomes or oppressed by drudgery is suddenly to find oneself in a different category. One has crossed the line between 'moral sensitivity' and 'political involvement' — a line quite non-existent, but which so many feel constrained to draw in order to keep the job of the teacher on the safe side of subversiveness. In certain areas this non-existent line assumes, ironically, the proportions of a barbed wire fence. The teacher who intervenes to prevent bullying or playground fights is doing no more than his or her duty. Thoughtful contributions to whole school code of conduct documents are wholly admirable. But the classroom discussions he or she conducts about the way in which conflicts develop in the family and in society and about ways of resolving them may begin to cause raised eyebrows. For the teacher is now on the point of crossing the line into peace education, an acknowledged subversive activity.

Teachers and pupils, everyone agrees, should do, or learn to do, things because they believe they are right and not simply on another's say-so. But moral autonomy is the enemy of hierarchy. It points towards everyone's having some say, given they are capable of this, in decisions which affect their lives. In the running of a school, it goes with collective decision-making among the staff, perhaps the rotation of offices, certainly mechanisms for controlling the exercise or abuse of power. Among pupils, it indicates as much participation as their level of understanding and self-control will allow, and preparation for an adult life in which they are wary of overt or hidden authoritarianism at work and elsewhere, and predisposed towards democratic alternatives. Once again, no line can be drawn around autonomy-promoting measures within the school, a line which hives off all considerations of the inequalities of decision-making power in the wider social arena in general and in such of its constituent institutions as the workplace and the family in particular.

Discontinuities between teachers' attitudes towards what goes on inside school and outside it are also instructive. Those who would strongly applaud efforts to stamp out cheating and other dishonest acts by pupils will not necessarily be vigorous advocates of a school policy which seeks to be honest about, or make transparent, the workings of the institutions of society, including schools themselves. Honesty is the best policy — between pupils in schools. Outside this context, some teachers may well unreflectively assume that a certain amount of secrecy and even cover-up are necessary to a smoothly functioning society. But this is only one *Realpolitik* view, and one which has increasingly come under attack, most recently in a number of well-documented and detailed challenges (see Bok 1978 and 1982; Michael, 1982). There is every reason, rather, for the teacher to make relevant links between personal and institutional issues of honesty.

Personal morality shades into public; its territory merges with the world of politics. If every teacher is to be a teacher of, and exemplar of, morality, then every teacher is a teacher of, and exemplar of, citizenship. Some teachers, certainly, will have a more intimate association with the teaching of politics than others. For reasons already obvious, pupils, especially as they grow older, will need a specialized understanding of the political, economic, socio-logical features of their society and of other societies across the world. But teachers of non-political subjects, of maths or music, say, cannot leave all political education to political specialists. They cannot draw a line around their responsibilities in 'moral' or (more frequently these days) 'personal and social' education: to do so would be to give their pupils a false picture of ethical reality. They cannot draw a line, either, around the subject they teach, imagining that it is something to be taught 'for its own sake', with all other considerations left outside. *Why* one teaches maths or music cannot — at least rationally — be divorced from visions of the 'good life' for the pupil or the 'good society' in which one sees him or her living. Once again, reflection spreads out beyond immediate objects of attention towards wider and wider horizons.

Teachers, according to this view, should not be ashamed of being branded as political activists. It is when they try to *disclaim* a political dimension to their work that their attitude becomes suspect. What characterizes them, and at the same time distinguishes them, from the dogmatic activists discussed in section II, is their appreciation of the diversity, or fragmentation, of values. They have no monistic attachment to a single value to which all else is at best instrumental. They are conscious that they must do justice to each individual child's right to follow his or her own projects, commit-ments, or plan of life. They will not sacrifice that child's unique life to the demands of a future utopia. But neither will they lead pupils to think that their lives are of paramount importance and to ignore their possible contribution to social improvements realizable perhaps only after their death. Utilitarian values, too, have a place — but not a dominating one — in these teachers' thinking. They have to be weighed against the values of personal commitment just mentioned, as well as against the rights of others than the pupil to be treated fairly, impartially, with respect. All these values, and others, too, like the obligations associated with one's various social roles or dependent on one's contracts, run in a gamut from the small-scale and face-to-face to the large-scale and clearly political. Among the many aspects of the complex job of teaching are both the need to be aware of the diversity of ethical values and of their private-to-public dimension in each case, and the disposition to weigh these different values and dimensions against each other in specific cases so as to reach considered and sensitive judgments. And this complex business of arriving at considered professional judgments is not, we have to remember, only a matter of the individual's making up his or her mind. It is also a matter of making collective judgments so that whole school policies can be framed.

Given the nature of these individual and collective judgments, we clearly could not be expected to produce a comprehensive set of principles which would absolutely guarantee to teachers following them that their conduct was within appropriate bounds and overstepped no limits of indoctrination or manipulation. We are dealing here with practical judgments which cannot be constrained by exhaustively specific principles detailing, for instance, what topics can and cannot be mentioned in school. What is important is that teachers make their professional judgments, having certain overall aims of education in mind — to do, for instance, with the development of the pupils' intellectual autonomy — and seek over time to refine and improve on these with the help of colleagues and pupils. There is more, of course, to be said about this process, but this is not the place for it.

A school in which teachers work and pupils are brought up on lines like those advocated above is a school in which political activism is all-pervasive (or, as its enemies would say, 'rife'). It is not a school in which moral and political education has been boiled down to a collection of life skills, which make no pretence at giving students a coherent picture of the moral and political community they might come to inhabit. It is not preparing children for a utopia which may never come. It is realizing in its own practices a small-scale and very present utopia of its own. Schools alone cannot change society, we are told. And this is true. But they might be able to do *something* to improve it. What they can do at their best is to serve their members and those outside them as a model of how a community can work relatively harmoniously together — not a tension-less or conflict-free community, to be sure, but one in which conflicts are contained and compromises struck within generally agreed procedures. In creating and promoting schools like these, teachers are *already* realizing, in part and imperfectly, their vision of the 'good society'.

Acknowledgements

We would like to thank Graham Haydon, Paul Hirst and Philip Stevens for their helpful comments on our first draft.

References

BOK, S. (1978) *Lying: Moral Choice in Public and Private Life*, Hassocks, Harvester Press.

BOK, S. (1984) *Secrets: On the Ethics of Concealment and Revelation*, Oxford, Oxford University Press.

HARRIS, K. (1982) *Teachers and Classes. A Marxist Analysis*, London, Routledge and Kegan Paul.

MICHAEL, J. (1982) *The Politics of Secrecy*, Harmondsworth, Penguin.

NAGEL, T. (1979) 'The fragmentation of value' in NAGEL, T. *Mortal Questions*, Cambridge, Cambridge University Press.

WHITE, P. (1983) *Beyond Domination: An Essay in the Political Philosophy of Education*, London, Routledge and Kegan Paul.

WILLIAMS, B. (1979) 'Conflicts of values' in RYAN, A. (Ed.) *The Idea of Freedom: Essays in Honour of Isaiah Berlin*, Oxford, Oxford University Press.

'The Values of a Free Society'* and the Politics of Educational Studies

Anthony Hartnett and Michael Naish

'... Now, then, where's the first boy?'
'Please, sir, he's cleaning the back parlour window,' said the temporary head of the philosophical class.
'So he is, to be sure,' rejoined Squeers. 'We go upon the practical mode of teaching, Nickleby; the regular education system. C-l-e-a-n, clean, verb active, to make bright, to scour. W-i-n, win, d-e-r-, der, winder, a casement. When the boy knows this out of a book, he goes and does it ... That's our system Nickleby; what do you think of it?'
'It's a very useful one, at any rate,' answered Nicholas.

Charles Dickens (1867) *Nicholas Nickleby*,
Chapter 8, 'Of the internal economy of
Dotheboys Hall' p. 88.

On the whole, the Conservative Party does not make a practice of issuing literature on educational theory, comparable to the work of Tawney and the Fabians, largely because of our reluctance to let a highly specialised subject escape from the hands of qualified educational experts into bedevilment by political theorists. (Conservative Party Archives, 1952–53, Box 509, unpublished letter from Mr. Chute of the Conservative Research Department, to A.H. Halsey, a student at Liverpool University, Bodleian Library, Oxford)

---

* Department of Education and Science (1984) *Initial Teacher Training: Approval of Courses*, Circular 3/84 p. 9.

But there is a crucial area which must be the province of both theory and philosophy: both should concern themselves with questions about what should be taught, to whom and with what in mind. And it is part of my purpose to argue that such questions should be raised and debated by teachers, not just while they are training, but constantly throughout their careers at school and university. In school as much as outside it, thought of a serious kind about what is on offer and why, is an absolute requirement of a rational and civilized society. (Warnock, 1977 p. 9)

Introduction

These are bad times for education. In schools the talk is of falling rolls, reduced resources, increased stress, low pay, low status, redeployment and early retirement. The areas in which teachers have traditionally been able to exercise their own judgment (for example, the curriculum and the assessment of pupils) are becoming smaller and smaller. The interventions of the Department of Education and Science (DES) and of the Secretary of State even extend down to curriculum content (the merits of capitalism) and to syllabus writing (Lawton, p. 29 and p. 30; and Troyna and Ball, pp. 37–8). Teachers may soon be subject to regular assessment, and this will bring an increase in the power of 'the management team'. They are being left less and less room to be principals acting in their own right and are constrained more and more to act as agents for others, to be 'no more than an extension of the agency' of their employers, without any purpose of their own in what they do except for that which arises from their desire to make a living (Langford, 1978, pp. 14–15). Scheffler (1964), in a discussion of similar trends in the USA in 1964, notes that they involve a 'view of the teacher as a minor technician within an industrial process. The overall goals are set in advance in terms of national needs ... and the teacher's job is just to supervise the last operational stage, the methodical insertion of ordered facts into the student's mind' (pp. 22–3).

In universities, too, declining resources have been accompanied by increasing central control, direct political pressure, and a severe diminution in autonomy. They are told to be more like Marks and Spencer's, to give good value for money, to provide what the market wants, and to implement 'top-down' management. Vice-Chancellors are to become 'chief executives', professors managers of 'cost centres', lecturers 'trainee managers', and students 'incomplete components' and 'providers of fee income'. The Secretary of State, through the University Grants Committee, is to be the 'chief share-holder' and the talk is of performance indicators, departmental profiles, and management information.

The institutions of teacher education have been particularly badly hit. Large areas of educational studies, particularly at the level of initial teacher training, have effectively been captured by a combination of the government and the DES ('national needs') and the local authorities ('management interests'). The talk is of 'squeezing theoretical studies out of the tube' and of what is taken to be practical relevance. This is the 'new vocationalism' in its teacher education form. At least some of the official leaders of teacher education (the profession's cutting edge) are now taken to be those who, like sheepdogs tamed to the whistle, are tirelessly alert to the demands of the Secretary of State and are ready to implement them, even when these are still corridor talk at Elizabeth House. They have, at best, only half-heartedly defended the independence of educational studies from central control and have failed to sup-port publicly those individuals and groups *within* the centre (in the Department of Education and Science and Her Majesty's Inspec-torate, for example) who are opposed to the fashionable currents of the time. Where initial training has led, the rest of educational studies will soon follow. Any independent critique (one as little compromised as possible by particular political or professional interests) of current educational policies and practices will increasingly have to be undertaken by a dwindling band of seemingly eccentric individuals, working within institutions whose orientations are largely determined by whatever set of external interests happen to be dominant at the time.

In general, the picture is one of greater centralization of power; of increasingly hierarchical management structures within educa-tional institutions; of a focus on the requirements of industry and commerce; of leaving politics to the politicians; of teachers as agents for others; and of consultation, where allowed, being given no serious political weight (Troyna and Ball, pp. 40–3). This is likely to lead to a restricted, controlled and manipulated agenda for public debate, and one that will permit the controversial political and other assumptions of official policies and practices to escape scrutiny. Such a manner of conducting the enterprise of education is likely to be highly damaging. It may work against any improvement in the quality of solutions proposed and implemented to meet educational problems; it is likely to work against the legitimacy of educational institutions in the eyes of their clients; and it is incompatible, in our view, with any adequate conception of democracy.

Our discussion focusses on the following five questions. Firstly, what are the characteristics of education's prior and central problems? We suggest that they are fundamental, political and enduring and, hence, are controversial and do not admit of closure.

Secondly, to what extent can an increasingly centralized educational system adequately address these prior and central problems? We suggest that such a system is likely to increase problems rather than reduce them.

Thirdly, to what extent do the content, organization and structure of educational studies, as they are at present, hinder or illuminate the debate about education? We argue that the restructuring of initial training, for and on behalf of the Secretary of State, has moved educational studies towards a classroom and school practice-focussed orientation which is conservative, damaging for students of educational studies, and for the quality of the debate about education. Given that the quality of the debate has some bearing on the quality of policy and practice in education, such an orientation is likely to be damaging to children in schools and to others in other educational institutions.

Fourthly, what are the implications of our answers to the first three questions for the control and management of the institutions of teacher education? We argue that educational studies require institutions which are independent, to some degree, from powerful interest groups (such as industry), on the grounds that such independence is necessary for autonomous academic enquiry into fundamental problems.

Finally, we suggest that our conception of education and of educational studies depends upon a particular conception of democracy and of the open society so that a defence of the one conception is, in part, a defence of the other.

Educational Problems: Fundamental, Political and Enduring

The central problems of education concern its general direction. Given that it is believed to benefit its recipients and society as a whole, what are these benefits? How are they to be identified? Are the conceptions of education available in society open to amendment and to radical overhaul, as groups within society change and demand to be taken seriously? Do the benefits of education primarily concern the development of rational autonomy or, as Jonathan (p. 138) asks, is this to be 'seen as an unrealistic, wasteful and dangerous aim for the mass of the population, for whom education should be merely a means of acquiring whatever skills and attitudes are appropriate to their allotted social role'? Such questions as these are not merely the central questions of education, but also the prior ones. Without answers to them, more specific educational questions about why we should teach this as opposed to that, or about how we should teach this or evaluate that, or about how we should organize classrooms or schools have little point.

There are three important features of these prior and central educational problems. The first of them is that they are what Maxwell (1980) calls 'fundamental problems' (p. 19). These are 'problems of living which we encounter in seeking to discover and achieve that which is of value in life'. Any conception of education and any policies and practices it sanctions embody an answer to the problem as to how individuals or groups in society are to be put in as favourable position as possible to live lives that are fulfilling, satisfying, and morally acceptable. They concern how the 'good life' is to be identified and lived, and how we are to know what Fred Inglis (1985) calls 'the good, the true and the beautiful' (p. 27). The papers by Acker, and Troyna and Ball (pp. 63–75 and pp. 37–46) draw attention to this aspect of educational problems. They show how, like the treatment of Cherokee Indians in the USA (Dumont and Wax, 1969), the educational system in the UK has traditionally only paid token attention to the kinds of answer that women, ethnic, and class groups give to the fundamental problems facing them. It has, in other words, not been responsive to diverse conceptions of education.

Further, as Maxwell (1980) argues, 'it is most improbable — perhaps even undesirable — that there should ever be general agreement as to what is to count as a correct acceptable solution' to any fundamental problem and that 'it is extremely unlikely' that any such problem 'will receive a definitive solution' (p. 33). This has important implications for the debate about education and for the nature and organization of educational studies.

The second feature of these prior and central educational problems is that they are political. Any solution proffered to fundamental problems makes political demands because it will involve issues about the nature, organization, quality, and direction of society; about citizens' interests; and about a just distribution of power, status, wealth and of life-chances in general. This is clearly seen in the chapters in this volume by Apple and by Jonathan. Apple shows how the political philosophy of an alliance of business, industry, and the New Right in the USA yields a view of education embodied in the slogan that 'what is good for business and industry is good for education' and how this has quite specific effects on curriculum content and textbooks. On this view, the 'good life' is possible only in a society predominantly organized on market economy lines. Jonathan (p. 136) makes a similar point about the UK, when she notes that the new vocationalism in education assumes that 'in an industrial society, the needs of society are to be conflated with the needs of industry, and that, moreover, the needs of each individual are best served by preparing him/her to serve the needs of society, understood in economic terms'. It is reflected in Sir Keith Joseph's remark, quoted by Lawton, (p. 29) exhorting schools to 'preach the moral virtue of free enterprise and the pursuit of profit', and the Chairman of the Conservative Party's view that schools 'ought to be places of useful learning where achievement was assessed according to accepted criteria'. (*Times Educational Supplement*, 22 November 1985, p. 10)

But whether a society predominantly ordered along corporate capitalist lines (and the conceptions of the good life for individuals it endorses) are to be preferred to those of other political traditions is a controversial matter and involves debating the criteria by which a justly ordered society is to be identified. To debate such matters is to engage in political theory. The importance of recognizing education's prior and central problems as political and as inseparable from those of political theory is not simply to claim that they cannot be remitted to experts for solution, since recourse to expert opinion is only justifiable where criteria for judging the adequacy of solutions are relatively securely established. It is to claim, in addition, that, in a democracy, the issues are the legitimate concern of all the members of such a society; that they are issues for public debate; and that the debate must have consequences for policy.

The third feature of educational problems is that they are enduring (Kekes, 1976). Kekes contrasts enduring problems with removable problems. A removable problem is one the successful solution of which leads to its abolition. Repairing a broken window by putting in a new pane of glass is to solve a removable problem. However, some problems cannot be removed but have to be lived with. Solving them is a matter of developing, often long-term, strategies of coping which might alleviate the most inconvenient and damaging effects of them. Problems of this kind are enduring problems. An example is having to cope with a deep and chronic tendency to depression or to migraine. Such problems present a series of ever changing challenges and any policy or strategy to cope with them has to be continually interpreted, adapted, revised, adjusted and perhaps even abandoned and replaced by another. The general problem to which the problem of education addresses itself — that of preparing members of a society for life in that society — is an enduring one since the circumstances and nature of any society are continually changing. The form education might take will be affected by such factors as how culturally diverse a society is at a particular time; how industrialized or technologically developed it is; and how high the level of unemployment is. The chapters by Coffield, Edwards, Jonathan, and Reid and Holt in this volume all raise issues about the adequacy of changes in the form education should take in response to current levels of unemployment.

Different individuals and groups will develop and advance different and competing conceptions of education on the basis of their different political and other beliefs, to take account of these changing circumstances (Naish, 1984). Just as believers in corporate capitalism or in certain kinds of liberalism will each endorse and demand the institutionalization of his or her particular conception of education, so will different ethnic, religious, or gender or class-based groups (see the chapters by Acker, Bullock, Jonathan, and Troyna and Ball). Much of the argument will be about how, only if this or that particular conception of education is institutionalized (whether for all children or for some group of them) particular groups will best be able to begin to seek 'to discover and achieve that which is of value in life' (cf. Jonathan, p. 143). The importance of noting that the central and prior problems of education are enduring is that arguments about the form that education should take are open-ended and admit of no last word.

Arguments, then, about the central and prior problems of education are arguments about inherently controversial issues in which the citizenry as a whole has a legitimate role. These arguments are also perennial. All of this has important implications for issues about centralization.

Anthony Hartnett and Michael Naish

The Limitations of a Centralized Educational System

The question we address here is whether a centralized educational system is, *prima facie*, likely to offer such best solutions as might be had to the prior and central problems of education, given that these are fundamental, political, and enduring.

One preliminary point is that, in any centralized system, the central authority's role and the role of its constituent institutions (for example, the DES) are likely to be put beyond critical scrutiny, even though they themselves may be part of the problem that needs to be tackled. As Lawton points out, in 1976 the DES was the subject of two critical reports on its own workings which drew attention to a number of serious failings. There have, however, been no scrutinies of its work since then. The control of the agenda is such that Sir William Pile (a former Permanent Under-Secretary at the Department) felt unable to mention these two critical reports, even after his retirement (Lawton, p. 24).

Moreover, most centralized systems of educational control are unlikely to be neutral between answers to education's prior and central issues. They will favour some set of political arrangements as opposed to others and, hence, some conceptions of education as opposed to others. This is well illustrated by Troyna and Ball's discussion (pp. 37–46). Where a system is centralized and where these prior and central issues are not on the public agenda, controversial assumptions and decisions may be put beyond critical scrutiny. And where this happens and where particular groups' views about education are not given adequate political consideration or weight, then general democratic values are threatened. Further, institutions begin to lose their legitimacy in the sense that those over whom authority is exercised cease to feel that the institutions and those who have authority in them, are speaking to their interests, even though it is these very interests that the institutions are, allegedly, there to protect or promote (cf. Reddiford, 1971, pp. 20–1). Where legitimacy is lost, and where there is no forum for or tradition of public politically effective discussion, there is likely to be withdrawal from the institutions (seen, for example, in truancy figures in schools). Where private finance or other resources permit, rival schools are likely to be established (Apple, p. 162; and Troyna and Ball, p. 42). Where they do not permit, there may be recourse to violence or intimidation as a way of gaining what cannot be gained by discussion (see the introductory essay p. 16). Any attempt at coercion and any exercise of power by the state in response to this will simply be taken to provide further evidence of the non-legitimacy of the institutions.

Another equally damaging objection to centralization is that it is incompatible with such problem solving strategies as we have for dealing with fundamental problems and problems in general. The general strategy is one of articulating the problem to be solved as well as possible and then of proposing and of critically assessing possible solutions against each other. This is a collaborative exercise and one which, in the case of political issues in a democracy, is one to be taken up by the public at large. To fail to put any proposed solution to public scrutiny is a poor way to treat it since its merits cannot be adequately determined in its absence. A willingness to test canvassable solutions to a problem by public scrutiny is a mark of a genuine interest in seeing a problem solved as well as possible as opposed, say, to simply exercising power or to maintaining, at any cost, a particular political position. Some implications of these points for curricular issues are discussed by Knitter (1985, especially pp. 388–90).

If all of this is true, then there is at least a presumptive case against the kind of centralization under discussion. The nature of education's central and prior problems are such that any solutions to them can only be reasonably judged as the best that can be hoped for if they pass the test set by public scrutiny. Such problems require a tradition of sustained public debate that speaks both to the day-to-day problems of the enterprise, and to the issues about the enterprise's point and purposes. This tradition has to flourish within institutions as well as within society as a whole. Unless this is the case, the practices of education, its policies, and discussions of them will not constitute what Reid and Holt (p. 91) call 'a second order tradition'. Such a tradition is alone in good order and is 'always partially constituted by an argument about the goods the pursuit of which gives to that tradition its particular point and purpose' (MacIntyre, 1981, p. 206). Education, rather, will consist either of an historical tradition whose ideological assumptions are set in concrete, or of a series of incoherent and unrelated lurches in policy and practice. In either case, it will be well beyond the reach of the better argument and hence better solution. A society with one or other of these kinds of educational system (particularly a society undergoing major social, economic, and political change) is a prime candidate for decline and internecine violence.

Anthony Hartnett and Michael Naish

Politics and the Control of Educational Studies

We now turn to the third question, namely the one about the nature and organization of educational studies. The intellectual and cultural resources on which a society can call in the debate about education include its political, social, and other related theories; its art and literature; its religious, historical, and social traditions. Any society should, above all, be able to call particularly on the traditions of educational studies, if these are in good order, as they are institutionalized within higher education. We suggest that educational studies are not, certainly at the institutional level, in good order and, hence, are unable to play the role that they might and should play in the debate about education.

Taylor (1985, pp. 42–3) suggests that, in England and Wales, about £30m is spent each year on educational research. A good proportion of this sum is used to support the research activities of academic staff in university departments of education. Even before resources were reduced and central control increased, these departments had not established a strong tradition of critical commentary on public issues along the lines of, say, the Frankfurt Institute of Social Research. This was established in the early 1920s with an initial endowment that produced a yearly income of about $30,000 US (Jay, 1973, p. 8). Why a critical institutional tradition has not developed is an issue which we explore in Hartnett and Naish (forthcoming). For present purposes we suggest a number of factors which may begin to provide an explanation.

To begin with, politicians are interested in educational issues in a way that they are not interested in, say, history, philosophy, music, or, until recently, football. Schools and other educational institutions provide them with ready scapegoats who can be held responsible for any number of social problems. As Halsey puts it (quoted by Troyna and Ball, p. 37) education can be seen 'as the waste paper basket of social policy — a repository for dealing with social problems ... where there is a disinclination to wrestle with them seriously'. Hence, although these institutions are of interest to politicians, this is often for reasons which have little to do with the prior and central problems of education or with the quality of solutions to them or with the quality of thinking about them in general.

Further, one way of controlling schools is to control educational studies. And a mechanism for doing this is available as Lawton (pp. 31–4) makes clear. The government can control the initial training of teachers in such a way as to threaten the survival of the training institutions, and this will have a profound effect on the nature of educational studies in them. This is most immediately seen in thinking and practice on the Postgraduate Certificate in Education course where some academics, apparently led by Professor P.H. Hirst (Hirst, 1985; for additional references see Hartnett and Naish, 1981), have played the Trojan horse to bring into educational institutions a view of educational studies which is incompatible with any adequate conception of independent academic enquiry; which takes no account of the political aspects of educational practice and policy; which is narrowly practice focussed; which has no adequate place for serious intellectual reflection on, or understanding of, the nature of the educational enterprise or of its central and prior problems; and which gives no serious weight to the views of student teachers, of children in schools, or of citizens in general (*ibid*).

Educational studies, lacking any rigorous intellectual tradition or resources to fall back on, are an easy victim to a demand to make them 'safe' and 'non-threatening' to governments and other powerful institutions in society, by focussing on issues of day-to-day practice. Educational studies have, to an unparalleled extent, 'taken in' government and other official views about the general direction of policy and practice. They have concerned themselves more with how what has been officially laid down might be better done at the expense of the issue as to whether it should be done at all, and whether it provides as reasonable a solution as can be expected to the problems to which it is allegedly addressed (Jonathan, p. 139).

To take this practice-focussed view of educational studies, however, is to leave unexamined the pattern of practices at any particular time. It is to leave unexamined the question of whether particular practices are compatible with each other; of what conceptions of education they presuppose; of how they relate to the wider societal contexts and to issues of the distribution of power, status and wealth; and of why it is that some sorts of schooling and schools have ceased to speak to some sections of the population (if, indeed, they ever did).

Moreover, practice involves working with simplified models of the social world and of solving problems under conditions of urgency. This leaves little room for reflecting on why the practices are as they are, and this may have an ideological function, in that it may shift attention for educational failure away from wider political issues about the nature and organization of society onto the practices of schools. Further, to focus attention solely on practice is to make it difficult to detect institutional drift, where the aggregate of practices has a tenor which is divorced from, or is even incompatible with, the avowed purposes of particular institutions. To take the particular momentum of an institution for granted and be indifferent to institutional drift is to be bound by an irrational conservatism that precludes reflection about what is going on, and makes adequate action in the face of education's central problems less likely. The weaknesses of this kind of conservative thought are well described by both Mannheim and Hayek.

Mannheim (1953, pp. 102–3) notes how conservative thought 'clings to the immediate, the actual, the *concrete*' and is opposed to 'speculation or hypothesis' and 'therefore does not really trouble itself with the *structure* of the world'. He contrasts this with progressive activity which 'feeds on its *consciousness of the possible*. It transcends the given immediate present, by seizing on the possibilities for systematic change which it offers'. Hayek (1960, p. 404) notes how conservative thought 'tends to harm any cause which allies itself with it' in that it 'fears new ideas because it has no distinctive principles of its own to oppose them; and, by its distrust of theory and its lack of imagination concerning anything except that which experience has already proved, it deprives itself of the weapons needed in the struggle of ideas ...' It 'is bound by the stock of ideas inherited at a given time. And since it does not really believe in the power of argument, its last resort is generally a claim to superior wisdom, based on some self-arrogated superior quality'.

Educational thinking needs not simply to see the practical but to see the practical in the light of the theoretical and the theoretical in the light of the practical — to see each of them in a way that allows them to illuminate each other. To have theory divorced from practice is, no doubt, as deplorable as it is conventionally taken to be. It is equally deplorable to have practice divorced from theory. Justifications of practice have to be taken back to the political theories out of which they have grown. Criteria of justification and assumptions related to them have to be open to scrutiny. Indeed, it might be argued that in a democratic society, which is opposed to change by violence, it is in its educational institutions above all that traditional, taken-for-granted, conventional answers to fundamental problems in general (and, in this context, the political and social ones raised by education) ought to be subjected to sustained scrutiny.

This is not to suggest there should be no place for practice focussed educational studies, or for some academics in educational studies working closely with politicians, local education authorities and others, in the current fashion. It is to suggest, however, that this is logically secondary to enquiry into education's prior and central problems, and that involvement with the powers should not make up the whole of educational studies. Institutional pressures on autonomous educational studies should be resisted so that the fundamental questions of education do not simply become the concern of a few scattered individuals working, without intellectual and other support, in institutions whose dominant concerns lie largely elsewhere.

A further reason for the failure of educational studies to speak to the fundamental problems of education is that academic careers and advancement are often closely bound up with having well-oiled relationships with central and local government. This would not apply to anything like the same degree in such areas as philosophy or history. Decisions about funding, access to institutions, membership of key committees and institutions are all likely to owe more to narrowly political considerations than they would in mainstream academic disciplines. All of this influences the content, characteristics, and structure of educational studies, and results in certain kinds of text-books, courses, ways of thinking about educational problems and in certain kinds of academic appointment. Some of those who are, formally, the intellectual leaders of the area listen to the views of the DES or of governments on what educational studies should be about; on what acceptable lines of research are; on what should be taught and then define the subject accordingly. The role of such institutions as the Universities Council for the Education of Teachers (UCET), the Council for the Accreditation of Teacher Education (CATE), the DES and the research committees are of particular importance here.

The dilemma between the intellectual demands of educational studies and the political dimension are made explicit when the term 'professor of education' (and 'lecturer in education') are examined. 'Professor of education' might be regarded as a 'character' in the sense that MacIntyre (1981) uses the term. MacIntyre takes a character to be one of those 'social roles which provide a culture with its moral definitions' (p. 29), they are the 'moral representatives of their culture' (p. 27), and they furnish their culture with a 'cultural and moral ideal' (p. 28). One important characteristic of a character is that 'the requirements of a character are imposed from the outside, from the way in which others regard and use *characters* to understand and to evaluate themselves' (p. 28). MacIntyre himself illuminates this idea with a discussion of the characters of 'the Public School Headmaster in England', 'the Professor in Germany', and, in current times, 'the Manager' and 'the Therapist'.

Fortunately, many professors of education are characters in a number of senses, and some of them resolve the dilemmas presented to them (as this book demonstrates) by either concentrating on the intellectual and academic aspects of the role or by consciously separating this from the narrowly political. But the issue of the PGCE discussed above (p. 193) does provide *prima facie* evidence for the complexity of the moral and intellectual dilemmas which are seen in the character 'professor of education'. Political pressures do, of course, exist in other academic areas or subjects but in education they may actually define what the subject is and this has implications for the notion of 'professor of education'.

Educational studies are also put at a disadvantage in the debate about education because they are specialist rather than fundamentalist in focus (Maxwell, 1980). Fundamentalism is the view that intellectual life and academic enquiry should be concerned with helping us discover the best solutions that there are to fundamental problems (see the section of this chapter entitled 'Educational Problems: Fundamental, Political and Enduring'). Specialism is the view that all genuine enquiry must focus on problems that can be sharply defined and that can have agreed solutions reached by the use of agreed procedures. But since the prior and central issues of education (questions about its nature, direction and so on) are decidedly of a fundamentalist and not of a specialist kind, much educational enquiry has simply passed them by. There is a relatively impoverished tradition of discussing them, and this means that much work in educational studies either loses its point, is trivial and isolated from any important problem, or is ideological in that it covertly supports one set of answers to fundamental issues in education, while it believes it is neutral between them. This can be seen in the largely specialist tradition of educational research which, in its search for intellectual respectability, has become empirical, positivist and, apparently, apolitical (see Hearnshaw, 1979; King and Melanson, 1972; Hamilton, 1983).

Specialism has other consequences. It leads to a development of subject areas that takes place independently of fundamental problems. These areas become hermetically sealed off both from fundamental problems and from each other. Within each of them academics speak to each other but not to their fellow academics. A consequence of this is that educational studies usually fails to make connections between social theory and educational research (cf. Coffield, p. 111); or between different levels of explanation — for example, between psychological or sociological explanations of what is commonly called 'learning failure'; or between psychology and the philosophical issues raised by and presupposed by much of psychology's view of human nature and of human action (see Schwab, 1978).

Specialism also plays a role (along with other political and cultural factors) in making sure that what audience there is for educational studies predominantly consists of teachers, academics, officials, and civil servants. It consists, that is, of professionals. As Maxwell (1980) points out, specialism is 'almost exclusively a view of professional, expert, scientific, academic inquiry' (p. 31). Hence educational studies are not seen as an intellectual resource which might nourish public discussion of fundamental problems but as a rare claret fit only for the palates of connoisseurs. Such a view restricts the debate in respect of those who can take an informed part in it, just as the emphasis on practice restricts the range of questions that are discussed.

Institutions that have given up any serious attempt to defend a view of educational studies as addressed in part to education's prior and central problems are likely to find that policies of trimming, of compromise, of institutional compliance and docility, and of public relations (no doubt all starting as attempts to survive) become a taken-for-granted way of life. This will produce a restricted agenda, a restricted audience, and growing damage to the quality of the public debate about educational issues, to the quality and legitimacy of solutions to them, and to educational studies themselves.

Implications for the Control of Educational Institutions: The Need for Autonomy

The fourth question which we raised concerns the implications of our answers to the first three questions for the control of the institutions of teacher education. It could be argued that, although educational studies might be compromised by the processes outlined above, no society and certainly no democratic society, can have institutions that are immune to the political preferences of elected governments; that in the UK universities are almost all publicly funded and she or he who pays the piper should call the tune; that it is better to have compromised educational studies (perhaps practice focussed) and institutions subject to state control than a non-compromised educational studies with their institutions immune from control. What is actually wrong in having universities and their curricula subject to the kind of party political control that Ten (1975) describes where

> before a student is admitted to the University of Singapore, he has, like students entering all the other institutes of higher learning in Singapore, to obtain a Certificate of Suitability from the Ministry of Education to prove that he is not politically subversive? (p. 149)

A number of things might be said about such an argument. One is that to argue for the institutionalization of autonomous academic enquiry is not to argue that universities and other institutions should be freed from the need to justify what they do. The question is rather why, if at all, societies and hence governments should create and sustain at least some educational institutions whose assigned main function is that of academic enquiry and teaching. In order to answer this question we need to say something about the notion of 'the academic'.

An enquiry is academic when its concern is to get to the truth of some matter, or as near to it as is possible, irrespective of the urgent demands and pressures of the world of practical affairs. As Minogue (1973) puts it, in academic enquiry 'no one has to come to a conclusion upon which a decision must be based' and a person 'can afford the luxury of allowing the evidence to dictate quite precisely what conclusion he will come to ...' (p. 86). In the world of practical affairs, by contrast, 'decisions have to be taken and minds made up ... on what are, in academic terms, inadequate grounds. There is about the taking of decisions in the practical world an irredeemable element of improvization which renders it necessarily, not contingently, subject to error'.

It is pointless to denounce the approximations, compromises, simplifications etc. of the world of practical affairs since, without them, timely action is impossible. It is pointless, too, to defend everything that goes on under the heading of 'academic enquiry'. Much of it may be trivial. We agree with Maxwell (1980) and with Popper (1963, p. 72) that academic enquiry takes its value from the importance of problems that have their origins outside it. To say this is to say that any defensible academic enquiry must be fundamentalist. It should, too, be clear from our earlier discussion that there are any number of political, moral, empirical and other assumptions required for action in the social (and educational) world whose reliability cannot be assessed, simply, if at all, by practice. No one can think that practice *tout court*, uninterpreted and without a sustained and unpressured investigation, will establish whether capitalist modes of societal organization and the educational programmes they imply are to be preferred to one or other of their competitors; or whether and to what degree parental attitudes affect school performance; or whether there should be a unitary system of schooling as opposed to different religious or ethnic groups having their own publicly funded schools and so on. What the examples show is that there are plenty of questions about practice which are amenable to academic enquiry and which are not questions of practice (as this is conventionally understood) and yet which are central to the understanding, elucidating, and improvement of it. Further, if such enquiry is to follow the argument wherever it leads, it needs to be free from not simply the pressures of time but from the pressures exerted by particular interest groups which might prejudice the nature of the enquiry and its conclusions, even before it starts. If such enquiry is to be as autonomous as possible, its institutions need to be socially located in such a way as to preserve this autonomy. Where there are a number of competing solutions proffered to fundamental problems, and to the subsidiary problems to which they give rise, institutions are required which are as little beholden as possible to the interest group linked to and advocating one particular solution as opposed to another. These institutions (and universities would be one example of them) need to be independent if they are to be free to follow the argument wherever it leads, to criticize and evaluate the responses of the various interest groups, and to constitute an arena and resource for serious public debate about them. These institutions are themselves interest groups and will expect to be judged by other interest groups. Universities and their departments of education should be judged, on this account, by the extent to which their assessment of ways of meeting fundamental problems in education and elsewhere is more sophisticated and is less adversely affected by particular sets of interests than the responses of the interest groups themselves.

The justification of institutions which are, to some extent, independent and protected from powerful interest groups is an area which is seriously underdeveloped. Some of the consequences of the general failure to articulate the case for such institutions is becoming clear now that many of them are under severe attack. Examples of such institutions include: (a) economics departments or departments

of political theory in higher education whose work is independent
of whatever happens to be the dominant economic or political views
of a particular government; (b) departments in universities or
research institutes concerned with human medicine which offer
assessments of the claims of drug companies about the efficacy of
particular drugs or of tobacco companies' claims about the consequences of cigarette smoking; (c) groups that attempt to examine, in
a scientifically informed way, the claims of the nuclear energy
industry; and (d) broadcasting institutions which are at least partly
true of direct government or commercial pressure.

The particular justification of universities (and hence of educational studies) is part of the general justification of institutions
which are independent of particular interest groups. What might be
called 'the institutional crisis of educational studies', discussed in the
section entitled 'Politics and the Control of Educational Studies', is
partly a result of pressures on the institutions of teacher education
which are forcing them to work hand in hand with a particular
government and its agencies and with particular sets of political,
social, and economic interests. To subject academic reflection to a
particular set of interests in the way that this has happened is both
to put some inherently controversial positions beyond scrutiny and,
in Jonathan's phrase 'to subvert the aspirations of one group so as to
serve the purposes of another' (p. 136). To be bound in this way
to the world of practice is for the academic world to make its
norms of epistemological respectability almost entirely political (cf.
Kolakowski, 1980, p. 129). It is to abolish any mode of enquiry or
any institutions that might play an independent role in assessing
claims about the priority or otherwise of particular sets of interests
and about the consequences and merits of particular educational
policies and practices.

If, then, academic enquiry is to follow the argument wherever it
leads, irrespective of time or particular sets of interests, it must be
institutionally separate from what we have called 'the world of
practical affairs'. Such a particular social location will not *guarantee*
that academic enquiry is uncontaminated by particular interests, for
universities and other institutions concerned with such inquiry have
their interests, just as their individual members do, but they make it
likely that their work will be less damagingly contaminated by such
interests and by the exigencies of action as they would be, had they
a different social location. Part of the value of academic enquiry for
practice, it might be said, consists simply in the fact that it is
institutionally separate from it.

Educational Studies and Wider Political and Moral Issues

The existence of institutions having the kind of independence discussed above presupposes certain political and societal values of democratic, liberal and non-totalitarian kind (cf. Kolakowski, 1975; and Taylor, C. 1975) so that a defence of fundamentalist educational studies is, in part, a defence of a certain sort of democratic society.

The general defence of such enquiry and the institutions it requires is that it is in the public interest to have institutions concerned with independent academic enquiry into fundamental problems, and to have such enquiry owing as little as possible to particular interests (Benn, 1972; and Maxwell, 1980). For example, a debate controlled by the tobacco industry, about the effects of smoking on health, is less likely to be in the public interest than one informed by considerations that owe something to independent institutionalized enquiry.

If all of this is true, then limiting the agenda of the political and educational debate and restricting those who are deemed fit to take part in it (whether by political exclusion or by giving them an education in schools or in the institutions of teacher education that precludes them from taking part [cf. Jonathan, pp. 143–4]) is a threat to democratic values themselves. If student teachers, teachers, parents, and the citizenry as a whole, or children (cf. Schrag, 1975; and Harris, 1982) are allowed, at best, only a token voice in the debate about education, and if the debate becomes the province of a smaller and smaller group of only indirectly accountable people (politicians, civil servants, and other administrators), to what extent is this compatible with a democratic society? Such a group can, in any case, have no special expertise on the matters in question. And because the central issues of education are political, they are issues on which the citizenry as a whole has a legitimate voice. A consequence of this is that the constituency for educational studies must be wider than politicians, civil servants, academics and teachers. To create such a wider constituency is, in part, to begin to create the political support that any institutionalization of the ideal of independent academic enquiry requires, if it is to be maintained. It also raises questions about access to educational institutions, particularly to those of higher education, by the citizenry as a whole.

Further, where the professional education of teachers (and the educational studies constituting it) are specialist; where the aims of such an education are determined elsewhere and are put beyond critical scrutiny; where such an education encourages intellectual and moral docility; where its content is determined by a particular political ideology (Parekh, 1982, p. 59) and so where professionals in education are ideologically dominated; where they are agents-for-others or alienated from their work; then professional education, far from improving practice, may actually make it worse.

We outline a defence of the kind of participatory democracy (within institutions and within society) that the general argument of this chapter presupposes in Hartnett and Naish (forthcoming). For current purposes it is, we hope, sufficient to note that our view of educational studies presupposes a political position, and one whose defence raises central issues in political and economic theory. It has been argued, for example, that any society organized along pre-dominantly capitalist lines needs to be a society run by a professional political élite with a largely apathetic citizenry, and that the distribution of status, power, and wealth in it will make any genuine participatory democracy impossible (see Pateman, 1970; MacPherson, 1977; and Levine, 1984). This view might be con-trasted with the DES circular 3/84 which forms part of the title of this chapter. The message of page 9 would seem to be that 'the values of free society' and their 'economic and other foundations' require capitalism. It may be, however, that they have been developed in spite of it. Whatever the case, this is enough to show that there are important questions here about whether capitalism and participatory democracy are compatible; whether capitalism is to be taken as a value that is prior to democracy (with democracy and forms of it permitted only to the extent that they do not seriously compromise capitalism's workings); or whether one form or other of participatory democracy is to be taken as the prior value with capitalism as a possible mode of societal and economic organi-zation only to the extent that it does not compromise the form of democracy in question. That our discussion leads to questions of this kind should not be surprising, if our view of the relationship between education and politics is correct. It would, rather, be odd if it did not.

Postscript

There is always the danger of thinking that intellectual criticism is itself sufficient to bring about fundamental change. We must learn again and again that it is not ... But we must also recognize that human beings are capable of bringing to consciousness the interpretations, evaluations, and standards that they tacitly accept, and can subject them to rational criticism. We are still vastly ignorant of the material conditions necessary for critique to play a role in the transformation of existing forms of social and political reality. (Bernstein R.J., 1979, p. 236).

References

BENN, S.I. (1972) 'Universities, society, and rational inquiry' *The Australian University*, 10, pp. 30–47.

BERNSTEIN, R.J. (1979) *The Restructuring of Social and Political Theory*, London, Methuen.

DUMONT, R.and WAX, M. (1969) 'Cherokee school society and the intercultural classroom' *Human Organization*, 28, 3, pp. 217–26. Reprinted in HARTNETT, A. and NAISH, M. (1976) (Eds) *Theory and the Practice of Education*, Vol. 1, London, Heinemann Educational Books, pp. 158–73.

HAMILTON, D. (1983) 'History without hindsight: Some reflections on British education in the 1980's' *Australian Educational Researcher*, 10, pp. 24–36.

HARRIS, J. (1982) 'The political status of children' in GRAHAM, K. (Ed.) *Contemporary Political Philosophy: Radical Studies*, Cambridge, Cambridge University Press, pp. 35–55.

HARTNETT, A. and NAISH, M. (1981) 'The PGCE as an educational priority area' *Journal of Further and Higher Education*, 5, 3, pp. 88–102.

HARTNETT, A. and NAISH, M. (forthcoming) *Thinking and Doing in Education*, London, Heinemann Educational Books.

HAYEK, F.A. (1960) *The Constitution of Liberty*, London, Routledge and Kegan Paul.

HEARNSHAW, L.S. (1979) *Cyril Burt Psychologist*, London, Hodder and Stoughton.

HIRST, P.H. (1985) 'Educational studies and the PGCE course' *British Journal of Educational Studies*, 23, 3, pp. 211–21.

INGLIS, F. (1985) *The Management of Ignorance: A Political Theory of the Curriculum*, Oxford, Basil Blackwell.

JAY, M. (1973) *The Dialectical Imagination*, London, Heinemann Educational Books.

KEKES, J. (1976) *A Justification of Rationality*, New York, State University of New York Press.

KING, L.R. and MELANSON, P.H. (1972) 'Knowledge and politics: Some experiences from the 1960s', *Public Policy*, 20, pp. 83–101.

KNITTER, W. (1985) 'Curriculum deliberation: Pluralism and the practical', *Journal of Curriculum Studies*, 17, 4, pp. 383–95.

KOLAKOWSKI, L. (1975) 'Neutrality and academic values' in MONTEFIORE, A. (Ed.) *Neutrality and Impartiality: The University and Political*

Commitment, Cambridge, Cambridge University Press, pp. 72–85.

KOLAKOWSKI, L. (1980) 'Why an ideology is always right' in CRANSTON, M. and MAIR, P. (Eds) *Ideology and Politics*, European University Institute, Publication 5, pp. 123–31.

LANGFORD, G. (1978) *Teaching as a Profession: An Essay in Philosophy of Education*, Manchester, Manchester University Press.

LEVINE, A. (1984) *Arguing for Socialism: Theoretical Considerations*, London, Routledge and Kegan Paul.

MACINTYRE, A. (1981) *After Virtue: A Study in Moral Theory*, London, Duckworth.

MACPHERSON, C.B. (1977) *The Life and Times of Liberal Democracy*, Oxford, Oxford University Press.

MANNHEIM, K. (1953) *Essays on Sociology and Social Psychology*, London, Routledge and Kegan Paul.

MAXWELL, N. (1980) 'Science, reason, knowledge and wisdom: A critique of specialism', *Inquiry*, 23, 1, pp. 19–81.

MINOGUE, K. (1973) *The Concept of a University*, London, Weidenfeld and Nicolson.

NAISH, M. (1984) 'Education and essential contestability revisited' *Journal of Philosophy of Education*, 18, 2, pp. 141–53.

PAREKH, B. (1982) *Marx's Theory of Ideology*, London, Croom Helm.

PATEMAN, C. (1970) *Participation and Democratic Theory*, Cambridge, Cambridge University Press.

POPPER, K.R. (1963) 'The nature of philosophical problems and their roots in science' in POPPER, K.R. *Conjectures and Refutations: The Growth of Scientific Knowledge*, London, Routledge and Kegan Paul, 1963, pp. 66–96.

REDDIFORD, G. (1971) 'Authority, education, and student power', *Educational Philosophy and Theory*, 3, 2, pp. 13–26.

SCHEFFLER, I. (1964) 'Concepts of education: Some philosophical reflections on the current scene' in LANDY, E. and PERRY, P.A. (Eds) *Guidance in American Education*, Harvard University Press, pp. 20–7.

SCHRAG, F. (1975) 'The child's status in the democratic state', *Political Theory*, 3, 4, pp. 441–57.

SCHWAB, J. (1978) in WESTBURY, I. and WILKOF, N. (Eds) *Science Curriculum and Liberal Education: Selected Essays*, Chicago, University of Chicago Press.

TAYLOR, C. (1975) 'Neutrality in the university' in MONTEFIORE, A. (Ed.) *Neutrality and Impartiality: The University and Political Commitment*, Cambridge, Cambridge University Press, pp. 128–48.

TAYLOR, W. (1985) 'The organisation and funding of educational research in England and Wales' in NISBET, J. and NISBET, S. (Eds) *Research Policy and Practice: World Yearbook of Education 1985*, London, Kogan Page and Nichols Publishing, pp. 42–67.

TEN, C.L. (1975) 'Politics in the academe' in MONTEFIORE, A. (Ed.) *Neutrality and Impartiality: The University and Political Commitment*, Cambridge, Cambridge University Press, pp. 149–64.

WARNOCK, M. (1977) *Schools of Thought*, London, Faber.

Notes on Contributors

SANDRA ACKER Lecturer in Education, School of Education, University of Bristol.

MICHAEL W. APPLE Professor of Curriculum, Instruction and Educational Policy Studies, University of Wisconsin-Madison, USA.

WENDY BALL Research Associate, Centre for Research in Ethnic Relations, University of Warwick.

ROGER BULLOCK Senior Research Fellow, School of Applied Social Studies, University of Bristol.

FRANK COFFIELD Professor of Education, School of Education, University of Durham.

TONY EDWARDS Professor of Education, School of Education, University of Newcastle-upon-Tyne.

DAVID HARGREAVES Chief Inspector, Inner London Education Authority.

ANTHONY HARTNETT Senior Lecturer in Education, Department of Education, University of Liverpool.

MAURICE HOLT Principal Lecturer, College of St. Mark and St. John, Plymouth, Devon.

RUTH JONATHAN Lecturer in Education, Department of Education, Edinburgh University.

DENIS LAWTON Director, Institute of Education, University of London.

MICHAEL NAISH Senior Lecturer in Education, Department of

Education, University of Liverpool.

BILL REID Reader in Education, Department of Curriculum Studies, University of Birmingham.

SALLY TOMLINSON Professor of Education, Department of Educational Research, University of Lancaster.

BARRY TROYNA Reader in Education, Faculty of Education, Sunderland Polytechnic.

JOHN WHITE Reader in Philosophy of Education and Head of the Department, Department of Philosophy of Education, University of London Institute of Education.

PATRICIA WHITE Senior Lecturer in Philosophy of Education, Department of Philosophy of Education, University of London Institute of Education.

Index

values
  diversity 180–1
  public schools 84
Victoria Ministry of Education 12,
  105–7
Vincent, D. 123, 127
vocational education 158
  Germany 117
vocational programmes 100
vocational training 111, 128–31
vocationalism 6, 99–101, 110, 136,
  138, 139–40
voluntary-aided schools,
  Muslim 39, 41
voucher plans, schools 163

Wakeford, J. 83
Walker, S. 64
Warnock, M. 184
Warnock Report 49, 54, 55
Warren Piper, D. 70
Watts, A.G. 113, 125
Wax, M. 187
wealth, distribution 81
Weiner, G. 67, 68, 69
Wells, J.H. 71
Wheeler, M. 48, 52
White, J. 3, 13, 15, 171
White, J.P. 22
White, P. 3, 13, 15, 171
Whyld, J. 68, 69
Wilkinson, R. 80
Williams, B. 11, 176
Williams, J. 43
Williams, R. 16

Williams, S. 80, 101
Williamson, B. 116, 125
Wilson, Harold 104, 148
WISE 69
WNC 68, 71
women
  education 8–9
  qualification levels 64
Women into Science and
  Engineering 69
Womens' Educational Resource
  Centre 69
Women's National
  Commission 68, 71
women's studies 67
Wood Report 51
work, preparation for 100, 124,
  142–3
work experience, guaranteed 122
workforce, deskilling 105
working class parentage, ESN-M
  pupils 54
Worswick, G.D.N. 117

Yellow Book 10, 31
Young, D. 12, 129, 130
Youth Employment Premium 119
Youth Opportunities
  Programme 102
Youth Training Scheme 92, 102,
  109, 112–14, 129, 130–1
youth training schemes 15,
  125–6
youth unemployment 37, 56, 105,
  126